ENTER THE
OLD PORTALS

ENTER THE OLD PORTALS

REMINISCENCES:

Fifty Years on a Seminary Campus

MURRAY AND DOROTHY LEIFFER

First Edition

I. Murray and Dorothy Leiffer   II. Title.

Library of Congress Catalog Card Number 87-90828

To

*Our Former Students and Colleagues,
Partners in the Community of Scholars
and Fellow Pilgrims Toward the Light*

CONTENTS

FOREWORD

Alasdair MacIntyre once said that we declare who we are by identifying that story of which we are a part. This holds for institutions no less than it does for individuals. The identity of Garrett-Evangelical is found in large measure in the story of those who have taught, served, and studied in its company.

Surely no one is better suited to tell the story of this seminary than the authors of this book. Murray and Dorothy Leiffer, as students, professors, and professors emeriti have linked their lifetime ministry with this institution. Their 45 years on our faculty mark them as the senior faculty in this seminary in the number of years of service, and it is doubtful that many can equal such length of service in any institution of higher learning.

Garrett Theological Seminary, of which the Leiffers write, was one of three institutions forming the present Garrett-Evangelical Theological Seminary. Joining Garrett in 1936 was the Chicago Training School. In 1974 Evangelical Theological Seminary of Naperville, Illinois, and Garrett Theological Seminary united to form Garrett-Evangelical Theological Seminary. Fred Norwood and Paul Eller have written histories of these institutions in their two separately published volumes.[1] The Leiffers have written a different form of history in this book. Aided by scores of students and faculty colleagues, they have told the informal history of the people and the issues which in a major fashion shaped the character of Garrett Theological Seminary. Those who read these pages will be reminded of the people who have been spiritual guides, teachers, and friends to them. Others will be able for the first time to get acquainted with those who helped shape the character of this institution.

Murray and Dorothy Leiffer have provided a model of partnership and ministry to successive generations of Garrett students. They were committed to rigorous standards of scholarship. At the same time they gave themselves so thoroughly to teaching and to their students that many graduates of the seminary think and speak of them in familial terms. Alumni/ae consistently speak of Murray's firm insistence upon intellectual honesty, of Dorothy's leadership in recreational classes and the gracious hospitality of their home, and the Christian commitment and character which rested as a quiet benediction upon

---

[1] *From Dawn to Midday at Garrett*, by Frederick A. Norwood. *Evangelical Theological Seminary 1873-1973: Shaping Ministry*, by Paul H. Eller.

all who worked with them. Characteristically they have omitted many of the personal references which came in the recollections of those who corresponded with them and have focused instead upon names of others and upon the issues which continue to remain uppermost in their concern.

The Board of Trustees of Garrett-Evangelical have honored the Leiffers through the formation of the Dorothy and Murray Leiffer Chair of Christian Social Ethics. On October 17, 1985, Dean Richard D. Tholin was named the first Leiffer Professor. At the installation, the following words were read:

> A theological seminary is an institution which unites scholarship and devotion. Here professors and students engage in discussion with thinkers of the past and present and seek to discern a fuller truth and understanding which God is disclosing in our midst.
>
> The institution of the Dorothy and Murray Leiffer Chair of Christian Social Ethics marks an important development of this seminary. It is stipulated that this professor is to be selected on the basis of personal integrity and character, demonstrated love of people, concern for the Church, and strong academic qualifications. The person is to be selected without reference to sex, race, or cultural background.
>
> Dorothy and Murray Leiffer have both served as professors at Chicago Training School and the former Garrett Theological Seminary. Both are graduates of this seminary. Dorothy Leiffer's degree is the Master of Arts received from Garrett and Northwestern University in 1926. Murray Leiffer's degrees are the BD from Garrett Biblical Institute in 1925, an MA from the University of Chicago in 1928, and a PhD from Northwestern University in 1932.
>
> The span of their involvement in the life of this institution includes 1927 to 1972, a total of 45 years, the longest tenure for any professor in the history of this institution. A son, Donald John, was born to the Leiffers while they were living in Evanston. Prior to his death in 1970, he taught at West Los Angeles College.
>
> Mrs. Leiffer's courses were offered in the field of recreational leadership in the local church. Dr. Leiffer's work was in the fields of urban ministry, social ethics, and sociology of religion. The Leiffer Bureau of Social and Religious Research was founded in 1941 and continues as a program of the seminary.

Dr. Horace Greeley Smith, who served as president of the seminary during 21 of the years that the Leiffers were on the campus, speaking to the inaugural gathering in 1932, said that there were two Garretts which should be recognized. Of the one, he said, we are the guests. Of the other, the Garrett yet to come, we are the hosts.

It is evident that any who serve and study at Garrett-Evangelical will be debtors to the hospitality of those such as the Leiffers who gave the substance of their lives for the sake of an educated and effective ministry. We know well that today we are the guests of the Leiffers and the co-workers whose lives they recount here. But what of those to come? Of these, we are genuinely the hosts. These pages will help us to provide that hospitality for those who will follow.

I am confident that the anecdotal history provided here will help acquaint us with our hosts. I am equally assured that it will give fuller grounding to the hospitality which we provide for those who are to follow.

Neal F. Fisher, President
Garrett-Evangelical Theological Seminary

INTRODUCTION

Similarities between different historical periods do exist. Yet each has its uniqueness, especially for those who are a part of the pageant of those years.

Under the tragedies and uncertainties of war, people seem to turn with urgency and hope to religion and the Church. It was surely so when we (Dorothy and Murray) were young, during and after World War I. Those years witnessed a swing back to religion, especially to what many elected to call the "Faith of Our Fathers." For them this meant accepting the verbal inspiration and literal interpretation of the Bible, belief in the creation of the world in six days, the Jonah story, and so forth. At the same time, also in battle array, were those dubbed "modernists," who proclaimed the gradual evolution of the world from primeval chaos, the historical development of the Bible, and the humanness of Jesus. Often the latter group coalesced with the earnest advocates of social reform, applying the teachings of Jesus to the injustices which they saw in the world around them.

Each of us had grown up in a church-going family where the ancient teachings of the Church were uncritically accepted. Now we were college students, and hard questions were raised in our courses in philosophy, psychology and religion. Naturally we were intrigued by the exponents of the various contending views of religious truth. They ranged from Billy Sunday and Aimee Semple McPherson to G. Bromley Oxnam (one of our university teachers), Harry Emerson Fosdick and Harry F. Ward.

It was in this mixed-up, confusing world of religious as well as secular ideological conflict that youth were endeavoring to find God's will for their personal lives and guidance in their struggle with vocational decision, we among them. A group of us at the University of Southern California (at that time a Methodist school, with a Methodist minister as President, and regular chapel-assembly periods) were much influenced by such campus lecturers as Sherwood Eddy, John R. Mott, Kirby Page, and Norman Thomas. Murray and his closest friend, Max Chamberlin, shared their "bag lunches" each noon in a small room at the university. Taking turns, the two ate, read aloud, and discussed Harry Emerson Fosdick's "Meaning of Prayer," or

Walter Rauschenbusch's "Social Principles of Jesus." We were intrigued by and perhaps a little scornful of a classmate who was heading for the ministry in another denomination. When invited to join us, he declared that Fosdick was a heretic and his books should not be read until one went to seminary (he elected a conservative one) and found out how to combat such dangerous views. Indeed, our courses did encourage skepticism.

Max and I attended the same local church and debated issues of theology with our patient, saintly, but not omniscient pastor. We undoubtedly troubled him with our questions about the historicity of the Bible and doctrinal points which he considered important.

Like a gleam of light into this confusing jumble of ideas and vague plans came Harris Franklin Rall, who gave a series of lectures at the USC School of Religion and spoke in the chapel. A few of us were privileged to meet with him in free-for-all "bull sessions." He was not disturbed by our toughest questions and had a faith and philosophy that were to us profoundly helpful. So five of the "pre-ministerial" men decided to go to Garrett for graduate work.

Three of us, Maxwell Chamberlin, Roy Mason, and Murray agreed to buy a car and drive back to Garrett, seeing the country as we drove. After much discussion we invested in an ancient four-door "touring car," a Ford Model T, known affectionately as a "Tin Lizzie," fully equipped with a hand crank (no self-starter) and side curtains, which could keep out quite a bit of the rain, but not much of the night-time mountain cold. Its horn was broken, so we bought a cheap tin flute to use instead. We planned our route with care—up the San Joaquin Valley, over the Sierras, across the desert, through Yellowstone National Park, and on to Evanston, Illinois, to enroll at Garrett.

Dorothy also was graduated in 1923. That summer we were engaged and she continued at U.S.C. as a full-time librarian, earning a little money to help us launch our new home. We were married the next summer and traveled together to Evanston. There we secured a little attic apartment in a private home on Sherman Avenue. In 1925, after Murray received his B.D. degree, we moved to the West Side of Chicago, to a Dutch-Polish community.

Yet in a sense we never left Garrett, for after two years of continuing our studies and two years of teaching at the Chicago Training School on the South Side, we were invited back to Garrett to teach, where we happily shared in the life of the school until retirement in 1972.

We have not attempted to write a formal history of Garrett but rather, with the help of reminiscences of scores of friends, to give an informal account of the people and events that constituted the dynamic life of the school which has meant so much to others and to us, and whose graduates have made lasting contributions to churches and communities throughout this land and in countries beyond the seas.

No two (or even four-score) persons, no matter how long their memories, can do full justice to the life of a school such as Garrett-Evangelical, whose story spans the generations and whose halls have echoed to ten thousand voices. Other persons could recount fascinating happenings, viewed from different perspectives. Some of our experiences have been included with reluctance and only under the urging of good friends. We hope that the reader will forgive the frequent use of first-person pronouns.

The two of us have written this book together. However, some items require us to distinguish which person is referred to. Sometimes it is Dorothy, sometimes Murray; more often, both of us—for that is the way we have lived. Occasionally, we simply say "Leiffer" because we want to stand off from the event and look at it with the reader. We hope this will not prove confusing.

The authors wish to acknowledge their deep indebtedness to scores of friends, colleagues on faculty and staff, and alumni/ae (most of them former students of ours). They generously shared their lives with us in years now gone. And literally scores of them have written within the past year to tell us of their memories of the "old school." Their participation, often with stories previously unknown to us, has added much vitality and humor to that which follows.

The idea of writing such a book was not ours. The credit, if credit there be, goes to Vance Rogers, a longtime friend and now President Emeritus of Nebraska Wesleyan University, and to Neal F. Fisher, President of Garrett-Evangelical Theological Seminary.

Rockwell and Frances Smith, Otto and Frances Nall, Vance and Barbara Rogers, and Neal Fisher read the manuscript and offered valuable suggestions in form and content. To each of them we are grateful. Our sincere thanks also go to three members of the G-ETS staff, Helen Hauldren, Linda Renaud, and Frances Shuford for their skillful editorial assistance and typing of the final draft of the manuscript.

Murray and Dorothy Leiffer

I

GARRETT: TRAINING FOR A PROFESSION

On a September afternoon in 1923 three travel-weary beginning students from California—Max Chamberlin, Roy Mason and Murray Leiffer—arrived in Evanston in an old Ford, after a 28-day camping trip, to attend Garrett Biblical Institute. Would anyone be there to greet us? Would the dormitory be available? (We had taken turns sleeping in the car or on the ground, and any real bed was a prize to be desired.) Would there be a job—any kind of job—at which we could earn some much-needed cash? The answer to all three questions was: "Yes!" Thank the Lord!

The Dean, Frederick Carl Eiselen, was in the front hall of the brand new Administration Building and greeted us, shabby in our camping-travel clothes as we were, with a hearty handclasp and a genial "Welcome!" that made us feel comfortable in our choice of Garrett. He took us past workmen who were still cleaning up after laying the concrete floors in the Museum Corridor (first floor hall) and up the broad stairs to the President's office to introduce us to Charles Macauley Stuart, a delightful, warm personality—quite unlike the new President at the University of Southern California whom we had considered a rather unapproachable "stuffed shirt."

Dr. Eiselen got the keys and escorted us to our dormitory. The three of us were to have a suite of three rooms in Building B, second floor—now Pfeiffer Hall. When we inquired about work, he assured us that temporary jobs would be turned our way, and suggested that we talk to the librarian, Samuel Gardiner Ayres. We soon moved in our modest assortment of luggage, such as could be carried in a Model T Ford in addition to three full-grown men.

After a much-needed shower and a quick lunch of "remainders" from our travel supplies, the three of us set out to find Mr. Ayres. He was a jolly person—elderly, ruddy-faced, and with more stomach than chest, but the sort of man you could not help liking. Of course he could put us to work—all three of us—and at eight o'clock the next morning. That evening we walked for the first time beside the restless waters of Lake Michigan, and knew that we had made the right choice of a seminary.

At eight o'clock sharp the next morning we were at the old library in Memorial Hall[1] ready to go to work. The job was simple but weighty: clearing out the books, shelf by shelf, from the old stacks in the basement, dusting them, lugging them upstairs and out to a two-wheeled pushcart in which we transported them to their new home, all 125,000 volumes of them, plus more than 20,000 pamphlets, of which Mr. Ayres was equally proud, and he loved every one of them. It was a dusty, tiring job; however, we were earning forty cents an hour!

For a week the three of us and one or two other men worked long hours to get "our" library out of Memorial Hall. Garrett was obligated to vacate the building so that its new occupant, the School of Commerce of Northwestern University, could move in. When President Stuart turned over the keys to the Dean of the School of Commerce, he remarked sententiously, "We've removed everything of worth to us except the Ten Commandments in the chapel's windows, and we think it appropriate for you to keep those."

Garrett's new administration building was easily the most beautiful and impressive edifice on the entire campus. Its Gothic architecture, stone walls, great square tower, and appropriate decorative features, its high ceilings and broad stairways made one think of the medieval cathedrals of Europe. Later we were to experience the thrill of watching or participating in processionals, with all the color of academic robes and hoods, and the dignity of organ music echoing through the large chapel. Clarence Tompkins ('26), a student at the time, reports that during the construction of the new Garrett building a visiting lady looking at the stone gargoyle finials, waiting for installation, asked: "What are those ugly things? Are they going to be used on the building?" Dr. Stuart smiled and said, "They thought they should have a statue of me in the building. I sat twice. Remarkable resemblance, isn't it?"

At the moment, however, the newness of the administration building was itself something of a problem. Not only were the workmen still putting finishing touches on the structure, but it soon became apparent that the concrete flooring on both first and second stories was not well laid, and President Stuart, a meticulous man who watched details and wanted things to be done correctly, insisted that

---

[1] It was a red-brick structure known to the students as "the little red schoolhouse," standing about two hundred feet northwest of the present Deering Library of Northwestern University. Fred Norwood in his book, *From Dawn to Midday at Garrett* (1978), aptly described its "mongrel architecture" and quoted an old catalog, "The architecture is peculiar but might be called Romanesque in its general outline."

both floorings be removed (it had to be done with jack-hammers) and relaid without the cracks that had become all too evident in a few short weeks. The noisy, messy work had to be done after the autumn quarter had begun.

It was a heady experience for us, getting started in a new—and graduate—school, in a new building, and in a new part of the United States. This was serious business, a privilege not to be taken lightly. To qualify for admission for the graduate degree, one was expected to have presented a suitable transcript, giving evidence of graduation from an approved college, and also a statement from a local church, testifying that one was "regarded as a proper person to study for the Christian ministry."

The normal academic load was three "majors" a quarter, a major constituting a four-hour-a-week course. Some "half-majors" (two hours a week) were also offered. Frank Orman Beck, Professor of Sociology and Urban Studies, was assigned to be my advisor. Since I entered with some graduate academic credits in the field of religion, I was excused from a few of the introductory courses. Hebrew and Greek were no longer required, but I thought it appropriate to have some knowledge of Greek, since I planned to enter the pastoral-preaching ministry. Dr. Beck signed me up for three courses: Introductory Greek, under John J. Rapp, Introduction to the Pauline Epistles, under Doremus Almy Hayes, and one on The City and Its Churches, under himself. It was interesting to observe that professors at Garrett, like professors everywhere, each regarded his own field to be of primary importance. I had had that type of experience before—and have had it since.

Getting Acquainted with a New Faculty

"Daddy" Rapp, as he was affectionately called by those who had taken work with him, loved the Greek language. The Gospel According to John was the subject matter for the course. Never before had I known a teacher so enamoured of his work. As we labored to translate, we learned quite a bit of Greek, more about New Testament theology, and a great deal about a person who loved his work and showed unending patience with us novitiates.

A fellow-student, Otto Nall ('26), recalls that Daddy Rapp "was most kind and patient with those who were studying the mysterious Hellenic tongue, but was given to knocking his glasses off his face as he twirled around in his desk chair and threw up his hands. 'Jumping Johnny Robinson, don't you know a second aorist when you see one?'"

Doremus Almy Hayes, a tall, spare, well-groomed person, had equal fondness for his field, but was as much in contrast to Daddy Rapp as two devotees of the New Testament could be. Hayes was a meticulous scholar, and had written several volumes of exegesis and interpretation on different portions of the New Testament. He was an exponent of the lecture method, and expected his students to take copious notes. In a letter written to my fiancee (Dorothy) at that time, which she recently unearthed, I commented:

> In class yesterday Hayes lectured. He gives it off very fast. He considers himself quite an authority and practically demands conformity on the part of his students. One must get all his lecture down as grounds for later questions, and it is almost impossible to get it all down. The fellow next to me murmured after an especially speedy flow, "Well, he may make me a parrot, but I'll be hanged if he can make me a racehorse!"

I later discovered that he was as precise in his grading as in his classroom procedure. A portion of each hour was reserved for questioning one student after another on particular items in the assigned text (his own book). For each response a grade was entered in his little book. The written examinations were of a similar type, and his term grades were stated in exact percentages. Since at that time I had a rather good memory, I did fairly well in reproducing his lectures. In fact, he recorded a grade of 98 for me in the second course I took from him, then later half apologized, saying privately, "Leiffer, you didn't make any mistake on the examination, but nobody deserves a 100."

Otto wrote:

> Doremus Almy Hayes was a tough marker. In the interest of fairness he usually quoted a dozen names of scholars who had one view of a Bible passage in the writings of John or Paul, and then as many authorities on the opposing side. But our teacher would say: "Now, *we* think" and if you wanted a good mark you had better side with the "we's."

This may make Dr. Hayes sound like a rigid, unimaginative dictator. Only later did I discover how faulty such a generalization would be. True, no student ever joked with him or played tricks on him. Yet, as I learned later, even though he recognized his inborn superiority, he had a wry sense of humor and was a delightful dinner-table companion. But commitment to his academic discipline was complete.

Dr. Beck, my third professor, was short of stature, and of broader build than either of the others. A friendly, approachable man, he obviously enjoyed talking with students and about his own experiences. His doctorate in sociology was from the University of Chicago, where he had specialized in urban studies. After fifteen years as pastor of city churches, and because of his special interest in Christian social service, he became Director of the Chicago Welfare Department and then Executive Secretary of the Chicago Inter-Church World Movement before coming to Garrett.

In conversation it became obvious that he had a thorough and intimate acquaintance with all parts of the city of Chicago and especially those of underprivilege, the social settlements and West Madison Street. In his best-known book, *Hobohemia*, published after his retirement from Garrett, he presented a fascinating set of vignettes of people he had known: handicapped, tormented, maladjusted people of "Bug House Square" on the Near North Side, and others on West Madison Street. He knew Emma Goldman, "Queen of the Anarchists," and Jane Addams, who established Hull House and almost literally gave her life for the impoverished immigrants of south Halsted Street.

Dr. Beck was always concerned for the "under-dog." In 1907 he had been one of the founders of the Methodist Federation for Social Service. Concerning him, a classmate of mine recently wrote: "Frank Beck gave me my first organized understanding of the social gospel."

Here was a man with whom I at once found rapport. At the end of my first year at Garrett, I decided to major with him. Eventually when he retired in 1929 I was elected to take over his work—but that is getting ahead of the story. It was indeed stimulating to start our studies at Garrett.

<>

An important part of the school life was the daily (i.e., Tuesday through Friday) chapel service, held at 10 a.m., after the first two classes. Faculty and students were "expected" to attend, and usually three-fourths were on hand. The faculty gathered in the President's office, and moved in informal procession into the chapel, occupying the small "stalls" on a long bench on the platform across the front of the chapel, facing the audience. Since the platform was about three feet high, students could easily note the absence of any faculty member. Generally all but two or three were present.

In addition to these brief corporate worship services, the students in each "dorm entrance" were encouraged to hold a prayer meeting once a week, in the room of one of them, commonly at ten o'clock on

Wednesday night, before retiring. The number attending depended on the devoutness of the several residents, the effectiveness and pressures of the sectional "devotional chairman" and the proximity of due-dates for term papers or exams. Incidentally, two of the twelve persons in our dorm section were Blacks,[2] one of them, Charles Blooah, from Liberia.

<>

In the winter quarter of my first year there was the joy of sitting under the tutelage of two other fascinating persons—Leslie Fuller and Harris Franklin Rall. Professor Fuller, whose field was Old Testament Literature, was as tanned and rugged as the Bedouins with whom he lived in Arabia for a year. Blessed with a lively sense of humor, well disciplined in the field of Biblical studies, and having experienced life in Palestine, he was able to quicken our desire to learn and enjoy the Bible. No one could ever accuse him of being a literalist, and indeed he seemed to enjoy shocking some of his fundamentalist students. (In odd contrast, Leslie's brother, Charles, who shared with him and their father the year of rugged living in Palestine, became a fundamentalist radio evangelist in California!)

He was famous for his "rainbow course," Outline of Old Testament Literature, that all were required to take. Using various colored pencils, we drew lines beside the text in our Bibles, designating the various historical literary sources, each in its distinctive color—blue for early Judean stories, red for "Late Priestly" sources, and so on. Hence the name: "rainbow course."

It was probably the most controversial course in the curriculum and Leslie Fuller reveled in the discussions which it produced. The very marking technique and the accompanying lectures destroyed (or at least threatened) the "finger of God" literalism which many students had brought with them. Thirty years later a minister in a western conference told me that "when I was in Fuller's class I thought that he was surely possessed by the devil. Two other students who felt similarly met in my room frequently to pray for his conversion. Indeed, we rather expected that on some terrible day the floor would give way and he would drop directly into Hell."

---

[2] In the 1920's, and for some time later, persons of African descent would have been offended to be called "blacks." The polite term then was "Negro" spelled with a capital. The situation now is reversed, and many Negroes regard Black as a race title and feel aggrieved if a lower case "b" is used. Therefore, in this book, as a matter of courtesy, we are using a capital "B" when the term clearly refers to a person of Negro ancestry.

The professor, who was well aware of such criticism, was never dismayed by it, but seemed to find satisfaction in "disillusioning the innocent." One friend recently wrote me about a conservative classmate: "He brought all his (conservative) prejudices to seminary, and I can still visualize Dr. Fuller jumping on him . . . to 'liberate' him. I thought Dr. Fuller was merciless, even cruel." However, the majority of us had heard enough concerning the "historical" approach to the Bible that we did not feel the sense of shock experienced by students coming from conservative homes and colleges.

Most remember Fuller with delight, recalling his lighthearted laughter and unforgettable wise quips. Olin Stockwell ('24), who was a fellow student when I took the course, wrote recently:

> Fuller was a creative teacher who always got a lot of fun out of his students and teaching. He always announced his favorite lecture well in advance. On the day he was to give it, one of the students passed his hat for a collection, and Dr. Fuller accepted our offering with his usual broad grin. A few weeks later when examinations came, he appeared with a sack of jelly beans, purchased with the money from the lecture. So we all ate jelly beans while trying to write our papers. It was good fun, and he was good fun.

One day a student inquired, "Were the prophets married?" He knew that Hosea was, but what about Amos? Fuller with a twinkle in his eye replied: "Oh he was married all right, but his wife lived on the charge."

When Olin and I were in the class it met immediately after chapel in the nearby large lecture room. Dr. Nagler taught a class in church history in that room before chapel and used as a makeshift lectern an 18-inch wooden box with no bottom, placed on the desk. The first thing Fuller would do when he entered the room was to sweep that off to one side while starting his lecture. A small dog had been wandering through Garrett's sacred halls, and two of the students caught the little fellow and put him under the reading box just before Fuller came in. With his usual aplomb Fuller put his hands on the box and started to move it to one side. But it did not slide readily. Cautiously he lifted up the box and there, facing him in eye-to-eye contact, was the little mongrel wagging his tail. The professor and the waiting class burst into uproarious laughter as the dog headed for the doorway. Fuller's classes were informal! But he always held the attention of the students.

Probably the most widely known member of the Garrett faculty at that time was Harris Franklin Rall. His numerous books on theology and his active participation in the Methodist Federation for Social Service accounted for the fact that he, rather than Leslie Fuller, was seen as the major proponent of "modernism" on the Garrett faculty.

After Frank's death Georgia Harkness wrote an incisive description (honoring Dr. Rall) of the conflict of "modernism" with the older and more acceptable orthodoxy of that day.[3]

> It was . . . in the twentieth century that the major growth and most rigorous testing of liberalism was to come. Little by little, the liberal emphasis on the historical and textual study of the Bible, on the ethical teachings of Jesus and the moral imperatives of a Christian society, on the need for Christian faith to find a working synthesis with science, began to [filter down to] clergy and . . . to the laity. It is difficult for anyone born within the past fifty years to realize the sense of shock with which these ideas were greeted. It is no exaggeration to say that the present horror of Communism in the churches is hardly more intense than the horror of "higher criticism" in large areas . . . [which] came to a head in the emergence of a militant fundamentalism about 1920. This was not the simple piety of an older orthodoxy but a fighting creed, of which the "fundamentals" were affirmed to be the virgin birth, the substitutionary atonement, the physical resurrection, and the imminent second coming of Christ, based on the complete and literal inerrancy of the Scriptures.
>
> It is against this background of Biblical and creedal literalism, often joined with a "die-hard" social conservatism in matters of racial and economic justice, that Dr. Rall for a half-century did valiant service in the cause of Christian truth as he had come to see it. In this connection I am reminded of a remark once made to me by President Henry Sloan Coffin of Union Theological Seminary. Said he, "The younger men who now so freely castigate liberalism have never had to fight, as their fathers did, for the right to believe and to say the things they now take for granted."

It was Dr. Rall's calm, objective approach to the Bible and to Christian theology that had attracted us to come to Garrett. Under his guidance we began to understand the significance of a vital, philosophically valid theology. His interpretations made the Christian faith fully acceptable to inquiring and skeptical youth. As my Garrett roommate Max remarked some forty years after we had been graduated: "Because I had the privilege of studying under Rall I feel that I was able to achieve a tenable life-giving faith with his guidance and did not need to revise my theology every ten years."[4]

[3] The Wesleyan Quarterly Review, August 1965, "The Theology of Dr. Rall," pp. 141-150.
[4] Dr. Rall was confident that there was no fundamental conflict between the Christian faith and the new science. It was probably in the early 1920's that he wrote "The Story of Creation." We do not know whether it was ever published, but have the permission of Mary Rall, his daughter, to include it in this book. It combines the ancient Biblical story with our present knowledge of cosmology in a beautiful, simple, poetic manner. (See Appendix, page 201.)

Dr. Rall was short of stature and slight in build, and always carefully dressed. His neatly trimmed gray goatee, and the way he stroked it when he was "thinking on his feet," caused quiet amusement among the students. When they sought to imitate Dr. Rall, that was often the revealing gesture. Another motion well remembered by his students was his holding one arm straight up, and pointing his other arm horizontally, as he declared, "Theology is a two-way affair—*upward* toward God, *outward* toward one's fellows." What caught attention was his evident alertness and zeal, as shown in his penetrating glance and quickness of speech. He enjoyed expressing his ideas with preciseness. His Bible, his dictionary and the thesaurus on his desk were well worn. Pausing before answering a student's question, his eyes would twinkle, he would stroke his little goatee with his right hand, and then a well-turned, appropriate answer would be crisply voiced.

He was a staunch exponent of the "social gospel," and he and his friend, Francis J. McConnell, were among the founders of the Methodist Federation for Social Service in 1907. Frank Rall credited one of his undergraduate professors at the University of Iowa with giving him "not so much a set of conclusions as an example of open-mindedness and of order and lucidity in thought and expression." So, good teachers look back to their good teachers.

Students soon recognized that both Dr. Fuller and Dr. Rall were not only widely read in their own fields but expected their students to spend many hours a week digesting Bible commentaries and scholarly works of persons with differing views, as well as relevant articles in the current professional literature. Their aim clearly was not so much to push the student to a specific set of conclusions as to develop his independent thinking, based on wide reading and careful analysis. To this end each of them required several substantial papers during the term. And, incidentally, both professors read and marked up the papers themselves.

However, these men, like others on the faculty, were primarily interested in their students as persons growing in maturity. They and most of their colleagues encouraged out-of-class discussions and conversations in their offices about the non-academic aspects of the student's life. Nearly every professor invited each of his classes to his home for an extra session or a social evening, but both the Fullers and the Ralls went beyond that. Max and I were surprised (and quickly accepted) when Dr. Rall and his wife invited a half dozen of us to enjoy a picnic with them in the forest preserve during my first spring quarter.

The Fuller home was always open, and those of us from the

southwest were invited to come over for an informal, family-type dinner on numerous occasions. The food was never elaborate, but it was good, hearty and ample. Then after the meal we would gather around their big dining room table and play "Michigan" with match sticks instead of poker chips, or "Jenkins Says 'Hands Up'" (to guess which hand covers the quarter). The fact that the coin might scratch the table top never bothered Leslie or Mabel Fuller. Never before had we found this type of cordial, open-handed friendliness on the part of university professors.

Each of the other professors had distinctive and important contributions to make. Frederick Carl Eiselen, German in background, a thorough Old Testament scholar, spoke with a fairly strong German accent and always with a voice that carried conviction. He was an authority in his field and had a number of books to his credit. From him we learned to love the Psalms and other sacred writings.

It was not until my second year, after Dorothy and I were married, that I was to take work with Dr. Nagler, and then Dorothy and I enrolled in the same class in the basic "History of the Christian Church," a survey course which required a great deal of reading. The first day in class he asked each person in turn to stand up, give his name, and tell where he was from. I was at the end of the row, and stood up and said, "I am Murray Leiffer, from California." Dorothy followed suit and said, "I am Dorothy Leiffer, from California." The class cheered and Dorothy blushed. Dr. Nagler had a cherubic smile on his face as he enjoyed the commotion. In those early days students were not encouraged to marry, and when a man married usually his wife lived on a student charge.

Dr. Nagler came from a pietistic German Methodist background and had a warm appreciation of people. He knew his field well, was a competent teacher and was enjoyable to listen to, but he was not a brilliant scholar. As many a student would testify, he was one of the kindest and most sensitive of human beings.

Another senior professor was Solon C. Bronson. He, like Stuart and Hayes, had joined the faculty in 1896. Two things I remember from his course in preaching: "Do not read your sermons; but if you feel you must read them, write them in such large script that, if a cross-wind should blow through the church while you are preaching and carry away your notes, you will be able to read the next item as it sails out the window." The other was derived from his long experience as a mentor at the Boys' Club in Chicago: "It is often wise to keep your eyes open as you pray. There is nothing in Scripture which says that you should not watch the congregation during your prayer."

Clarence Tompkins has a more appreciative remembrance: "Over and over Dr. Bronson would declare: 'In your preaching— 1. Make the truth plain. 2. Make the truth pleasing. 3. Make the truth persuasive.' We rascals mimicked the old fellow." He was doubtless a good minister and rather effective speaker. Yet with all his self-assurance he did little to increase our preaching skills or our appreciation of his lectures. The Board of Trustees had recently established seventy as the age for retirement of faculty members. Bronson and Stuart were the first to be retired under the new rule. Bronson deeply resented this, but I did not hear of others who mourned his retirement.

Probably the youngest member of the faculty was Irl G. Whitchurch, with whom I had a course in "Philosophy of Religion." Over the decades of my acquaintance with academia, I have been impressed by the wide diversity of students' attitudes toward any given professor. Dr. Whitchurch undoubtedly had an excellent command of his teaching field. The incisiveness of his lectures and the sharpness of his analyses of the contributions of predecessors in the field elicited almost an attitude of discipleship on the part of some students. Others were estranged. The acidity of some of his remarks, untempered by humor, caused a few to avoid him after one course. An alumnus remembers a comment of his to the class on one occasion: "You shift your brains into neutral, and let your tongues idle."

Meeting Our Expenses

Fortunately student fees were low and presented no problem to us. We were delighted that there was no tuition or dormitory room rent. We were our own housekeepers and none of us objected to that. The incidental fee for a person occupying a room was $15.00 per quarter, with an additional fee of $4.25 to cover "bedroom equipment and laundry charges." There was also a quarterly library fee of $1.25, and a fee of $2.50 which was turned over to the student organization, the Dempster League; this covered a subscription to the school publication *The Garrett Tower*.

Although school charges were minimal, the necessity of earning enough money to cover the cost of books and meals remained. Before coming to Evanston I had written President Stuart to ask about the possibility of doing some tutorial work. His reply was kind but not encouraging. However, since I was a person not easily discouraged or turned aside, when the term was well started I asked for an appointment to see him. Afterwards I wrote my fiancee: ". . . not much chance at present. He surely treated me nicely; he is a real gentleman, though slightly effeminate in manner and voice. Told me to come in and see him often, and in case of any trouble to go to him directly. Well, today he himself called me out of my Greek class and said that Mrs. Stuart had some work she would like me to do tomorrow."

The other men and I did many odd jobs for people about town. In fact, we found that Garrett students had a good reputation with the homemakers of Evanston—taking down screens, washing windows, doing yard work. The going pay rate was fifty cents an hour. Our friend Roy soon got a job tending a coal-burning furnace. He had to get up not later than six o'clock in the morning and check on the furnace two or more times during each day. The pay—$2.50 a week. I was more fortunate, snaring a job which involved sweeping out an electrical goods store on Davis Street each afternoon and washing the windows at least once a week: five *big* dollars a week.

That left the little problem of eating to be reckoned with. There was no lunchroom or "commons" at Garrett and, on the basis of prior unfortunate experiences, the administration had forbidden eating in the dormitories. That rule was surreptitiously broken by some of the men, especially those with student charges who brought victuals from home. Others ate at one of the little lunchrooms on Foster Street, most favored because of its low prices. With a degree of justification, it was dubbed "The Dirty Spoon." The really popular meal job was at the Evanston Hospital, over a mile from Garrett if one cut across a few vacant lots. About eighteen of the fellows were fortunate enough to get jobs there. Serving the nurses in their dining room two of the three meals each day—or working in the kitchen—qualified one to receive three meals a day. Those on the breakfast shift had to be on hand by 6:30 a.m., and returned for either the noon or dinner shift. They could get the third meal by showing up for it.

This resource was one day brought abruptly to a close. One of the "regulars," unable to be present, arranged for a fellow student, who happened to be a Black, to substitute for him. The hospital dining room manager refused to let him serve tables, and suggested he could work in the kitchen. The Garrett men all walked out that day over the issue; the nurses had to serve themselves. The manager soon set up a cafeteria line and the white men lost their meal jobs permanently. That was in the winter of 1924-25, over sixty years ago.

My friend, the President, called me to his office one day and informed me that he was buying a car and had never learned to drive. Would I be willing to teach him? I agreed somewhat hesitantly, because after all he was the President and I just a student. On several afternoons "we" practiced on the empty streets in northwest Evanston, until he felt some confidence. Two weeks later he told me he had sold the car! It seemed that he had on one occasion run over a section of a neighbor's hedge, and later had smashed a hole through the back wall of his own garage because he went forward instead of in reverse! He could not bear the thought that he might injure someone. Dr. Eiselen was right in referring to his "sweetness and graciousness, a man who in a unique way typified the perfect Christian gentleman."

<>

There was always plenty of spice in life at Garrett, a good deal of bantering and friendly gossip. During my first year we had a thoroughly enjoyable Halloween party in the autumn, and an April Fools party in the spring. Schuyler Garth, then a senior, with a good committee to help, planned them both.[5] There were about 120 at the April Fools party, some twenty of them women, chiefly wives of students. We were not a particularly sophisticated lot, and enjoyed various types of relays and intellectual competition. Many of the games were developed by the committee and we all had a delightful evening of fun and fellowship.

No Room for Complacency in a Sick World

There were plenty of serious social issues to challenge us also. Only a few years had passed since Armistice Day, which closed World War I, and many of the students had seen service in the Army or Navy. Their commitment to the cause of peace was registered in the large number who joined the Fellowship of Reconciliation, an international peace organization. There were numerous meetings addressed by peace-minded speakers. One of them was held on Thursday, March 6,

---

[5] Schuyler Garth ('24) was one of the natural leaders in the student body. On graduation he began his ministry in Florida. After serving many years there and then in Pittsburgh, he was elected to the episcopacy in 1944. He was much loved as pastor and bishop, and the manner of his death was mute witness to his self-sacrificing love of others. He and Lola, his wife, on an episcopal visit in Mainland China in January 1947 were aboard a small plane, in company with a missionary family. Engine trouble developed. The pilot warned them that a crash could not be avoided. At Schuyler's suggestion, he and the father of the children each took a child in his arms and dropped backwards through the open door of the plane, knowing that they themselves would be killed, but hoping to save the lives of the children. One of the children was the only person to survive and he told the story. All the others, including the pilot, died in the crash.

1924 in a little restaurant in the basement of a building at the corner of Library Place and Orrington. On Friday morning I wrote Dorothy:

> . . . Something happened today. The morning Chicago *Examiner* came out with a black one-inch headline—"Mob Student Pacifists in Evanston Cafe." It told how the Northwestern football captain and a number of letter-men and "huskies" came over to the restaurant about ten minutes after the others had arrived, and challenged them to come out. The pacifists invited them in—sent a delegate who was pelted with rotten eggs, tomatoes, and bricks. The rest of the pacifists were wise and withdrew (but the writer failed to find out that there was only one entrance to the place!). The article closed saying that "the pacifists decided they would hold no more meetings in Evanston."
>
> And every bit of that is a lie. The meeting was entirely undisturbed and quiet. Not a thing was thrown, no one was bothered. It broke up and all went home without being accosted by anyone. And we talk about an unpolluted press! A headline article and not a bit of truth in it, except the fact that Northwestern and Garrett students concerned about peace gathered in a restaurant to hear a man named Fletcher talk.

The determination of Garrett students to witness for peace was a dominant motif in the life of the school throughout the 1920's and into the early 1930's. The Fellowship of Reconciliation conducted a study of the opinions of clergymen and seminary students in 1930 concerning their attitudes toward issues of war and peace. The replies from four seminaries, one of them Garrett, were reported separately. To the question "Are you personally prepared to state that it is your present purpose not to sanction any future war or to participate as an armed combatant?" 99 out of the 134 Garrett men who replied (or 74%) answered "Yes." This figure is in contrast to 53.8% for all responding clergy.[6]

A similar study, made by the same organization three years later,[6] used the same question and reported on eight seminaries, one of them Evangelical in Naperville. At that time, 38 out of 46 responding students also said "Yes." While recognizing that there is an unmeasurable selectivity and possible skewing in this method of data gathering, one nevertheless gets a feel for the intense opposition to war in that period on the part of seminarians.

---

[6] *The World Tomorrow*, May 1931, p. 151, and May 1934, p. 225. Our thanks to David Himrod, Assistant Librarian at GETS, for furnishing the above data.

Another issue which aroused students' ire was the propaganda of the Ku Klux Klan. At that time the KKK had the loyalty and financial support of many respectable people in all parts of the country. It was particularly strong in Indiana and Illinois. One student pastor was preaching in his rural Indiana church when a group of local people wearing Klan robes but no hoods marched up to the altar with a sizable sum of money to apply on the debt of the church. Completely surprised, the pastor voiced a weak protest, and afterwards asked to be relieved of that pastorate.

There were several large gatherings of Klansmen in open fields in northern Illinois. My employer, Mr. S., attended some of them and sought to convert me to the cause, which he averred was certainly Christian. Again I benefit by the fact that my wife saved some of my letters. I wrote in March 1924:

> Had a great argument with S. and one of his staff. Feel quite sure now that the whole bunch of them are KKK. They gave some very interesting information. The reason that no Catholic has ever been President of the US is "because in taking the oath of office he would have to kiss the Bible and a Catholic dare not do that." . . . Of course I dissented vigorously to all this. Another very interesting "secret" is that the birth rate of Negroes is 17 (according to the supply-man three days ago) or 19 (according to Mr. S. tonight) times that of American whites. I believe I showed the utter absurdity and impossibility of such a figure, said it was a lie, and that an organization using such propaganda had no justification for its practices, and its methods were wrong. I offered to bet my week's pay that he couldn't prove those figures. He did not take me up. Please don't be surprised if I lose my job there.

<>

Student days at Garrett were richly rewarding, and I owe the school a debt that I can never fully repay. The professors gave of themselves as well as their learning. Of them all, Frank O. Beck influenced my professional development most deeply. He shared his own love of the city and opened for me the position of counselor to the white Protestant boys (aged 17 to 20) who were brought before the Boys' Court of Chicago.[7] Beck also encouraged me to apply for a Laura

---

[7] Others in comparable roles were a friendly Black layman who, with me, represented the Chicago Church Federation and who counselled the Negro Protestants; a genial elderly man from the Holy Name Society for the Catholics; and a competent, sophisticated Jewish social worker, dealing with the Jewish boys.

Spellman Rockefeller Fellowship in urban sociology at the University of Chicago, instead of returning on graduation to California or Arizona to serve as a pastor.

With that two-year fellowship in hand, we decided to move to the Near West Side of Chicago and continue with our staff positions at the St. Paul Methodist Church, while Dorothy carried forward her studies for the Master of Arts at Garrett and Northwestern and Murray worked for his at the University of Chicago. We rented a little apartment on 14th Place, in a Polish-Dutch neighborhood, and on weekdays took the "L" to the Loop where she went north to Evanston and he turned south, or spent the morning at the Boys' Court. Dorothy sometimes substituted for me at the Court. Sundays and some evenings we spent at the church. So passed two busy, fruitful years.

Our Years at Chicago Training School

In the spring of 1927 Dr. L. F. W. Lesemann, the President of the Chicago Training School, invited Murray to teach "full time" at that institution. That was an unexpected opening of a friendly door and, after consulting with our mentor, Frank O. Beck, we were glad to accept the invitation. We soon learned that CTS, as everyone called the school, was an unusual institution, with a small but highly dedicated faculty and students deeply committed to "giving their lives" in Christian service.

The school had been established in 1885 by Lucy Rider Meyer, a Christian woman of amazing energy and determination. She was confident that many young women longed to serve their Lord and that the Church had provided no means for their training and placement. With the loyal support of her husband she worked diligently to get an adequate training school started and to raise money to keep it going.

Such an enterprise always has difficulty in raising sufficient funds to meet its needs. But the determination of Mrs. Meyer surmounted all obstacles, and when we became acquainted with the school it was located in an excellent set of buildings on the south side of Chicago, an area which at that time was undergoing rapid population change. CTS was essentially a two-year vocational college with a strong Christian commitment. For its first forty years its student body was entirely female. In 1925, when Dr. Lesemann became President, men were invited to join the student body, which was cosmopolitan in many respects. There was a wide age distribution, and students of different races and cultural backgrounds were included.

Frances (Mahaffie) Nall, who taught at CTS from 1925 to 1931 recalls with nostalgia, "It was the most Christian environment in which I have ever lived. In that wonderful spirit everyone was accepted for what that person was—whether man or woman, dark or light skinned, American or foreign . . . Each student had a desire to help others." Out of necessity the school operated on a very modest budget. Administrators and teachers gladly carried heavy schedules. Salaries were small. "We had devotions in the dining room at 7 p.m. Everyone had to stay for prayers. It became a game with students and faculty alike to make a frugal dinner of one hot dog and a baked potato last a whole hour. One night a student giving the devotions thanked God for the plentiful meal. Everyone laughed, for most of us left the dining room hungry."

That autumn Dorothy, our little boy and I moved to a small apartment owned by the school. For two years Murray taught courses in Sociology and Social Problems. Dorothy also taught some courses in English Composition and Church History. Our two-year-old son, Don, enjoyed playing with the children of other members of the staff. Murray continued to study part time at the University of Chicago, which was now much closer. It was an excellent learning experience for us and a valuable preparation for teaching at Garrett.

II

A NEW POST IN A FAMILIAR ENVIRONMENT

Great was our curiosity when, in January 1929, we received a letter from Frederick Carl Eiselen, who had been elected President of Garrett when Dr. Stuart retired. It was an invitation to have lunch with him at the Chicago City Club. His purpose we discovered was to invite Murray to join the faculty of Garrett. This proposal came as a complete and rather overwhelming surprise. It would involve taking over the work of Dr. Beck, our close friend and mentor, who had asked for early retirement. We told Dr. Eiselen that before accepting the invitation we would like to talk to Dr. Beck. This we did, and were assured by him that he hoped we would accept. Never from that day to this have we regretted the decision. Dr. Eiselen said that the invitation came from the Board of Trustees, on the unanimous recommendation of the faculty. He added that, if we should decline, their second choice was an urban minister from New York City. Subsequently that man was elected a bishop, and we were doubly sure we had made the right decision.

During the conversation Dr. Eiselen observed, somewhat sadly, "There is something about the students that troubles me. They view their ministry too casually. They are neither hot nor cold—just lukewarm." (That was in January 1929. The signs of impending economic collapse were already rising above the horizon, and we thought of the words to the church in Laodicia [Rev. 3:15-19].)

In the spring quarter of that year I taught my first course at Garrett: Urban Sociology. The students dealt gently with the new instructor, and asked me to speak at a student forum in May. This I did, selecting as my topic "The Coming Depression." The evidence to me was clear: farm income had been dropping catastrophically for much of the decade;[1] farm mortgages were being foreclosed by the thousands; International Harvester and other industrial companies selling to farmers were laying off employees; rural banks were being closed in increasing numbers. The one "bright spot" was the stock market, which was enthusiastically vaulting from one new high to another;

---

[1] Two rather extreme examples: the retail price for potatoes dropped from 6.3¢ per pound in 1920 to 3.2¢ in 1929; sugar from 19.4¢ to 6.4¢ per pound.

speculation was rife. The situation, I asserted, foretold that a depression was inevitable within a year or two. My rather naive reading of the signs of the times proved uncomfortably correct. The stock market crash occurred on "Black Friday," October 29, 1929.

The spring of 1929 was for us quite hectic. I was teaching full-time and Dorothy part-time at the Chicago Training School. My schedule also involved one evening a week at a University of Chicago seminar, as well as four round trips per week by "L" (we had no car) to Garrett to teach a three o'clock class. In addition, while Dorothy took care of our home and our small son, I tried to prepare for new courses which I would teach at Garrett in the summer quarter. We also continued our weekend work on the Near West Side, at St. Paul Methodist Church, but we were able to drop our responsibilities at the Boys' Court.

President Eiselen and his wife, knowing that our resources were quite limited, graciously invited us to live in their home that summer. She and their daughter Elizabeth planned to spend most of the summer at their lake cottage in Indiana. He was at home during the week and with them over the weekends. Living with him four days a week gave us an opportunity to catch up on Garrett happenings in the four-year interval since I had been graduated.

One sad (but amusing) occurrence during that time involved a rash of thefts from dormitory rooms and professors' offices. Typewriters, radios, and clothing had been stolen over the past year. Bicycles began to disappear, including the old reliable one belonging to Gus Freeburg, our Garrett maintenance man. The police were called in on several occasions, but could not solve the problem. The President decided that the only way to stop the depredations was to have all the locks in all the buildings changed.

There was a man in the student body, D.K., who was skilled in the use of tools and had done many repair jobs for the school. He was asked if he would undertake the project. Objects continued to disappear, even from rooms where locks had been changed. After Gus Freeburg lost his bicycle he asked K. if he could find a used bicycle which might replace it. K. obliged, and the next day showed up with one. Gus, giving it a trial run, said he liked the bike, but the seat wasn't comfortable. So K. brought him another seat, and Gus pronounced it perfect. It then occurred to the police that they should check K.'s apartment. (He and his wife lived off-campus.) There they discovered a dozen typewriters, and in K.'s storeroom many bicycles and parts. It turned out that for a year K., a confirmed kleptomaniac, had been accumulating the stolen items and hiding them in his apartment. He had not sold many of them. Subsequently Gus realized that he had bought back his own bike, repainted, but with a seat replacement. Later, K. had produced the original seat. No wonder that Gus found the reassembled bicycle comfortable!

The summer conversations with Dr. Eiselen helped us to get acquainted with him and to gain insights on an informal basis concerning teaching on a seminary faculty, as we started what proved to be forty-four years of residence in Evanston. Joining a faculty of scholars, many of whom had been my respected teachers and all of whom were my seniors in terms of years, was a little intimidating. Debates in curricular matters demonstrated that each of us was quite aware of the pre-eminence of his own teaching field. Dr. Hayes, on more than one occasion, remarked that in a theological seminary obviously the foundation for the whole curriculum had to be the Bible. And, since this was a Christian school, pre-eminence must be given to the New Testament. He did, of course, smile when he said it, but there was no doubt in his mind as to the validity of his comment. Dr. Fuller replied that there would have been no New Testament without the Old Testament, to which Dr. Rall would add that, while a thorough grounding in the Bible was necessary, a tenable Christian faith—which was essential in the world today—could only rest on the development of a rational theology. Others (professors of Preaching and Religious Education) were impressed with the fact that the local church is where the alumnus will have to carry forward his ministry. The novice whose field was Sociology of Religion and Urban Community Studies felt that it was wiser for him to stay out of these debates—at least for a time. Yet he was aware that these professional dividing lines did not disrupt the essential Christian amity of his colleagues and their common concern for the welfare of the students.

Toward the end of the spring quarter, the Garrett administration and faculty decided on a new venture in faculty evaluation. At the time of final examination in each course, the students were furnished with a sheet of paper, with a set of questions concerning the course that had just been completed, including teaching methods used, assignments, type of participation, the professor's mastery of his subject, and the student's own learning experience. The professor, at the time the exam was given, read aloud a brief statement, furnished by the administration, as to the purpose of the evaluation. He distributed the question sheets to the students, then gathered up the answers and put them into an envelope which he sealed in the presence of the students and turned in at the President's office. Naturally a new instructor at the end of his first course felt somewhat nervous about such an exercise. I was never informed by the administration as to how I "rated," but the grapevine indicated that I had passed.[2]

It was gratifying to have a good registration for each of the two courses that I offered in the summer quarter. Incidentally, some of the students enrolled in the spring and summer courses kept in touch with us over the years, and one of them, Merrill Abbey, thirty years later joined the faculty. He and his wife Lucy have been cherished friends of ours even until now.

It was not until the autumn that we fully appreciated the warm faculty fellowship into which we were privileged to enter. There seemed to be a genuine concern and respect for one another such as one might expect within a small Christian community. And this extended to the wives of the professors as well. We felt no condescension on the part of those who were our seniors. All of the professors were ministers. All had seminary degrees and most had had graduate professional training in their teaching fields. Nearly all of the faculty families lived within walking distance of the campus.

We soon learned that here was practiced the pleasant custom of Sunday afternoon calling. If the callers found no one at home they left their calling card—which put the next responsibility on the couple that received the card. Informal as the relationship was, it still was expected that "juniors" would not call the seniors by their first names until they were invited to do so. Sunday calling was an enjoyable way of getting to know one another in the congenial atmosphere of the home. Unfortunately it is now outmoded and in most homes the time seems to be occupied with watching TV.

When it was clear that we would be at Garrett for at least a period of years, naturally an important question for us was—"Where would we live?" Clearly we could not afford a house. Some kind person suggested that we get in touch with Thomas A. Stafford, the General Secretary of the Methodist Board of Pensions, who owned an apartment in a co-operative housing project at the corner of Simpson

---

[2] During my long years of teaching such a rating of professors was administered only once more. I felt that this might be an excellent procedure, perhaps once every four years, provided the President or some highly trusted senior member of the faculty talked over the results frankly with the teacher involved. This could prove quite valuable, especially to the younger members of the faculty and others whose minds were open to the learning process. I have been informed that such faculty evaluations are now conducted regularly.

and Sherman. Happily for us, when we called on him we found that a small one-bedroom apartment in the 18-unit co-op was for sale. After inspecting the apartment and making a careful audit of our resources, we determined that we could risk the purchase. Our memory is that we paid less than $4,000 for the equity. The monthly assessment on the apartment at that time was about $45, which did not cover telephone, electricity or gas. We lived in that apartment for seven years. Dr. Stafford continued to be a wise counselor and valued friend.

At first it seemed advisable to continue to work for my doctoral degree at the University of Chicago. However, even though the administration kindly assigned favorable teaching hours, it proved too much of a strain to go by "L" from Evanston to the South Side of Chicago to arrive for an 8:00 a.m. class and return in time to teach at Garrett at 11:00 each morning, with a second class from 2:00 to 4:00 on Monday and Wednesday afternoons. After two quarters of such commuting, in addition to preparing lectures for classes of alert students, I decided to transfer to the Sociology Department of Northwestern University. This proved a wise move. It saved a vast amount of commuting time and strain, and also permitted me to get well acquainted with the professors in the fields of Sociology and Anthropology at Northwestern. After I had completed my doctoral degree these men invited me to sit in on their thesis and other seminars—which I did, in limited measure.

A major benefit of living in Evanston was the privilege of joining First Methodist Church. Only rarely could we attend there when we were students, because we were on the staff of a church in Chicago. Now, however, we rejoiced in sitting under the seminal ministry of Ernest Fremont Tittle and, with our Don, participating in other aspects of that church's program. While people of all economic strata were in the church's fellowship, the general tone there (as in the Evanston Congregational, Presbyterian, and Episcopal churches) was that of a dignified "upper class" congregation. The ushers and collectors (all of them men) wore formal morning attire.

Illustrative of this general tone is a story told by Rosalie Farwell ('42). Belle James, who joined the Garrett-CTS staff in 1934, was a proper person, who wanted the girls to follow suit. Rosalie writes:

> When we first arrived, she told us that we were expected to attend "First Church." We did that but did not wear hats or gloves since it was still warm. She called us in and asked if we had hats and gloves, and said that if we did not and could not afford to buy them, she would help us to do so, but that we must wear hats and gloves to church.

Evanston was a pleasant as well as stimulating residential community. The area where we lived near the campus was particularly attractive. The three of us on many a Saturday had a picnic lunch on the beach. Or we would take the streetcar to the end of the line in northwest Evanston and hike out to the forest preserve. Our Don, small as he was, always enjoyed the exercise as well as the lunch at the destination point—an old railroad bridge. We sat on a couple of ties with our feet dangling over the stream, enjoying the spring or autumn foliage. After a tramp through the woods, we hiked back to the end of the car-line.

It was always enjoyable to walk along the streets in our part of town, particularly under the great arching elms along Orrington Avenue. Occasionally on Sunday afternoons we would catch a glimpse of family activities through big front-room windows, perhaps a group surrounding a piano, singing popular songs and hymns. Sometimes when it was raining we put on our rain gear and walked out to enjoy the wind and the storm at the lakefront.

Sundays in Evanston were different than in most cities of America. Until the mid-40's no stores except drug stores were permitted to be open in town. If one needed groceries one had to go to Howard Street at the north edge of Chicago. Also, no liquor could be sold in Evanston at any time. That was one of the stipulations when the University was chartered. Further, no movie theaters were open. However, a committee of distinguished citizens including a few prominent ministers arranged for occasional lectures, one or two a month, on Sunday afternoons at the Varsity Theater. Persons like James Breasted, Director of the Oriental Institute, and Lorado Taft, the noted sculptor, were invited to speak. There was no admission charge, but a collection was taken to cover expenses. We frequently attended. To live in Evanston, we felt, was a privilege.

However, Chicago with its amazing variety of problems and opportunities, was almost literally next door, and we maintained contact with its many facets, enjoying the Art Institute, the symphony and ballet, and also visiting often with our friends in settlement houses and the areas of underprivilege.

III

THE DEPRESSION
YEARS . . . YOU WON'T
BELIEVE IT!

A large proportion of Garrett students came from rural backgrounds—especially the great Midwestern farm belt, and were fully cognizant of the economic tragedy that had been engulfing farming communities for almost a decade. The families of several had lost their farms through mortgage foreclosure. Few of them could expect any parental financial assistance. Odd jobs were increasingly hard to find in Evanston. The collapse of the stock market did not directly affect the students or most of the faculty, but the psychological effect on us all was significant. More banks were failing (659 in 1929, 1,352 in 1930, and 2,294 in 1931). In those days bank failures created a sense of panic in the local community. There was no federal insurance to protect depositors, and few large banks—which had their own serious problems—were prepared to take over smaller ones.

Garrett, its faculty and students, were not catastrophically involved at the start. Bills were met and salaries paid, even though the Board of Trustees needed to borrow additionally from their bankers. However, the situation became increasingly ominous. Unemployment spread, the repeated assurances of government and business leaders that "prosperity is just around the corner," instead of bringing confidence, soon evoked derisive laughter. It is interesting that, even though the Department of Agriculture regularly gathered statistics on the number of hogs and cattle, and the Department of Labor tallied the number of persons employed in the civilian labor force, there were no official statistics as to the number of unemployed until about 1942. However, the Department of Labor estimated retroactively that while a million and a half were unemployed in 1929, the number rose rapidly to 12 million in 1932 and over 12.8 million in 1933, approximately one-third of the labor force.[1]

The Depression had become a painful reality and all of us felt it. The Evanston *News Index* reported numerous suicides of local men who had once been prosperous business leaders. More than one had a home on Orrington Avenue or in Wilmette.

Responding to a knock on the rear door of our apartment might disclose a man or woman who politely asked if we had some work to be done to earn a little money. Since our answer was necessarily, "No, thank you," there was occasionally a follow-up request: "I'm hungry. Could you let me have something to eat?" When a sandwich or two had been prepared, the person sometimes sat on the steps and ate it at once—or said, "I'll take these home and share them."

Even small children became aware of the atmosphere of worry and strain. Dr. Harvey DeBra was Director of Student Pastoral Activities at Garrett. He and Mrs. DeBra lived in the same building with us. Our son Don frequently visited them. Mrs. DeBra reported to us that one afternoon when he was in their apartment a delivery man brought some goods for which she paid. Later another man knocked and asked if she could give him and his family some help; she handed him a dime. Don exclaimed, "My, you and Dr. DeBra must be rich," to which she replied, "Yes, Donnie, we *are* rich. We have lots of good friends and enjoy good health, and Dr. DeBra and I have each other." To which, she said, Don answered, "Oh sure, we're rich *that* way too."

Inevitably the weakening national economy began to affect the churches and Garrett. There still was no tuition fee at the school, and only a small amount came in from the incidental fees. Most of the school's income was derived from endowment funds which had been invested in property in the Chicago "Loop." As the Depression worsened, many of the renters in these properties declared bankruptcy or moved away. The entire Garrett faculty salary budget, which had been a modest $72,350 for 1930-31, was first cut, then dropped to $44,512 by 1932. And much of that was not met.

Dark as the picture was for us all, those in leadership positions with higher salaries accepted the heaviest cuts—and did it without

---

[1] Two additional sets of data add vividness to the economic tragedy: Tables from the *Statistical Abstract of the United States* showed that the total value of all farmlands and buildings dropped from $30.7 billion in 1920 to $14.8 billion in 1935. This meant that farmers lost more than half the value of their property in those few years. And these values dropped faster than did the farm mortgage debt. The value of all bread grains produced in the US dropped from $1.7 billion in 1929 to $220 million in 1932.

publicizing the fact. All needed to make such economies as we could. (My class roll book for 1932-33 was made of old ledger sheets cut to size, which Dorothy sewed into a book, using heavy wrapping paper for a cover. I still have it! Standard roll books sold for ten cents.)

We decided to try our hand at a little redecorating of the dining area and sun porch in our apartment, which were badly in need of redoing. One morning when Murray was away, Dorothy set up the stepladder in the sun porch, whose large windows gave a clear view into the interior, and began to work, paying no attention to passersby. After an hour or so Mr. F., the President of our co-op, rang at our back door and informed Dorothy that the "walking delegate" of the painters' union had observed her activity and was threatening to stop all unionized services to the building (such as milk delivery and laundry pickup) unless the non-union decorating in our apartment ceased. Mr. F. was evidently able to persuade him that the owner of an apartment could not be prevented from using non-union labor (i.e., his own) to freshen up his own place, but Dorothy (who came from non-unionized Southern California) was indignant.

Accustomed to reading the signs of the times, I had remarked to a colleague on the faculty that almost certainly Garrett would be forced to let some of us go, and added that he and I—the new members on the faculty—would probably be among those who would be dropped. I was amazed to find that such an idea had never occurred to him.

I was scheduled to be "off" in the spring of 1932.[2] So in early March before we were to leave for California, I asked if I could visit President Eiselen at the hospital, where he was slowly recovering from a series of operations. He invited me to come. I frankly said to him I guessed that Garrett's financial situation would force the cutting of the faculty. If that was the case I would appreciate knowing, since we were leaving for the west coast and if I were not to be retained at Garrett it would be wise for me to ask Bishop James C. Baker if he would appoint me to a church in my annual conference (Southern California).

It was evident that the situation at Garrett was more painful for Eiselen than his physical condition. He informed me that some professors would indeed have to be dropped but that I was not one of them. Then he confided to me that he had requested his secretary to come to his hospital room to take dictation, including the notices to go to faculty men who would have to be dropped, and she had refused to

---

[2] The accepted pattern was for each professor to teach three quarters each year, with the fourth quarter free for study, travel, or vacation. Naturally, juniors like myself tended to be given the spring quarter off (the pleasantest season in Evanston).

take the dictation! For a man as sensitive to the hurts of others as he was, this was another traumatic experience.

Dr. Fuller and Dr. Rall, two senior colleagues, were on the committee that had to make the difficult decisions. Unknown to each other, Dr. Rall invited us to his home the evening before we were to leave for the west, and Dr. Fuller invited us for breakfast the following morning. Each told us the same story—the great difficulties they faced but the compelling necessity of the committee decision.

With this distressing news ringing in our ears we headed south and west, and soon were in a heavy snow-storm—literally as well as figuratively. We were sadly aware of the consternation and shock of our colleagues when they would receive those letters—for we knew that most did not recognize the necessity for some such action. Incidentally, we discovered later that several of them felt that I must have had a hand in the action—because I had talked about the inevitability of matching the budget to the reality. To meet part of the sharp retrenchment, five faculty members were notified that they would be dropped at the end of the next quarter. (The ones who remained almost envied them because those departing at least received their full back salary, plus three months' quit-pay.) In addition to the five, one man retired; two others accepted openings immediately available elsewhere.

While he was still in the hospital Dr. Eiselen resigned. In May of 1932, at the urging of the Board of Trustees, Horace Greeley Smith accepted the presidency. He had been serving as pastor of the Wilmette Methodist Church, which had recently erected a beautiful new sanctuary under his leadership. This he gave up in June 1932, with its assured salary, to try to steer Garrett out of the deep morass in which it found itself.

He conducted the first chapel service of the summer quarter after his election. There was much anxiety and bitterness among students and others over the dismissals and the precariousness of the future. He briefly and forthrightly described the financial plight of the school and the uncertainties that lay ahead. Then he spoke words of faith and assurance, and before the benediction requested that all remain seated until he and Mrs. Smith could reach the door, because they wanted the privilege of greeting and shaking the hand of each person in attendance. A memorable service and a brave beginning.

That autumn the faculty carried forward the revamping of the curriculum—a perennial faculty activity!

Perhaps it was the sense of urgency of our total situation that pushed us to agree on the three-group system, which was summed up in the catalog of 1933-34 in three sentences:

1. Christianity is a great historic movement (Bible and History)
2. Christianity is a faith, a conviction, an interpretation of God and the world, of people and life (Theology, Philosophy, Social Ethics)
3. The Christian religion is a way of life (Preaching, Church Administration, Religious Education, etc.)

Under these three rubrics all the courses were grouped; some were reorganized. Dr. Rall was the chief craftsman of the new structure.

Overriding curricular matters was a feeling of economic urgency. It was amazing that during this period of financial pressure and faculty and staff insecurity Horace Smith was able to maintain (at least outwardly) a calm and confident manner. Pressures on him were acute. At the first faculty meeting in the summer of 1932 Dr. Smith told us that there might not be any salary checks for the next two months but he hoped that beginning in the autumn it would be possible for Garrett to pay its personnel regularly, although at a reduced level. This was indeed good news, for we had been receiving less than half our reduced salary, and checks had come irregularly. Beginning with October 1932 all on the faculty, the President included, received the same stipend—$225 per month. The following June we all received a $25 per month raise, to $3,000 a year—and were grateful.

The administration (i.e., Horace Greeley Smith) cut expenses in every direction. The main building usually was locked, except to those of us who had a key, on Saturday and Sunday. During the week the library, as I recall, was closed at 8:00 p.m., to save electricity and staff time. Smaller wattage light bulbs were used wherever possible. The third floor of the main building, where my office had been from 1929 to October 1932, was vacated, with all radiators turned off and the windows sealed as well as possible against the coming winter cold; the stair doors at the north end of the hall were fastened shut.

I was reluctant to have my office—the only one remaining on the third floor—moved downstairs, because it had become almost a second home for us. We spent several evenings a week there, working on research projects, Dorothy typing and I studying. Our Don liked the "spookiness" of it, and enjoyed drawing on the blackboard or reading his books. We usually planned on quitting by 10:00. Long before then all the building lights had been switched off. It was then as, holding hands, we slowly groped our way to the head of the stairs and carefully descended, that we really sensed the mystery and wonder of our old monastic home, rejoicing (but with care) in the beauty and awesomeness of the arches and the impressive front hall. Yet it was always good to step out into the fresh air and lock the doors behind us.

Dr. Smith continued to urge economies on us all. Al Eliason, entering Garrett in the autumn of 1948, remembers his "welcoming the new class with a subtle nudge: 'I once appealed to students to turn off the lights, but I discovered it was easier to go forth and raise additional funds!' which made me feel so sorry for the aging-but-active Smith that I became a missionary for turning off the lights."

During the Depression years there were three persons on the secretarial staff: the secretary to the President, the secretary to the registrar, and the secretary to the editors of the publications. The positions of registrar and librarian were filled by faculty members who had supervisory responsibility. Mabel Gardiner, with the title of assistant librarian, was the only full-time person on the library staff.

Faculty as Fund Raisers!

In the autumn of 1932 President Smith suggested to the faculty that some of us might try our hand at raising money to help meet the school budget. There had, up to then, been no direct solicitation of support from alumni, so several of us volunteered. It was not a strong forte of any of us. One pair of faculty men rang the doorbell of a prospect in Evanston and the senior of the two was so flustered that he burst out, "We are Mr. and Mrs. X. We've come to talk to you about Garrett." Then, realizing his mistake, he quickly corrected himself, but after that was in no condition to make a good "sales pitch."

Nenien McPherson and I teamed up, seeking to raise funds for "the old school." Nenien was Assistant Professor of Theology, an alert go-getter Southerner, short of stature and trim. We would leave early on Monday morning, drive out perhaps a hundred miles, and make several calls on alumni pastors en route back home for afternoon classes. The effort was to elicit contributions from them or their churches. We tried, but found that the alumni were having the same kind of problem raising the money for their own salaries.

Far more helpful than the rest of the faculty in this matter was Harris Franklin Rall, whose longtime friendship with Mrs. Henry Pfeiffer resulted in her giving $250,000 to apply against the school's gargantuan indebtedness.

The one successful call I made in Evanston was not on an alumnus but on Mrs. John Morava, who gave me a check for $100 for the school. After expressing real gratitude, I remarked that it would take much more than that from lay persons who could afford it—and regularly—if Garrett was to keep functioning and young men were to be trained for our future ministry. Months later she phoned and invited me to come to tea. Perhaps she "might be able to give a modest amount each year." It was a delightful occasion for me. I suggested that perhaps she could give $500 as a fellowship in memory of her husband, John Morava. This she did for several years, writing a check each year. It was not until 1938 that the John H. Morava Fellowship was announced in the catalog, because she had not been entirely confident of her own finances. Later she endowed the fellowship, and their son, John H. Morava III, subsequently added generously to that endowment and also served for many years on the Garrett Board of Trustees.

An Innovation: The Five-Week Summer Term

With a smaller faculty it was deemed essential for all of us to teach in each of the three heavy-enrollment quarters—autumn, winter, and spring. There was considerable debate as to whether Garrett could offer any summer program. The issue was resolved by organizing a five-week summer session, with the explicit understanding that it had to be self-supporting. Nenien McPherson was Registrar in 1933, and I was named Director in 1934. We had one visiting professor who, of course, had to be paid. The other six of us agreed to teach, with the understanding that each would receive $200 for the five-week term, provided that the incidental fees[3] would cover that. Fortunately they did, with a very small amount left over to meet other expenses.

That was the beginning of the Garrett Summer Term program, which soon became a popular institution. It was publicized as an opportunity for full-time pastors to come back for refresher courses. The term was short enough so that they could attend during their vacation, and the curriculum was enriched by bringing in an increasing number of visiting professors to join the summer faculty.

In 1939 an Interdenominational School for Rural Pastors was also initiated; it ran concurrently with the Summer Term, bringing the total summer faculty that year to 15, of whom six were Garrett professors. In some courses two teachers collaborated. One such was titled "The Pastor Preacher" and was taught by Charles R. Goff and Ernest Fremont Tittle. Years later Carl Keightley ('46), now retired and living in Texas, wrote:

> I used to say that reading the summer school schedule was like
> reading a Sears Roebuck catalog. You wished you could take

---

[3] The special bulletin read: "Garrett charges no tuition. The *total* incidental fees for the summer school are: Outside of dorm, one major, $7.50, two majors $11.25. In the dormitory, two majors or less, $22.50.

everything. They had such good teachers and such interesting courses. If I skipped a quarter, it was never the summer.

One of the most interesting courses that I took was on preaching, taught one-half by Charles Goff and one-half by Ernest Fremont Tittle. Those were real contrasts; each had a contribution to make. Tittle told us that illustrations were substitutes for thinking. Charlie Goff told us to use illustrations. Once Goff could not come, and sent George Crane to substitute. He told us how to be successful preachers. He told about a preacher who was having a hard time, needing to move all the time, and was ready to give up. And he [Crane] said: "I'll tell you what you do. Use the narrative method. Illustrations are like a string of beads. A little exposition and another illustration. In every section of your sermon, rise to a peroration; name three persons out of your congregation every Sunday. He went home and did that, and the next year they were asking for him back. You don't have to say anything that isn't true. You just say, 'I walked by Mrs. Jones' house and saw her beautiful irises.'" Well, you know, that does help.

A number of special events were planned for the enjoyment of those attending the summer term. We had a reception for faculty and students on the first afternoon. The evening before, there was a social occasion, perhaps a buffet supper at our home, for the summer faculty and their spouses, to provide an opportunity to get acquainted. Two or three special lectures and a couple of field trips were usual features of the five-week period. We rented three or four buses to carry the people on those trips, and visited various points of interest in and near Chicago. There was also an outdoor picnic for everybody, with plenty of food and outdoor games to suit all ages.

Dr. Kraft's son Robert recently told us how he and his sister enjoyed the Garrett summer school picnics. "Sometimes there was entertainment. I remember Jim Whitehurst with his line of magician's tricks . . . Dad also on some of those occasions would give a little of his humorous stuff, like "Three Blind Mice, from the Old Testament Perspective."

The Art of Living in Tough Times

Financially pressed as were the faculty, the students were hit even harder by the Depression. Virgil Kraft ('35, MA '41) recounts an amusing story:

It was a cold, lonely Thanksgiving day in Evanston in 1933. As a Garrett student, I was ambitious, idealistic, but hungry and a bit disillusioned—a victim of the Depression. Actually I was the son of a Methodist minister whose mostly unschooled parishioners believed that a tenth of their income was too small to give to the church, so they were giving a twentieth.

A few other students and I could not afford a trip home. Several faculty members heard of our plight and, ignoring their own shortages, began inviting us to their homes. Dr. Frank McKibben asked me if I would like to join their family for a dinner at 11:30. I accepted. Dorothy and Murray Leiffer invited me to another dinner. Fortunately this one was at 4:00. I accepted. Dr. Horace Greeley Smith and his wife asked me to share their Thanksgiving dinner at 8:00. I accepted.

Never since that day have I been so full of good food, and never have I lost my thankfulness for what that day illustrated—Garrett's grand benevolence and humanitarian spirit!

It was on "an otherwise dreary Sunday afternoon," recalls Julian Hartt ('37), "that we met on appointment." Julian was looking over the main building when I greeted him and asked if he was planning to enter Garrett. "Well, no," he responded. "I'd like to, but I can't afford it. I'm hard up." To which I replied: "We're all hard up here. Come on in and join us." And that is what he did, graduating with honors three years later. After securing a doctorate he was invited to join the faculty at Yale Divinity School, where he taught with distinction for many years. We had forgotten all about the incident until in 1983 he was invited back to receive an honorary degree from our school, and told the audience this story.

There were hardships aplenty in the 1930's. Understandably, toward the end of the decade people longed for assurance. Church folks were glad to hear sermons that brought solace and comfort and avoided the controversial. A number of members of First Church, Evanston, transferred their loyalty to other local churches because they were unhappy that Ernest Tittle "kept harping" on such subjects as economic justice and social righteousness.

Alumnus Howard Carey ('37) recalls in detail a relevant question raised in one of Dr. Rall's classes and Frank Rall's indirect answer to the common desire to avoid controversial subjects. The professor was setting forth some position which a member of the class questioned: "But, Dr. Rall, isn't that a dangerous position to take?" Dr. Rall paused, cocked his head as he was wont to do, stroked that special Van Dyke beard, then replied: "Well, you know, I have found that LIFE is dangerous." He then recounted the following story:

Deacon Jones of Central Church in Central City died and went to heaven's gate. St. Peter met him and inquired: "What can we do for you?"

"Well, you know who I am?"

"Yes, you are Deacon Jones from Central Church in Central City. What can we do for you?"

"Well, I think I deserve something as comfortable as I had on earth."

"All right, come with me." Peter led him down many twisting paths and finally turned in to a pleasant house on a pleasant street, and showed the deacon all around. The deacon explored the library, the art work, and everything. Then he said:

"This is very nice. I think I will be very comfortable here."

"Now is there anything else we can do for you?"

"No, I don't think of a thing. I believe I will be perfectly comfortable here."

Peter left, but came back after a thousand years to inquire: "How are things going, Deacon Jones?"

"Just fine, just fine."

"Now is there anything else we can do for you?"

"No, I am perfectly comfortable here."

At the end of another thousand years Peter came back, with the same results. But at the end of the third thousand years, when Peter made inquiry, the deacon replied: "Well, you know, things are getting a little monotonous; I never thought heaven would be that way."

"Heaven? Oh, this isn't heaven."

"Well, what is this anyway?"

"This is hell."

"HELL—How could you do this to me?"

"Didn't we give you just what you asked for?"

"Well . . . yes, I guess you did."

Startled, the deacon asked: "WELL, where is heaven then?"

Peter took him on a long journey, where they could look off across a vista and see people praising God. The deacon looked and looked. Finally he asked: "Near the back there, isn't that the janitor of our church?"

"Yes, it is."

"Isn't that a vacant seat just behind him?"

"Yes, that's right."

"Do you suppose I could have that seat?"

<>

Some of us, realizing that the students—especially those who stayed in town over the weekend—were both lonely and impecunious, also invited a few at a time to our homes for a meal or a social evening with refreshments. Dorothy enjoyed entertaining as well as cooking and baking, and had developed the fine art of making a little go a long way. We also delighted in listening to semi-classical and classical music on our record player. So at one time we initiated a series of "musical Friday nights," inviting any who wished to come and join us, sitting quietly listening to music. We boned up ahead of time on the composers and simple interpretations of the music, which we shared with the students. We often asked the young men and women to name the composer they would like to listen to. One replied that he "liked any composer, provided it was Mozart."

It was surprising how much milk, cocoa and cookies they were able to consume; yet we were aware that some of them had probably eaten no supper. In our early days at Garrett, the favorite drinks were cold milk or hot cocoa—accompanied by substantial sandwiches or large squares of gingerbread—perhaps reflecting rural background as much as appetite. Twenty years later those beverages were "out," and students preferred coffee or tea, accompanied by less nourishing snacks. Always there was a good market for Dorothy's cookies, especially brownies.

Nearly all members of the faculty lived within easy walking distance of the school, at least until the mid '50's. This of course made it much easier (and less expensive) for students to visit us in our homes, since half of them did not own cars.

More important than food was the fellowship which both students and faculty found heartwarming. We have been amazed at the comments made years later by alumni concerning their enjoyment at being in faculty homes. One alumnus, Ed Fuller ('38), now retired, recently wrote:

> Some of us from back in the late 1930's remember with great
> feelings of nostalgia the evenings when we fellowshipped and had
> creative games in the apartments of Dr. and Mrs. Harris Franklin
> Rall and of the Leiffers. It was in these informal hours that we
> learned much to enrich our theological and sociological outlook
> as we saw teachers live consistently with all they taught, showing
> care, which is often lost in professionalism and pride.

The faculty was aware that many if not most of the students lived
under financial stress even greater than their own. Students commonly
had difficulty paying the very modest school fees. Ministers' salaries,
as well as parishioners' incomes, were drastically cut. One student told
us of his experience. He served a two-point charge in Indiana. His
small salary, like those of others, was not fully paid, and his wife
seriously needed dental care, but they could not afford it. A member
of his church, a farmer, suggested an interesting barter arrangement.
He told the student pastor, "We can't pay our church pledge because
we just do not have the money. But the dentist in town owes us for milk
we have been supplying him for the last two months. How would it be if
the dentist would care for Sally's teeth, you give us credit on our
church pledge, and we will mark his milk bill paid?" And so it was
agreed.

A member of the faculty suggested that a barter arrangement might
be worked out involving Garrett. Possibly students could bring in farm
produce and get credit for it on their fees, and faculty could accept it as
part of their salary. There was general concurrence, so he distributed
slips of paper, asking if there were some farm produce which faculty
members could use. I well recall the hilarity when he was handed a slip
from Will Schermerhorn which read, "One load of good manure. I
need it for my front lawn." That particular request was not met, but for
a time quite a few eggs, dried corn, and some vegetables filtered in.
The idea was not an overwhelming success.

Christian commitment showed up in many ways in those dire days.
One of my advisees, Sidney Dillinger, completed his Garrett work in
1938. He had been serving a student charge in Illinois at a salary of
$700 a year. His people said if he would stay on a full-time basis after
graduation, they would try to raise the salary to $1,000. But Sidney
said to me, "As you know, I grew up in western Kansas. Now it's a dust
bowl. The DS wants us back to serve a two-point charge at $800 a year.
So we're going back." He, his wife, and their new baby returned to the
dust bowl. Years later he told me that the people of his churches were
unable to raise the full $800 for either of the next two years, but he and

his family did not have an empty larder. They grew some vegetables and their members kept them supplied with flour and meat.

Richard Miller ('39, MA '49), who was in Dr. Nagler's class, recalls the following poignant story:

> Church history is of interest to me, but my major interest in the subject was the professor who taught it. His last-minute announcement yesterday had attracted much attention: "No assignment for tomorrow—you won't even need to prepare to take notes—just be on time, please." And we were, all eighteen of us.

> The room looked unlike its usual self. The desk at the front was covered with a tablecloth which apparently concealed several objects. On the walls were a dozen or more paintings by Professor Nagler and he sat playing the foot-pedalled organ. He played quite well.

> We distributed ourselves in our usual places and when he had finished his musical selection he turned and greeted us: "Why don't we, on this occasion, sing a few hymns? Hymns say a great deal about church history. Who has a favorite hymn?" We suggested and he played, some from memory, some from the hymnal. We all sang. He was so relaxed and the room so free of tension, I felt good about being there.

> After the hymns Dr. Nagler said, "I've taken this hour today to do several things. We have sung hymns that remind us of our faith and its roots. I want you to see some of my paintings. I'm not a great artist, and I know it, but I enjoy painting. It is a way to appreciate the beautiful and to share it with others." He explained his understanding of the beauty he had captured for us to share. It was evident to us all that he wanted us, too, to see the creation about us and appreciate God's gifts we perceive with our eyes.

> He then lifted the cloth from the desk to disclose several dishes of candy and cookies he had made. He invited us to help ourselves and then to sit down and eat the candy while he told us of a matter he wanted to explain.

> He said, "Tomorrow the newspaper will carry the announcement that I have lost my home in Evanston. The bank is foreclosing the mortgage which I cannot continue to pay. This foreclosure is not uncommon in these days. [It was in the early 1930's.] We have several obligations that, to us, are more pressing than the payments on our house. We will rent another house. Incidentally, the bank must give us continued occupancy for over a year beyond the date of foreclosure because of the equity we have in

the property. I want you men to know all is not lost when you lose some material wealth. I can still enjoy music, paint pictures and make candy for my friends—yes—and possibly write a little more and teach."

I don't recall more of that day except for the fact that I had a higher regard for the church in history that had so affected this man as to give him such balance in an unbalancing experience.

The Chicago Training School Joins Us

Under the pressure of economic necessity long-delayed changes are sometimes precipitated. When President Eiselen talked with us in the winter of 1929 about coming to Garrett, he mentioned the possibility of the Chicago Training School being transferred to the Garrett campus in Evanston, and remarked that our moving to Garrett after our having been on the CTS faculty for a couple of years might help bring this about. However, it was not until March of 1934 that the discussion stopped and the Chicago Training School did merge with Garrett, bringing its entire educational enterprise from the South Side of Chicago to Evanston. With this action, Dr. L. F. W. Lesemann, who had been President of CTS for 16 years, became Professor of Practical Theology at Garrett, and three faithful women who had been on the CTS staff for many years assumed similar positions in the new Garrett-CTS program. Esther Bjornberg was added to the teaching staff and became Instructor in Social Service and Field Work. Belle L. James became hostess of Dorm D, later renamed Lesemann Hall, and general counselor to the women students. (Most CTS students had been women.) Gladys Lummis, a gracious, devoted and hard working alumna of CTS, had responsibility in the Registrar's Office, including maintaining the alumnae files. Seldom has there been a school with a more loyal alumni/ae clientele. Each of the four was able to make substantial contributions to Garrett-CTS.

An alumnus of both CTS and Garrett, Oscar E. Link ('40) tells in charming detail his first impression and growing appreciation of L. F. W. Lesemann:

He was one of the first men I met at CTS in 1928. To me he was a very impressive person. His body looked so round, firm, and fully packed. He was always dressed very neatly and well-groomed. His white hair and rimless glasses gave a special touch to his mature looks. . . .

In the late 20's, his (first) wife was in poor health and each year was getting weaker, requiring more care as time went on. Dr.

Lesemann took care of her with tenderness and gentle concern. One Sunday morning he preached in our church. Driving back to school, after the service, I asked him how he was able to carry on day after day with his work and caring for his wife. His answer was a simple statement, "One does what he has to do." That seemed to be a typical attitude of the man.

The late 20's and early 30's were the time of the Depression, but Dr. Lesemann . . . managed to pinch and squeeze wherever he could to save a few dollars to keep the school going. (He was) a man of strong character and determination.

He was an individual who could pray under almost any circumstance. At the end of a school party, the beginning of a class, an athletic event, a birthday or patriotic celebration, in the presence of a crisis, he could find the right words to express the significance of the occasion.

One had the feeling at CTS that he was the one who kept everyone in line . . . He had a way of coming directly and quickly to the problem. He wanted to be fair and really worked at it. He had a way of instilling hope, courage and faith in us. He could be tough at times and very understanding on other occasions. . . .

Some of Dr. Lesemann's friends were disappointed when he left the pastorate to become President of CTS. One observed, "You are burying yourself." The school was his mission in life. He endeavored to keep the founder's spirit alive, set goals for our lives, gave direction to our ministry and a faith to live by.

Belle James, white-haired, always carefully attired, having a cheerful, alert visage, a calm and mild expression—was nobody's pushover. The women soon learned that Belle James knew about their problems even before they confided in her. She was a sensible, practical person, not easily embarrassed. One morning in 1928 she entered the CTS chapel after the service had started. It was her birthday and, unknown to her, the person who was presiding was expressing the students' appreciation of "our dear Belle James," with an enumeration of some of her virtues. When Miss James entered the rear door she tried to hear what was being said and, not being able to, called out in her strong voice, "Say it again and speak up louder! We can't hear back here." A ripple of laughter greeted her before the speaker could repeat.

The following wonderful character vignette from Rocky Smith tells a great deal about Belle James—also a little about the wearer of "bow ties on Tuesdays"!

During the war years in one of our summer sessions a young woman in Lesemann Hall suffered a psychotic episode. She became quite unable to take care of herself and it was necessary to arrange for her return to her parents' home in the east. Under wartime conditions the only transportation available for such a journey was the railroad, but she obviously was quite unable to make what was an overnight trip alone. While several of us were considering alternatives Belle James, then an old woman, said, "I'll go." And that settled it. No amount of argument to the effect that the journey and care were too much for her would shift her purpose: she was going. We did manage to get a Pullman bedroom . . . and off Belle went with her charge.

Before she left I elicited . . . a promise that she would inform me as to the time of her arrival back in Chicago so that I could bring her back to Lesemann from the Loop. She argued that she could readily return on the "L," that gasoline was rationed, that I couldn't afford the trip, that I was busy and she couldn't trespass on the time of so busy a man, but she finally agreed to let me know so that I could meet her. I received a telegram on Saturday, saying that she would arrive at the Central Station on Sunday morning and giving me the train number and time of arrival. I was there at the gates waiting for her when the train roared in. A stream of passengers came at me: service men on furlough home, travel-weary young wives returning from a goodbye to their soldier husbands at the east coast piers, business men returning from a trip east—a stream of persons seeking to be out of the train and home again!

In that mass of hot and tired travellers I could not see Belle; but her quick eyes saw me and she called out "Rocky." No wonder I had missed her. In one hand she was carrying her small suitcase, the other was holding fast to the hand of an obviously handicapped boy. Close behind her was a travel-stained young woman carrying a small infant. "Here, Rocky," Belle called out, "Hold on to this boy. He's feeble-minded and walks off if someone doesn't hold him, but he's a good boy. His sister is taking him home with her because there's no one else to care for him now." And with those instructions Belle left me holding the hand of the feeble-minded boy in the middle of the reception hall of Central Station while she helped the young mother secure a porter, and collect her luggage. I suspect that many of those who saw us there were not at all sure as to which was feeble-minded.

When Belle saw that her party was all assembled, she led us to the taxi stand, the amazed porter, stack of luggage, mother and baby, and the two of us so authoritatively and efficiently joined following our marshal. There Belle ordered the policeman on duty to secure a cab immediately, which he did, she gave the cab driver the address to which the young mother was going, asked him if he knew where it was, and instructed him in the best and most economical way of getting there. Under her supervision the little family and their possessions were loaded into the cab, farewells and "God-bless-you's" were said, and the cab rolled off, whereupon Belle thanked the policeman for his help, turned to me, and said: "Now, Rocky, you can take me home." It was Belle at her Christian best.

When she retired from Garrett, faculty and students organized a dinner in her honor. After the President of the school had made a somewhat lengthy statement praising her contributions she arose and, a little overwhelmed, replied, "I know I deserve the kind words you have said, but I certainly don't appreciate them." And we were never quite sure whether Belle James had committed a malapropism or was intending to be cute!

Gladys Lummis was a petite woman, always attractively dressed even though she lived on a deaconess' salary. She was a quiet, unpretentious woman of faith. For her, God was always in control of her life. During her last ten years at Garrett and also in retirement at Brooks-Howell Deaconess Home, she suffered acutely from arthritis—but without complaint.

Esther Bjornberg was an alert, serious-minded person who had a Master's degree in social work from the University of Chicago. For a number of years she gave cheerful assistance in the lab of our Bureau of Social and Religious Research. She was a generous and determined "liberal," an active member of the Methodist Federation for Social Service, and also a charming hostess in her home with her sister, both of whom were proud of their Swedish heritage.

Dr. Lesemann's leadership of the Chicago Training School, with the status as President of an educational institution, had brought him considerable satisfaction, even though it was essentially of a junior college rank. To accept a subordinate position at Garrett did require a measure of grace. But he was a genial, open-hearted spirit and a faithful, unswerving servant of the Church. In many respects he was similar to Horace Smith. The two men were close friends, and they worked together harmoniously. I had good reason to be grateful for his presence on the Garrett faculty when, in October of 1934, I had to be hospitalized with a serious duodenal ulcer, which had been causing increasing trouble for several years, and I was forced to cut down on some of my workload. He assumed full responsibility for supervising the approximately ninety student pastorates—a job I had carried for two years along with my regular teaching schedule.

Something of Dr. Lesemann's Christian spirit is revealed in a story told by Richard Miller, an alumnus and later a member of the faculty (1946-57). It was 1935. Dick was married and had a small child. With hesitancy he decided to make the venture, bringing his family from Nebraska and starting seminary training at Garrett. He arrived at the Rock River Annual Conference with his family, where he met for the first time Dr. L.F.W. Lesemann who was in charge of student pastoral work at Garrett.

Dr. Lesemann was a total stranger to me. But when we arrived in our broken-down Chevrolet, with a very sick little boy who had contracted something on the trip, we of course had no money or, to be accurate, had $10 to our name, no place to stay and the weekend before us. And the Conference would appoint us to the church on the following Tuesday. I happened upon Dr. Lesemann, told him who I was, and told him of our predicament, asked him if he could tell us a place where we could stay—we would be able to pay for it later.

"Why," he said, "of course. You're going to stay with us." And to my great amazement and joy, he took the three of us to his home, introduced us to Mrs. Lesemann, who immediately fell in love with our son, Dickie. And we had a very pleasant two or three days with these good people. They treated us like their own children. This was my first learning experience at Garrett, and it was a good one.

IV

A CHANGING FACULTY
(TO 1945)

Change is an inevitable ingredient of life. Surely Heraclitus was not the first to announce that "all things flow, nothing abides. . . . You cannot step twice into the same river. . . ." Yet, fortunately, although it too undergoes changes, a well-established institution may survive and transcend the individuals whose life and work at the moment seem all important. If one lives long enough—and can keep reasonably clear-headed—one can perceive continuity through changes and, benefitting by even his own limited tenure on life, may achieve a degree of perspective.

We on the Garrett faculty in the 1930's, if we were to survive, had to look forward to the future as well as be reconciled with the past. Following the loss of a total of eight professors in 1932, Doremus A. Hayes, who had joined the faculty in 1896, retired in June of 1933. Ernest Burch, Professor of New Testament, died of cancer that same autumn. Leslie Fuller, probably the most popular and controversial member of the faculty, died in the summer of 1936. He had gone with his two teen-age sons and two friends of theirs on an eight-week canoe and camping trip in the Canadian Northwest Territory and into Alaska. He had said to me before they left that he felt he would not make it back—and he did not. His death was a great shock to us all. Will Schermerhorn, another stalwart, was forced by a heart attack to retire in 1939. That left only four persons on the faculty (Nagler, Rall, Hollington, Whitchurch) who had been teaching when I arrived ten years earlier.

New members, of course, had gradually been added. First, and of primary importance, was Horace Greeley Smith, who had previously taught an occasional course in Preaching prior to becoming President in 1932. In spite of his administrative load he also did some teaching after that date. Otto Justice Baab joined us in 1934, in the field of Old Testament. Dr. Lesemann moved north with the Chicago Training School in 1934 as Professor of Practical Theology, alias Church Administration. Paul S. Minear arrived in 1935 to teach New Testament Interpretation. Edmund Soper in History of Religions in

56

1938, and Georgia Harkness in Applied Theology in 1939, completed the roster for that decade. These persons presented a great variety in terms of personality; however, they were united in their deep Christian commitment and genuine appreciation of the importance of the pastoral ministry. So, even though the composition of the faculty was changing, there was a continuity of the rich fellowship and the sense of common purpose in the faculty as a whole. But first, a few additional comments about those who left us.

<>

Doremus Hayes was a fascinating personality—austere and peppery, quickly aroused by criticism of either his scholarship or his methods of teaching. Nevertheless, he was a firm supporter of peace, even if he had to fight for it! In one of his chapel addresses which I clearly remember, he chose a text from the Sermon on the Mount, Mt. 5:9, and translated it: "Blessed are the pacifists, the peace-seekers, for they shall be called the children of God." He insisted that peace-making is what the Gospel is all about. This interpretation received warm support from students and faculty in the 1920's and 1930's, but it was also the view which Hayes had maintained throughout the First World War. In fact, he told me that strong pressure had been brought on the Garrett administration in 1917-19 to have him dismissed from the faculty because he was "unpatriotic" and should not be permitted to teach his views to young ministers. He confided that those exerting the most pressure were two Methodist ministers who were operating a "diploma mill" (i.e., selling academic degrees) at the time. Hayes was proud of the protection given him by President Charles M. Stuart, and others on the faculty, even though some of them did not agree with his interpretation of the Sermon on the Mount.

Hayes was well acquainted with Edgar Goodspeed, who taught New Testament at the University of Chicago, but forthrightly objected to the latter's translation of the New Testament. In writing a review of it for the *Christian Advocate*, Hayes protested that Goodspeed had "put pants on the Apostles." Goodspeed was furnished a copy of the proof to read before printing. Goodspeed responded that the comment was cute and appropriate, but he would appreciate it if the editor (T. Otto Nall) would delete the expression, since his mother had just died. With a silent smile, Otto obliged.

<>

Ernest Ward Burch rarely thrust himself forward or initiated a conversation. He was a quiet, introverted sort of man, with a strong scholarly bent. His doctorate, as I recall, was from Yale. In a little book that he always carried in his pocket, he kept his own record of the happenings in faculty meetings. Actually, we depended informally on his memoranda. Our procedures under Dr. Smith were rather casual, and no file of official faculty minutes was kept. On one occasion, not directly related to the faculty, the President remarked to me, "Better to *say* it than to write it, for then it will not haunt you."

Harriet, Ernest's wife, was a "Yankee" and proud of it. She kept the family financial records and supervised Ernest—for his own good. They had no children. One day, after he and I had been talking in the hall near his office at Garrett, he pushed back his door and beckoned me to come in and take a chair. Then, sitting in front of his desk and casting a glance to see that no one else was in the hall, he opened a drawer and pulled out a box of chocolates. "Take one, Murray. Sometimes I feel the need of a bit of refreshment. Harriet doesn't know that I have them!"

His students remember him as always being well prepared, thoroughly conversant with his field. His lectures were gems of art and timed precisely to fit the fifty-minute periods. Four decades later, one of his students wrote, "Burch helped me achieve a clear, coherent understanding of the life of Christ." A high compliment indeed.

For some reason the Burches seemed to feel particularly warm toward us; after Ernest's death Harriet came to look on Dorothy practically as a daughter. We helped her get established at a nice retirement home, and Dorothy spent an afternoon with her almost every week. She lived to be a hundred and two years old. One other story about them goes back to 1933.

That autumn a student fell ill with a high fever and skin eruption. He was taken to the Evanston Hospital and the doctor concluded, "It may be a case of smallpox." The Evanston Health Department immediately went into action. The next day it set up a small clinic in Room 205. Everyone in the student body, faculty, staff, wives and children, and others who might have had contact with the sick man were to be vaccinated at once. A complete list of all of us was furnished to the Health Department, and as we went along the line, names were checked off. Ernest Burch had reported the situation to his wife and asked her to go with him the next day for vaccination. She, with New England vigor, insisted she would not go. Ernest, a mild-mannered man, phoned this fact of life to the Health Department. He was told that if his wife promised not to leave their house and would have no contact with anyone but himself for two weeks, she would be excused. Twelve days later Harriet commented, "Just another two days and I'll be a free woman, able to go where I want." "Oh, Harriet," Ernest said, "Didn't I tell you? They found that George had measles, not smallpox!" The story went around and after a decent interval even Harriet was able to laugh about it.

<>

Leslie Fuller was as unconventional and casual in dress and manner as Burch and Hayes were neat and fastidious. However, this never was true in matters of personal integrity or scholarly research. He was an expert in his field and demanded high quality work from his students. One of them recounts:

> Our beloved Dr. Leslie Fuller, sometimes impatient with students' stupidity, would speak out a bit sharply. Once, after he did so, another student rose in protest, calling it unfair, and walked out of the room. The protester expected the Rainbow Bible teacher to take it out on him. Instead, as he entered chapel later, he felt Dr. Fuller's hand on his shoulder. "Good for you, X," he said. "You are the first student since Roy Smith to walk out on me, and I deserved it both times."

We who knew him were deeply saddened by his tragic, untimely death. On our office wall was a picture of Leslie, with his hand on his cherished companion—a happy mongrel named Kim. A year after Leslie's death a new student noticed the picture and asked, "Who is that fellow with the dog?" The question brought a deep twinge of pain. It is sad, yet true, that we are soon among the unknowns except to those who loved us.

<>

There was an open friendliness about Will Schermerhorn that attracted people to him. When I was a student at Garrett I much enjoyed a course in early church history under his direction. He also taught courses in Christian art and architecture. He and his wife, May, served for a term of five years in Hyderabad, India, but much to his disappointment they could not return on account of May's health. He was above average height and, when I knew him, had a deeply lined, kindly face, indicative of the fact that he had been confronted with many a problem over the years. He was a man whose "yea" was "yea" and "nay" was "nay." He was frank and outspoken, and had no patience with those who were devious or self-seeking.

One faculty meeting stands out clearly in memory. We were considering whether a certain student should be permitted to continue in residence. His academic work was unsatisfactory and he had been told that in the next quarter he would have to make at least a "C" average. He did not meet that requirement and in the faculty meeting his advisor urged that he be given one more chance. After considerable discussion, Will spoke up: "I have one question to ask. Did we promise him that if he did not make a "C" average, he would be dropped?" "Yes," replied the advisor. "Then I move that we keep our promise!" said Will. His motion prevailed.

A student in one of his classes remembers that: "two college professors from a conservative school heckled him in class. We [other students] booed them. But Schermerhorn treated them with loving gentleness. He put his arm around one of them and said, 'I don't believe your theology, but I do believe in your religion.' And he asked the other to serve as toastmaster at a closing dinner at the end of the quarter." The writer added, "Schermerhorn opened up the world of cathedrals, symbolism, Christian art, missions—God's world—to me."

James Uhlinger ('34) recalls Will's deep sensitivity to "the human situation": "One memorable morning in Dr. Schermerhorn's class remains in my mind across the years. He paused before beginning his lecture, to say wistfully, 'A man on my floor at the apartment died this morning—and I didn't know his name.'"

We have recorded elsewhere some of our memories concerning Frank Rall and Art Nagler, and it is appropriate that we speak briefly of the two other professors who continued on the faculty after 1940 and were seniors to me, Richard D. Hollington and Irl G. Whitchurch.

<>

Dr. Hollington was Professor of Preaching, and he looked the part—tall, slim, generally serious of mien. He was quick of wit and ready of speech. His resonant voice and usually austere demeanor seemed to fit him for the role. He had come to Garrett in 1927 so I did not have the privilege of studying with him. One of his students recollects:

Day after day we heard about "my church in Providence." By the
end of the year we decided that the White House must be some
anteroom to "my church in Providence." Well, one salient maxim
Dr. Hollington left with me to carry through half a century:
"When you are seated on a raised platform without a screen or
curtain in front of you, NEVER cross your legs. Sit with both feet
planted firmly on the floor!" Through these five decades I have
been amazed at how many ministers never had Doc Hollington's
class or heard about how he handled himself in Providence.

As a colleague, Dick was a delight. His wry sense of humor and large
collection of stories made the Hollingtons delightful dinner guests.

<>

Irl Whitchurch was an unusually interesting person. His students
tended to be either ardent disciples or quite critical of him. It was true
that if anyone disagreed with his hypotheses Irl was likely to become
sharply aggressive in their defense.

Les Palmer ('42) recounts that one evening he dropped in at the
dormitory room of Kim, a Korean fellow-student, who was having
some difficulty with the English language:

. . . I noticed the look of confusion on Kim's face as he sat
studying his notes from Dr. Whitchurch's class and thumbing
through his dictionary. "Kim, what's the trouble?" I asked. He
replied, "I can't find this word *piffle*. What does it mean?" I
explained to him that *piffle* was a derogatory slang word that Dr.
Whitchurch frequently used to express his opinion about an idea,
a bit of logic or a proposition with which he did not agree.

On the other hand, Les remembers a social occasion in the
Whitchurch home when Irl put on a stocking cap and clowned a bit to
entertain Les's five-year-old daughter. Irl was often generous of spirit
and during the wartime signed a note for one of the students so that he
could borrow $750 at the bank in order to buy a used car.

On a few occasions he criticized his colleagues by name in the
classroom or, by implication, even in a chapel address. At one time
several on the faculty "waited on" the President, urging him to speak
to Irl about professional courtesy. Yet even those of us who felt the
sharpness of his tongue appreciated his cordial manner when we were
off-duty. However, when he resigned in order to accept a deanship in
Southern California, his colleagues wished him well and shed no tears.

Old Problems, New Friends to Help Resolve Them

The deaths of Leslie and Ernest left us with a deep impression of our
human mortality. Concern was felt as to pension provision for their

widows (and perhaps potentially for our own wives) and also for retiring teachers and their widows. One can understand the sensitivity of the administration when pressed on this point. There had been no pension fund. A relatively small and utterly inadequate stipend was available for those who were ministerial members of Annual Conferences (and an even smaller amount for their widows).

Samuel G. Ayres, who had been our librarian for nineteen years, came to my office two months before his retirement, to share his deep distress. He and his wife had lost their life savings in the Depression and he had not heard a single word as to what his pension, if any, would be. As I recall, he later told me that he hoped he would receive $90 a month.

Being something of a "pushy," irrepressible person, I asked the President for permission to write to the Teachers' Insurance and Annuity Association, which then carried the pension funds of most American universities, to inquire whether a seminary might use their services. He was sure that (a) T.I.A.A. would not include a school such as ours, and (b) there was no money now available for pension purposes. After two years of my pestering he gave me permission to write, and in 1938, with the approval of both the Board of Trustees and the faculty, we signed up. At the start three percent of our modest salaries (which by then were up to $3,600 a year) was contributed by the school and a like amount was deducted from each pay check. A small but important beginning, it was raised to five percent in a few years.

<>

New professors obviously had to be secured. For example, catalogs of 1933-34 and 1934-35 carried the names of only two full-time professors in the Biblical fields—Fuller in Old Testament and Burch in New Testament. That was quite a contrast to the year 1931-32 when we had five full-time professors: Eiselen, Fuller and Voigt in Old Testament and Hayes and Burch in New Testament.

Otto J. Baab, who had been teaching Old Testament Interpretation at Illinois Wesleyan University, was invited to join our faculty in 1934, and shortly after that Paul S. Minear came in the field of New Testament. But once again, after Fuller's death in the summer of 1936, we were left with only one professor in each of the major Biblical fields. It was not until 1942 that a third member was added in Bible—Edward Payson Blair, to offer work in Intertestamental and New Testament subjects.

Otto J. Baab

Otto had his doctoral degree from the University of Chicago. He was a scholarly, thorough teacher who prepared his lectures with much care. He, like his predecessors, expected his students to maintain high standards. One of them said, "He gave us difficult tests. We joked that in the final exam, he instructed us to 'Outline the Old Testament and tell why.' We had three hours to do it in."

George Weber ('58) recalls:

> Our Old Testament professor Otto Baab was not one to laugh very often. One time he was beside himself and laughed so hard that he cried for five minutes.
>
> The class had been divided into groups to work out and dramatize some of the stories in our Old Testament study. Our group selected the story of Haman (Esther, 6 and 7). We made a "scare-crow" dummy out of some old clothes and tied a rope around the neck. As some of the class, in a very matter-of-fact fashion, narrated the story, friends were positioned upstairs in a classroom. At the appropriate time on a signal, down came "Haman" swinging on the rope outside the classroom window. It hit Dr. Baab as extemely funny. We all in the group received an "A" for that assignment.

The Baabs and Leiffers soon became intimate friends. For a number of years we lived within a block of each other. Our Don, accompanied by one or two of his friends, would push Mary Bea Baab in her baby carriage around the long block between Foster and Emerson. On several occasions each family took care of the youngster of the other family when parents had to be out of town.

Paul S. Minear

Paul Minear, tall and trim, with excellent training in the New Testament field at Yale, turned out to be a congenial colleague as well as an able teacher. The faculty was startled when, in 1944, he accepted an invitation to return to teach in the Yale Divinity School. So far as we can recall, he was the first professor who had been with us for more than a couple of years, who responded to an invitation from another educational institution, except for those who left during the tragic Depression years. All of us had felt it a privilege to teach at Garrett, and siren calls from other schools had little appeal. I, and I think the others, had regarded the invitation to teach at Garrett as a call to professional commitment, a distinctive life vocation.

Paul was and continued to be interested in the ecumenical movement, and participated in a number of inter-church and inter-faith conferences. This, of course, enriched his teaching. We had the feeling that his move to Yale was in the direction he wanted to go. And so we bade Godspeed to Paul and Gladys, his wife, and their two delightful little boys. He later returned as a visiting professor for a couple of summer terms.

As a matter of fact, it was not until in the mid-1950's that anyone at Garrett, so far as I can recall, talked about academic tenure. Then, some of the younger men, nervous about teaching security, asked me when I had been given tenure, to which I replied naively, "I have always assumed that I had tenure." When later the President asked me if I wished assurance as to tenure, I replied—perhaps indignantly— that I had all the tenure I needed, and was not at all pleased that it was thought that I might feel the need for reassurance. I had joined the American Association of University Professors prior to 1940, not for self-protection but because some teachers in a number of colleges and universities were being dismissed, or threatened with dismissal, because of their political or economic views and I wished to add my support to the "professors' union."

<>

Others who joined our faculty in this period included Edmund D. Soper who came to us in 1938 from the presidency of Ohio Wesleyan University, Georgia Harkness who had been teaching at Mt. Holyoke College, and accepted a position at Garrett in 1939 where she taught until 1950, and Rockwell C. Smith, who began his teaching career with us in 1940.

Edmund D. Soper

Prior to 1919 Edmund Soper began his career as a missionary in the Far East. In 1919 he became Professor of History of Religion at Northwestern University and also lectured at Garrett until 1925. Subsequently, he was elected Dean of Duke Divinity School, from which post he was invited to become President of Ohio Wesleyan University. He resigned that position to join the Garrett faculty on a full-time basis for his last ten years of teaching. It was a joy to have him return to Garrett as a faculty colleague. A jolly, rather rotund man, he was an excellent lecturer. Students enjoyed his lively sense of humor and his gracious hospitality.

His wife was in poor health when he came to Garrett, and died shortly thereafter. Two years later a woman missionary, Moneta Troxel, who had served several terms in Korea, enrolled at Garrett during her furlough year. She had a course with Soper and toward the end of the quarter asked for an appointment to discuss her term paper. Following their conversation, Ned asked her, "How does it happen that a fine person like yourself never got married?" To which she replied, "I was never asked." As she was leaving and stood at the door, Ned said, "Consider yourself asked." Moneta made no reply. About a week later, when they were passing in the hall, she paused and said to Ned, "The answer is 'Yes'." A few months later they were married. And many of us remember with delight the evenings we spent in their home and they in ours.

An advisee of mine, Walter MacArthur ('43), like others, appreciated Dr. Soper's thoughtfulness and wise counselling:

> My first few months (at Garrett) were not going well, grade-wise. It seemed that so many of my childhood and adolescent understandings of the Bible were being swept away by oceans of new and strange, even contradictory information. I was defensive and somewhat rebellious. Thus, when the first grades of the year were issued I was dismayed and ready to throw in the towel. Two wonderful people kept me from doing that, my wife and Dr. Edmund Soper.
>
> Dr. and Mrs. Soper invited my wife and me to dinner, where we got to know each other better. He learned of my background in woodworking and crafts, and he shared some of his mechanical interests and skills with me. While we were in his work-space and the women finishing things in the kitchen, he expressed his concern and alarm at my grades and apparent struggle with the new disciplines of seminary studies. In short, he said: "We appreciate, and are impressed with your knowledge of the Bible and understanding of things. You have a positive and valid faith. We are here, however, to open some new doors and windows of thought, to expand your horizons and deepen the springs of understanding. Now we really do not care whether you believe or accept any of this new information, but we need to know that you have been exposed to it, that you have listened and read faithfully. That is all we are asking of you at examination time. Just write down the answers to the questions with that in mind; your growth and our satisfaction will come naturally."
>
> It was the inspiration and wise counsel that I needed. I performed comparatively well the rest of my years in seminary. I will always be grateful to a caring and gentle, yet persuasive professor, who became a good friend.

Georgia Harkness

When Georgia Harkness came to Garrett she was the first full-time tenured woman professor on any American theological faculty. Esther Bjornberg was a full-time instructor in Social Service and Field Work, and two women on the Northwestern faculty in Religious Education—Blanche Carrier and Amy Clowes—also had offered a few courses at Garrett. Georgia first taught in our summer school in 1939, joining the faculty on a full-time basis in the autumn of 1940. She soon felt very much at home, and rejoiced in being part of the Garrett faculty. She would explain to her students why she believed she "had the most important job in the world." Don Williams ('48) remembers her saying (with a twinkle in her eye):

> If the world is to be saved, it will be by the influence of the Church, and the strongest part of the Church (in 1946 to '48, when I was in her class) is the American Church. She felt that the Methodist Church led the Christians of America in its influence for social good and, within the denomination, the training offered by its seminaries was the critical point. Of these seminaries, Garrett Biblical Institute was the largest. Theology is the heart of the curriculum, and applied theology the place where this discipline comes to bear on the needs of the world. Therefore, the professor of Applied Theology in Garrett held the most important job in the world!

Yet the greatest contributions that a seminary professor makes are frequently not those in the classroom, but in direct, one-to-one relationship with his or her students. Vance Rogers ('41), who later became President of Nebraska Wesleyan University recalls:

> My own gratitude goes to Dr. Georgia Harkness. It was in the winter of 1940—my father had suffered a severe cerebral hemorrhage. . . . We took him to Mayo Clinic; the doctors advised that he was terminally ill.
>
> I was in a serious dilemma—one of my family asked that I drop out of school, come home and take over the responsibilities of operating the family farm. I was driven by frustration and motivation to be loyal and helpful to my family and yet, somehow, to remain at Garrett and continue my education.
>
> My father died later that spring and the hard choices continued. It was during that period that I established a very meaningful relationship with Georgia Harkness. She counseled me as to how one should approach the reality of death and what is the

responsibility of a son to his family. Suffice it to say, that because of her guidance and the environment in which I found myself, I did make the hard decisions, remained in school, and finished my education.

Students were agreed that Georgia "was thorough and thoroughly organized. You knew where she was going, and she did, too. In addition and perhaps even more important, she was interesting." Her office was next to ours on the second floor, and she would often drop in for a bit of conversation. "It is the one place in the school," she said, "where I can let my hair down, and if I shed a few tears you never act as though you thought the less of me." At times she found the going a little tough. For one thing, she did not feel particularly comfortable with the President and, as a matter of fact, he didn't with her.

Georgia had a nice sense of humor and enjoyed playing games and participating in light-hearted group activities. This was delightfully displayed at a pre-Christmas banquet. But let Robert J. Payne ('50) describe it:

> In my younger years, I would sometimes impersonate individuals whom I admired, respected, and found fascinating.
>
> During my first year at Garrett, I began to impersonate Dr. Georgia Harkness, who became a warm friend. I had the vocal tone, pitch, and inflection to imitate her speech, even to its nuances. That first year, I confined my impersonation to clandestine, private conversations with friends.
>
> In those days, it was the custom for the students to present the entertainment for the Christmas banquet and for the faculty to present it for the spring banquet. I was asked by the Christmas banquet committee if I would give my impersonation of Dr. Harkness. With some trepidation, I agreed. (We have never known another school where there was such a close "family" relationship between students and faculty as there was at Garrett during those years.)
>
> That evening, Carlyle Mason was Santa Claus. Several persons appeared before him to present their "Christmas wants." Then I came on stage (wearing my wife's long coat and hat with a veil over my face) and Santa said, "Well, if it isn't Dr. Harkness! And what would you like for Christmas?"
>
> Using my best Harknessesque (or "Georgian"), and following the orderly style and substance of her lecturing, with which by then I was familiar, I replied, "About that—three things can be said: First of all, I want more faith for the Garrett students. Now faith means three things; two we want and one we don't. (A direct quote from her Theology I lecture.) The second thing I want is

clergy rights for women. At the Amsterdam Conference last
summer (1948) I had a debate with Karl Barth. It was called the
"Barth-Harkness Encounter." Karl Barth said that if Jesus had
wanted women in the ministry, he would have had some women
disciples . . . whereupon a Scottish professor, more brilliant than
your teacher, responded, "On the basis of that kind of reasoning,
out of every 12 ministers, there would have to be a Judas."
(Verbatim from her report to the Garrett community on the
Amsterdam Conference.) The third thing I want for Christmas,
Santa, is some red ink to use in marking the students' papers. I
just ran out last week and had to mark the last papers with
pencil." (That was true; I was in the class.)

(I had given Santa Claus in advance a bottle of red ink.) He
thanked me (i.e., Georgia) for my Christmas list and then
produced the bottle of red ink from his bag. I took it down to
where Dr. Harkness was sitting in the front row and handed it to
her. She was laughing as heartily as everyone else. She was a good
sport.

After the program, President Horace Smith approached me and
said, with a twinkle in his eye and voice, "Young man, I hope
you've completed your work in applied theology!" Later that
evening, Dr. Harkness came over to me and said, "I want to meet
my alter ego." I replied, "If you want to stay home tomorrow
morning, I will be glad to meet your classes for you." She said,
"Oh no, I wouldn't miss that!" The next day, everyone was
waiting to see what she would say when she came into class. She
began by saying, "I come before you this morning with fear and
trembling, but 'when duty calls or danger, be never wanting
there.'"

During my last year at Garrett, Dr. Harkness left to go to the
Pacific School of Religion. I was honored to be called on at her
farewell assembly to bid her goodbye and extend best wishes on
behalf of the student body.

We remained in touch with Dr. Harkness and saw her several
times through the years. The last time we saw her was at the
General Conference in Atlanta in 1972.

She was an active leader in her own Annual Conference, which
elected her quadrennially as a lay delegate to General Conference.
There she was an outspoken representative of women's rights in the
Church. For about two decades it was she who regularly introduced,
and spoke from the floor in favor of, the right of women to be full
ministerial members of an Annual Conference. At the first she was
one of the few women who could speak with a strong voice from the
floor of the General Conference and be heard clearly in every corner

of the house. And she always received a good round of applause even from those who would not vote for the position she advocated. When in 1956 her favorite cause carried, a great cheer went up, and she received a standing ovation. Happily, her birthday almost always fell during the sessions of General Conference, and in the latter part of her life someone was apt to ask for the floor and announce, "Today is Georgia Harkness' birthday," and the great gathering would rise and sing, "Happy Birthday, dear Georgia."

Garrett and the Rural Church

From as far back as we can remember, Garrett has been firmly committed to training students for ministry in town and country communities. Clare J. Hewitt had been an effective pastor of rural churches before he was called to teach at Garrett in 1920. Albert Z. Mann followed him in 1927, as Professor of Sociology and Home Missions, giving primary attention to the rural church. When, under the straitened financial condition of Garrett, Mann was no longer retained, the responsibility for rural courses fell to me. Since I was already teaching a spread of courses in Social Ethics and Sociology, as well as those in the Church and the Urban Community, I was able to offer only one major each year in the rural field. (Each member of the faculty was expected to conduct such reading courses as were needed, in addition to 10 quarter-hours a term of regular class and seminar work.) However, after Dr. Lesemann took over responsibility for supervising the students who were serving pastorates, I was able to develop more work in the rural field.

Seeking to strengthen our town and country program, I conceived the idea of establishing a five-week summer school for rural pastors, operating concurrently with the regular five-week summer term, for which I was the Director. The problem was how to get the money to finance it. Careful and prayerful cultivation developed two resources—the Sears Roebuck Foundation and the Farm Foundation, each of which agreed to cover the stipend of one visiting professor for the term ($500) on condition that we would provide a like amount in scholarships for rural ministers to attend the school who could not otherwise afford it. The first Interdenominational School for Rural Pastors was held in 1939. An interesting paragraph from that bulletin read:

> Fees and expenses have been cut to the lowest possible point in order that a maximum number of religious leaders may benefit by this Rural School. The registration fee for the five-week term is

$15.00. Dormitory accommodation will be available at $12.50. Meals can be secured in the Garrett Commons for the entire period for $22.50 by purchasing a meal ticket. In other words, $50 will cover all expenses for the five weeks. A limited number of scholarships are available for men who cannot readily come without such assistance.

Dr. William Stacy from the Iowa State College of Agriculture, Ralph Felton, Professor of Rural Sociology at Drew University, Mark Rich of the Department of Town and Country Work, American Baptist Home Missionary Society, and Aaron Rapking, Superintendent of the Department of Town and Country Work in the Methodist Episcopal Church, constituted the "rural faculty" for the first year. The students could also audit one course offered in the regular summer term. In 1940 our visiting professors were George F. Wehrwein, Professor of Agricultural Economics, University of Wisconsin, and Ralph Felton from Drew University. In the afternoon a half-major course (i.e., four hours a week) in rural recreational leadership was conducted by Lynn Rohrbaugh, of the Co-operative Recreation Service, and Dorothy Leiffer.

There was a certain amount of guile in my seeking to develop the rural emphasis in our Garrett curriculum. It seemed to me it was high time for someone else to be brought on to the Garrett faculty to share the work with me. Unforeseen help in bringing about this development arose that autumn, when I again became seriously ill with a long-standing ulcer, and the doctor said I must have a period of complete rest. Under that pressure, I approached the President, who opined that I might be allowed a sabbatical quarter in the coming winter, and asked me to locate someone who would be suitable to take over my classes.

Rockwell Carter Smith

Several leaders in the rural church field were asked for the name of the most promising young man with an earned doctorate in Rural Sociology and Economics who was also a committed Christian. One name was suggested—Rockwell C. Smith, who was completing his work for the degree at the University of Wisconsin. Correspondence and an interview convinced me that the recommendation was an excellent one, and I invited him to participate in the Merom Conference in Indiana that November. Professors and graduate students in the rural field from several seminaries held an annual meeting there in a genuinely rural setting. He, Dorothy and I together drove down to the conference. That weekend trip and conference gave us an excellent opportunity to become acquainted.

After a two-weeks regimen in the hospital in January, Dorothy, our son Don and I bade a grateful farewell to Garrett and to Rocky and Frances, and headed south in our car for Florida. By the time we got back in March, we learned that students found Rockwell Smith's teaching stimulating and that he had already won a place in the hearts of the faculty. He was outgoing, cheerful, proficient, and a consecrated Christian. So, when I broached with President Smith the subject of his being invited to membership on our faculty, I found a cordial reception of the idea. However, Dr. Smith asked whether I saw anything against his coming. I said, "Only one thing. Since he has the same last name as you, would you find that any embarrassment to you?" "Why, of course not!" "Well then, I would surely like to have him invited."

"Not so fast, Murray. We simply do not have enough money for another full-time man."

"Well, if Garrett can cover half of a reasonably satisfactory salary for him, I will see if I can find some money from another source."

I at once got in touch with Henry J. Taylor, Executive Director of the Farm Foundation in Chicago and asked if his organization could use the help of a good man on a half-time basis. And so it was worked out. That deal lasted only one year. But when Dr. Taylor notified us that their part of the half-time arrangement could not be renewed, Rocky had proved himself so invaluable that he was brought on our faculty on a full-time basis. (Later we learned that a number of students had petitioned the President that he be added to the faculty.) Our continuing friendship with Rocky and Frances from then until now has been one of the most precious experiences of our lives.

It was not surprising that, when recently we asked former students for their memories about faculty and staff, Rocky was mentioned more often than anyone else. His informality (for example, addressing everyone—almost—by first name) and his open, joyous spirit won him friends wherever he went. Well, there were a few exceptions: Mrs. Burch, who also hailed from New England, was shocked "that anyone who had been reared in New England *and* was a professor *and* a minister should act in such an undignified way." We don't believe that he ever called Harriet by her first name to her face.

Three years after Rocky joined us, Dorothy and I invited Frances and him with the others on the summer school faculty to our home for a social evening. I remarked that since we would all be working together rather closely for the next five weeks, we might feel free to call one another by first name. So, for that evening, anyone who addressed another member of the summer faculty formally by last name would need to pay a penalty at the end of the evening for each breach of informality. George Wehrwein, from the University of Wisconsin, was again one of the group, and he had been one of Rocky's major professors in his graduate work. When as the evening wore on Rocky needed to address George, he gulped, hesitated, and then said "Dr. Wehrwein—," grew red in the face, and blurted out, "I just can't do it!" Everyone else, including Frances, enjoyed hugely his quite temporary embarrassment.

Some years later, at one of our autumn Garrett banquets held in Great Hall at First Church, the students put on a skit kidding and caricaturing various faculty members. In one scene St. Peter with an assistant stood at the entry gate to Heaven. Among the characters who sought entrance was one looking remarkably like Rocky, who came to the gate and cheerfully burst out, "Hello, Pete! I'm Rocky." This brought down the house.

Robert Wilson ('55, PhD '58) remarked that Rocky's jocund manner may have obscured, at least sometimes and for some students, the depth of his learning and scholarship. But those who took work with him or shared in professional debates in his office soon discovered how well he knew his field. There was always a coffee pot plugged in at his office, with a brew so strong that no one could doze in class after imbibing a cupful.

Sam Wong ('66, MA '67), whose home was Singapore, writes:

> "Hello, Brother Sam, I am Rocky Smith. Welcome to America! I have heard a lot about you from Brother Murray." Those were about the first words I heard from Professor Rockwell Smith. It took me several weeks before I was able to call him simply "Rocky." Calling everyone by his first name with the prefix "Brother" was a trademark of Rocky. Badgering people about wearing bow ties on Tuesdays was one of his favorite pastimes. Every verse of Scripture to him was "John 3:16," and anyone who did not drink coffee was a suspect in his office, not to mention the seminary.

Rocky for several years led a summer seminar group studying the rural programs of European churches. One year they spent time at Chateau Bossey Ecumenical Center, Celigny, Switzerland. Sam Laeuchli, who was well acquainted with the Bossey personnel, reported that: "Rocky is very well known; they mention him the way a zoo-keeper speaks about a much-beloved and precious specimen which, however, has two signs on the cage: 'exotic' and 'bites.'"

Yet it would be utterly unfair to give the impression that Rocky spent most of his time joking or "being a character." He was and is a deeply devout and caring person, open-hearted and concerned for the welfare not only of his students but also for any other human (or canine) person with whom he might come in contact. A retired faculty colleague, Richard Miller, remarks:

> I saw many students talking with him about the work of the pastorate and he inevitably served as something of a pastoral model . . . . In my own conversations with Dr. Smith I could readily see his value to the student who has confided in him. The fact of the matter is, the student body when I was teaching at Garrett was searching for a father figure, even more diligently than when I was a student there.

> One of the stories which Rocky told me, and which I know he told to the students, undergirds this parental figure: Rocky had a relationship with his father and mother which was most helpful and in some cases very interesting. For example he told us the story of how he and his brothers lost interest in bread pudding. It seems his parents were not wealthy people. Little was wasted, and bread pudding frequently appeared on the menu. When the brothers' daily inquiry, on coming home for supper, "What's for dessert, Ma?" was answered too frequently, to their way of thinking, with "Bread pudding," they approached their mother with a complaint and ultimatum: "No more bread pudding." Mrs. Smith replied, "All right, boys, no more bread pudding." For several days there was no dessert at all. Then one night the brothers' question "What's for dessert, Ma?" brought the astounding reply "Queen of the May pudding." To the hungry boys it seemed that their mother had outdone herself. They hastened through the main meal in anticipation of this new delight. When the supper plates were cleared, Mrs. Smith went into the pantry and returned with dessert—Queen of the May pudding. She served the new delight, passed the plates around the table, and the brothers found themselves facing—bread pudding. Rocky said, "We ate it with great gusto. Thus ended the bread pudding boycott. We had a great deal of bread pudding from then on, and never said a word against it."

Rocky was a scholar, thoroughly conversant with the literature in the field of Sociology. He and Murray frequently shared a seminar, usually a thesis seminar. To the delight, sometimes the consternation, of our students one would challenge the other sharply on some point of sociological theory or methodology: "Murray, you're crazy. That shows your University of Chicago bias." To which he might reply: "You'll have to get more specific in your challenge. And then present a better 'Wisconsin' technique."

It was a sheer joy to turn over to Rocky Smith full responsibility for all rural courses and the Inter-denominational School for Rural Leaders, as well as some of the courses in Sociology of Religion. Through all of our 33 years together on the Garrett faculty, we cherished him as an academic colleague and a person with whom it was a pleasure to be professionally associated.

Other New Colleagues: 1941-1945

There were several important additions to the faculty before the close of World War II. In the autumn of 1941 a committee was formed to consider development of a joint doctoral program between Northwestern University and Garrett. It consisted of three from Northwestern—the President, Dean of the Graduate School, and Dean of the School of Education, and three from Garrett—the President, Irl Whitchurch, and Leiffer. After three meetings two sets of decisions were made. The first was: the University would regard Garrett as its Graduate School of Religion. Garrett would form a Committee on Graduate Studies to supervise MA and PhD candidates seeking the University degree. The policy agreed on remained essentially the same at least until I retired in 1970. Leiffer was named chairman of the Garrett committee, was placed on the University Senate, and his name and those of two other Garrett faculty were listed as Northwestern faculty members. Amicable arrangements for cross registration in either direction between the schools was ensured.

The second set of agreements provided that Frank McKibben would be transferred from the University to the Garrett faculty, and all courses in Religious Education on the campus would henceforth be taught at Garrett.

So it was that in 1942 Frank McKibben shifted his office and primary "loyalty" to Garrett, and was placed on our payroll. He was well known to us as he had been teaching one or two courses a year at Garrett. The students nicknamed him "Mimeograph McKibben" because of the large quantities of mimeographed materials which he distributed. Frank rejoiced in the change because, he said, he felt much more at home at Garrett.

Frank and Helen McKibben ran what might be called an "open house" at their home on Noyes Street. Students, especially those in Christian education, were always welcome. Often there were festive occasions when a dozen or more faculty people with a good sprinkling of students would be invited for an ample dinner and an evening of games. In the late 1940's the McKibbens bought and moved to a farm near Delavan, Wisconsin, primarily because they thought it would be a better place than Evanston to rear their youngsters. Frank commuted to Garrett, living in the dorm during the school week. The McKibbens frequently invited groups of Garrett people to "come up for a Saturday," to enjoy a bountiful picnic, a swim in the nearby lake, and a rich fellowship.

In 1942 Edward P. Blair came from the Biblical Seminary in New York to be the Harry Kendall Professor of New Testament Interpretation. He was well equipped, with his doctorate from Yale and work at the American School of Oriental Research in Jerusalem, to teach in both New Testament and Intertestamental Fields. A quiet, well-groomed man of good height and a scholarly mien, thoughtful and conscientious, he soon became a highly valued member of the faculty. His steady eye and open countenance gave assurance of his personal integrity. A colleague has commented on "Ed's sense of the reality of God, and his genuine warmth and concern for his students. He not only taught the Bible, but so obviously loved it."

His students remember him with profound appreciation. "He really knew his field." "His lectures were carefully organized and gave us the knowledge we needed. The depth of his Christian faith and conviction impressed us." "He really made the New Testament come alive." Ed Blair retired in 1971 in order to carry forward his research and writing, although he subsequently taught an occasional course as an adjunct professor. And 16 years later he is still writing and lecturing. His authoritative *Abingdon Bible Handbook* is in its third edition.

John Capps Irwin joined us in 1944 in Preaching and Church Administration. John had grown up on the West Side of Chicago and early decided to enter the ministry. After graduating from Garrett he had served on the staff of the Methodist Board of Education and then as pastor of churches in Northern Illinois and South Dakota. An alert, dynamic, quick-moving man, he had a mobile countenance and penetrating eyes. The word "debonair" is an apt description for him—affable, courteous in manner, and characterized by grace and lightheartedness. He was a friendly, outgoing person, blessed with a ready wit and an excellent command of the English language.

Stan Fixter ('51) was one of his advisees who spoke of his loving concern for his students, even after they had left the seminary. Stan said that Dr. Irwin and other members of the faculty were "just like parents—they never give up on their kids." John and his wife Edna lived in our co-operative apartment building, across the hall from us after the Ralls moved downstairs, until their departure from Evanston. He decided to resign from Garrett and to accept a position at Vanderbilt Seminary one year before he would have needed to retire under our rules, because he could continue to teach for five years longer at Vanderbilt. We were very sorry to see him and Edna leave because they had been wonderful caring and sharing neighbors. His wise counsel and cheery voice were sorely missed at Garrett after he left.

Albert E. Barnett came in 1944, replacing Paul Minear in the field of New Testament Interpretation. His doctorate was from the University of Chicago. He and Lucy, his wife, were Georgians, but were soon completely at home in Evanston. He was an able teacher whose students responded to him warmly. Charles Klosterman ('48) remembers Albert's enthusiasm for his summer garden, especially his peas. "I seem to remember his giving all his students an extra daily grade of A because his pea crop came in so well."

When an invitation came from Candler School of Theology in Atlanta, Georgia, the seminary on the Emory University campus, he accepted after much soul-searching. Both he and Lucy wished to stay at Garrett, where they enjoyed the fellowship. Nevertheless his strong social convictions, especially concerning racial justice and the cause of peace, pushed him to accept the Candler invitation. Albert was convinced that only a man from the deep South could be effective in bringing about needed changes in racial relationships in Georgia. He was a confirmed writer of "letters to the editor" on the subjects of race and peace. Two-page, single-spaced missives commonly came from his typewriter when he was "worked up" about a subject.

David C. Shipley taught at Garrett from 1945 to 1955 in Historical Theology. As we recall, his doctoral work was done at Yale. He and his wife Mildred were Californians. As a result of two serious operations he was never in robust health from the time we first knew him. This probably accounted for his sedentary habits and may have been associated with his quite stocky appearance. He was an able teacher and expected that those in his classes would industriously pursue their academic work. A student jokingly remarked that "Dr. Shipley never used a one-syllable word when he could find a polysyllabic one to take its place." He was uniformly patient and gentle and his lectures were replete with "gracious wisdom."

Carl Keightley has referred to Dave's manner of dealing with a man who had a student charge in Michigan and was a belligerently conservative person.

> He was a more mature student. I don't remember exactly what he
> said that upset Dr. Shipley, but Dr. Shipley answered him in a

curt way, which was not characteristic of him, for he was usually so gentle and considerate. After the session was over, he called the student up to the desk, and said, "I'm sorry. I didn't mean what I said. And if I did, I'm sorry."

Dave was humble in manner, and his keen perceptions were not always valued as highly as they deserved. "Just Dave," he would sign his letters. "Let recognition come from others," he would counsel. "Let him that glories glory in the Lord!" This was no pretense or self derogation. It was the real, loving, "You first, dear friend," Dave Shipley.

Some illuminating comments come from Lee Scott ('48), one of his long-term and dearly loved students:

> There was in Dave Shipley a passion for ideas which I found extremely contagious—a concern that students of the Christian heritage (and especially students of the Wesleyan heritage) participate experientially in the quest for the roots and branches of our faith-tradition. His theological mission was . . . to help American Methodists rediscover the Wesleyan theology of grace! In one of his letters to me . . . while I was preparing to begin my Yale dissertation on "Methodist Theology in America in the Nineteenth Century," Dave wrote:

> "Wesley's view was assuredly theo-centric. The redemptive process was inaugurated by the prevenient grace of the Divine initiative. Somewhere the emphasis changed to an anthropo-centric description of the redemptive process. The concern for defending *what* the grace of God does *in* man and *for* man somehow occasioned the loss of awareness that it was God's grace which made possible the redemptive work. Please help us discover at what points this deadly change-over to anthropo-centrism occurred."

> Dave Shipley's easy, genial style—celebrating the tentative insights of his students, caring about our personal lives and loves, including us in his own family life with his beloved wife Mildred—these are the pictures I retain in my memory of Dave Shipley. (His relaxed hallway conversations, often resulting in his starting a class late, were, literally, his hallmark!)

Since neither he nor Mildred possessed good health and the winters were particularly difficult for them, they decided to accept an invitation to teach in a warmer climate at the Perkins School of Theology in Dallas. We deeply regretted their going.

There were others who taught at Garrett for a year or two, whom we also cordially remember. But this concludes the roster of those who came before the close of World War II.

V

RELIGIOUS AND SOCIAL LIFE AT GARRETT IN THE '30's AND '40's

Quite appropriately corporate worship and private devotions have been a natural as well as a nurtured aspect of life in the community of Garrett. Those who enrolled in Garrett did so because they had, to some degree, an interest in entering a religious vocation. Attendance at the daily chapel service was never required during the time that we have known the school, but it was as regular a part of the total program as the academic. Usually various members of the faculty were in charge of the service Tuesday, Wednesday and Thursday, and students on Friday. Dr. Smith preached several times a quarter. He was our pastor. There were, of course many visiting church leaders, lay and clerical, who were invited to speak from time to time.

As noted earlier, the faculty walked in to the chapel together and sat at the front. President Eiselen (in 1931) told the faculty of an amusing experience. He and his wife were entertaining the Monica League[1] at their home. He asked if any of the women had suggestions for "the good of the cause." One young lady raised her hand and volunteered: "It bothers some of us that during the chapel service when the faculty sit on the platform facing us, they cross their legs in different directions and someone is always shifting right to left or left to right. Would it be possible for all to cross their legs in the same direction (and at the same time!)?"

Horace Smith continued the practice of holding a communion service at the first chapel in each quarter. On those occasions the faculty wore their academic gowns, but not hoods or hats. A fond memory of Al Eliason ('51) is "the dignity of the faculty processional at the first chapel service each quarter, robed and singing, and sitting in a semicircle back of the altar." Some of them assisted in the service.

---

[1] The Monica League was the organization which included all women students and wives of students and faculty.

This communion service was always a meaningful ceremony. Commonly the President would use the time-honored sentences, dismissing each table of communicants with the words, "Rise, go in peace. As these depart, let others come." It was for us all a significant experience, binding us—younger and older, students, staff, and faculty—in a common expression of dedication and purpose. Several alums still remember some of Dr. Smith's chapel talks in amazing detail. Walter MacArthur ('43) wrote, "President Horace Greeley Smith helped me immeasurably in a chapel address about midway through my first year," and he then proceeded to give an outline of that talk. The President had the great gift of using homely illustrations in an effective, emotionally sensitive way which called forth a universal response. Bob Holmes ('51) has said,

> One of the things that endeared President Horace Greeley Smith to me was the way he wore his robe. It was never fully buttoned (or zipped) but rather hung just barely over his shoulders, as if to communicate a certain uneasiness with wearing any garment that completely concealed his humanness.

Dr. Smith was at all times primarily a pastor, not an academician. He was deeply concerned about the spiritual life of students and faculty. He was that rare administrator who was always available, standing around in front of his office for a time after chapel was over and between classes. Years later alumni still recall how available he made himself. One commented: "I don't remember that I ever had need to counsel with the President, but I'll always remember how he came out directly into the hallway—he was the most approachable of people."

Largely through the encouragement of Horace Smith, Evaline Howes, whose husband had been a member of the Board of Trustees before his death, became increasingly involved in the life of the school. She was a woman of wealth and culture, who had maintained from her youth a simple and deep commitment to the Christian faith. After her husband's death she was elected the first woman member of the Board of Trustees, and sought to carry forward his interest in Garrett.

When the President suggested that she might consider building a prayer chapel on the Garrett campus in memory of her husband, she responded enthusiastically. In January 1937 the beautiful Howes Chapel was dedicated. It was designed for private or small group devotions. Again and again as I passed the chapel, the door commonly standing open, or entered it myself for a moment of renewal, I have found one or more students quietly seated in meditation or kneeling at the altar. It has the exquisite simplicity and also the beauty of a medieval chapel, with its stone walls and arches, its stained glass windows, carved woodwork, altar and kneeling bench—a symphony of architectural skills and artistry. A small but excellent organ is in an inconspicuous loft. Uncounted weddings and baptisms and not a few memorial services have been blessed by its atmosphere of peace and beauty.

Preparing for the Centenary

Dr. Smith looked forward with eagerness toward the centenary of Garrett. It was on December 2, 1853 that Eliza Garrett, the widow of a Chicago business man and two-time mayor of the city of Chicago, signed a will which set aside nearly two-thirds of her fortune for the founding and endowment of a school for the training of ministers.

With this centenary of Garrett coming up over the horizon, the President felt the need (and the Board of Trustees concurred) for a proper celebration. That was a major factor in the determination to enlarge and beautify the main chapel in the administration building, and at the same time to increase the size of the library—both reading room and stacks—which was much needed. The enlarged chapel, with three lovely lancet windows in the chancel, was dedicated in 1952. These windows furnished the outline for the memorable address President Smith gave in June 1953, at the time of his retirement: the first, on the left, the invitation window, "Come unto me;" the one on the right, portraying Jesus teaching, where the key word is "Learn;" the central and tallest, the witnessing panel, "Go ye into all the world." These, he said, are what Garrett is all about—"Come, Learn and then Go."

On a sunny day, the chapel is beautifully illuminated through these and the side windows, also made with stained glass, depicting the great characters of the Old and New Testaments and of church history. Each of them is dedicated to the memory of one or two individuals named by the donor. Our favorite window is dedicated simply to "The Unnamed Faithful." For us that symbolically carries out the message of the chapel windows. We like to envision each new graduating class venturing out to the ends of the world, and also the homes from which they came; and to think of the dedicated church stalwarts who, without any fanfare, have borne witness to the faith day by day, supporting institutions such as seminaries, as part of the great outreach of the Church.

Gerald McCulloh, who taught Systematic Theology, 1946-53, and has continued to be a good friend of the school ever since, had a memorable experience connected with the expansion of the chapel and library:

> When (the work) was in progress the topmost stone of the west front, the pelican on her nest, was carefully taken down, leaned against a convenient tree, and covered with a tarp. One of the workmen asked a professorial bystander what the significance of the pelican was in Christian symbolism. The legend of the pelican was recounted, with its portrayal of the parental sacrifice of life blood, dying that the young might live.
>
> > "In famine it feeds them
> > what love can devise;
> > The blood of its bosom,
> > and in feeding them dies."
>
> As the time approached when the architectural work was nearing completion the workman saw the professor again watching the progress. The workman said, "Doctor, we're putting the ol' she-bird back on her nest today. And Doctor, like the story you told me, I just hope that she will build her nest in the heart of every preacher boy who goes out from this school to ministry in the Church."

Some years after the Howes Memorial Chapel had been built, the President and Mrs. Howes had the lovely idea of developing a Prayer Garden in back of the chapel. In it are four attractive small prayer stations or "altars," each with an appropriate verse:

1. VISION - "I saw the Lord, high and lifted up"

2. CONFESSION - "All we like sheep have gone astray"

3. RENEWAL - "They that wait upon the Lord shall renew their strength"

4. DEDICATION - "Here we offer and present unto Thee, ourselves"

The entire area, with its green lawn, well-kept blossoming shrubs and hedges, is a thing of beauty. Over the years tens of thousands of visitors have quietly walked around the circle, pausing before the several stations.

Garrett and First Church Fellowship

It is not by chance that we include First Methodist Church under the rubric of the Garrett fellowship. Actually First Church, Northwestern University, and Garrett were all established by the same group of persons and with much the same motivation—a deep Christian commitment and a powerful interest in education, and not just education in general but "higher" education with a Christian perspective. Early Evanston grew up around the three institutions, Northwestern University, Garrett, and First Church. Professors gladly gave leadership time to different aspects of the church program. The senior minister of the church was regularly a member of the Board of Trustees of the University and of Garrett. A considerable part of the congregation consisted of faculty people, students and their families. After the early '50's, with the rapid increase of a heterogeneous population and growing diversity in University personnel, this close relationship may not have been as evident.

For at least two decades, under the leadership of Gene and Mary Durham, there was a strong Methodist Student Foundation, sponsored by First Church, which ministered to both Northwestern and Garrett students. Stan Fixter, who was quite active in the organization, remarked that this was especially appreciated by—

> those who did not have student charges. An informal but perhaps inevitable division of the student body existed between those who spent their weekends on student charges and others—primarily single men and women—who were able to hear Tittle preach and participate in the various organizations of that and other churches, and in the Student Foundation, in which much of the non-professional leadership was provided by Garrett young people.

A Happy Thought: Church Night

During the Depression years Evanstonians who had been accustomed to a good standard of living often found themselves pressed just to pay the food bill. Restaurants lost clientele and some had to close down. Few persons could spend money for travel or entertainment. Television was not even on the drawing board. People felt insecure and worried. A happy inspiration led to the development of the "Church Night" program in First Methodist Church, beginning in the autumn of 1932. For a "term" of eight consecutive weeks on Tuesday evenings people were invited to gather in the Church House for an intellectually stimulating and socially enjoyable program. Able volunteer leadership was secured from church members and university professors. Classes were offered in sketching, Bible studies, music appreciation, current events, orchestra, and several other activities. The program was designed for adults (over 18). There were no prerequisites or requirements, and no tuition fee.

Frances Nall, who came to play clarinet in the orchestra, told us after the first session that the man seated next to her did not use his instrument during the first "warm-up." Then, with slight embarrassment he asked her, "How do you play 'A' on the clarinet?" Frances demonstrated, and for the rest of the hour he bravely played each 'A' as it showed up in the music!

For those who could afford it, a good supper was available for 60 cents. Others could come at 7:00 for the first class. At 9:00, after the second class, people gathered in Great Hall for an informal "sing," conversation, and plenty of apples to munch (a dollar a bushel for a good grade of Jonathans). Over 400 attended regularly.

In the spring and for the next two or three years, the same pattern was followed, to the great benefit of the fellowship and the strengthening of the church. Particularly do we remember the appreciative comments of several older women who lived alone: "It is just great to have a program where men participate. Usually we women just meet with other women!"

First Church did not escape unscarred from the Depression. Many of its members were reduced from affluence—or at least a comfortable standard of living—to privation. Comments frequently heard were: "They had to sell their house (or lost it to the bank) and are renting a smaller one on the edge of town." Or "They have gone home to live with her parents." The church budget was not immune; one cut followed another.

Yet in many respects, in spite of economic hardship, we think it may truly be said that the spiritual life and the fellowship of the church were strengthened. For many whose worldly security had been seriously undercut, the fellowship of the church became a shining asset. Perhaps, as Leslie Fuller often said, it takes hard times and tragedy to bring out the best in us. And the fellowship of First Church was more vital in 1940 than in 1930.

In similar fashion Garrett gained strength through adversity. The school learned, painfully, the importance of maintaining closer ties with its graduates and of stressing its central reason for being: training persons for the ministry of the Church. The loyalty of its alumni/ae was quickened and, out of their limited means, they began to give more generously to the support of the school.

The Monica League and Women Students

When the Chicago Training School came to Evanston and joined with Garrett in 1934, it brought far more women into the student body than had been previously enrolled. For a number of years it was generally assumed that in their social life these women would participate in the program of the Monica League. However, their perspective tended to be quite different from that of the wives of student pastors. The "CTS girls," as they were often referred to, were in the main interested in professional preparation for some type of full-time work in the Church—as director of Christian education, youth work, or full-time ministerial or missionary service. Incidentally, they resented deeply the facile assumption of some Garrett male students and professors that "they came to Garrett to find a husband." They also objected to being considered members of the Monica League. That is, they were members of the general student body and wished to participate in the Dempster League along with the men, rather than being in a separate female organization or "caucus."

Quite understandably they resented being urged to join in the social and educational program of Wives' Week, designed for wives of student pastors. Surprisingly, the administration was quite slow in recognizing this rather obvious difference in perspective. When Frances Nall, following the retirement of Belle James, was asked to assume responsibility for directing the field work of some of the women students, she was instrumental in opening the eyes of the administration to this situation. Of course it should be added that when a professor invited a class to his home for a social evening, women students were included, as naturally as were the men in the class; wives of male students were also invited.

The Wives on Student Charges

The traditional concept that seminary students should postpone marriage until after their graduation was rather thoroughly abandoned before mid-century. The availability of "charges" in which the "student pastors" could earn a modest living was an attractive feature of the seminary. Usually the church preferred a minister who was married and whose wife would live on the charge during the week and assume some responsibility for the church program while her husband was in Evanston. This worked out very well in the case of a wife who was enthusiastic about her husband's choice of career and who was mature enough to give leadership to the people when necessary. For some of the new brides who came to Garrett with their husbands, fresh out of college and bashful, the situation might seem quite formidable. One of our faculty wives, who remained petite and pretty after many years in a parsonage, enjoyed telling of her first Sunday, along with her husband, on his first charge. She had determined that she would play her part, so she walked along the aisle after the service, shaking hands and introducing herself, until a rather deaf elderly lady said, "And whose little girl are you, my dear?"

The Monica League, an organization originally designed to include all women related to the school, usually had as part of its annual program a discussion of life in the parsonage, for the benefit of those wives who were "learning by doing." It was not easy for a young woman who lived perhaps a hundred or more miles away from Evanston, and whose husband "had the car," to attend these meetings at Garrett. It gradually dawned on many of us that the welfare of the wives of student pastors had been more or less lost sight of. A wife on the charge had little chance to share in her husband's educational experience, or to know his professors, friends, and fellow students.

Someone, perhaps a couple of faculty wives, had the bright idea of planning a "Wives' Week," when wives of student pastors could accompany their husbands on their return to Garrett for a four-day visit in autumn or spring. They attended classes with their husbands and enjoyed some special functions which were planned by students and faculty. This proved highly popular. Faculty people with an extra room and several lay families in Evanston opened their homes for the three nights that wives were in town. (If the couple had children, kindhearted lay people on the charge often undertook to care for them.) A reception for the wives was usually held, and a party or, more often, a banquet and program were enjoyed on Thursday night in the Great Hall of First Church. This pattern was continued for many years and was greatly appreciated by both the wives and their husbands. It gave the young women a favorable acquaintance with seminary life which proved valuable in many ways, not only at the time but also in future years.

A major event in the Wives' Week program was an afternoon tea held in a faculty home for them together with some of the faculty wives. The program consisted of an informal practical talk by one of the faculty wives and an opportunity for the visitors to discuss and ask questions about the problems they faced on the charge, and their own personal adjustment to their roles as wife of the minister with responsibilities during his absence and as a potential community leader.

Thursday Night at the Commons

Before Loder Hall was erected, with its superior accommodations for serving meals, the Garrett "Commons" was located on the foundation floor of the administration building where the Religious Education Library is now housed. The space was quite limited; the ceiling was low and the noise level high. Nevertheless, from the late 1930's until Loder Hall was constructed in 1960 it was the best we had. For many years Thursday night was "special" at the Commons, the meal was often a little more festive, outside friends were invited, and usually the students or guests put on a short program. It might be a musical half-hour furnished by friends from the School of Music, or a cluster of songs by those notable improvisors and free-lancers, Dick Miller and Rocky Smith. Or the "Chapel Octet," led by Joe Bell. Or a comedy skit by Bob Holmes and Helen Terry or Don Marsh. Occasionally a guest was invited to give a more or less serious address.

Frances Smith remembers Charles Kraft, respected Old Testament authority that he was, imitating an "eminent biblical scholar." His props were a podium and an old corded floor mop. He stood behind the podium, which concealed the long handle, rested his chin on the thickly-bunched, floppy corded "working end," and—

> looked for all the world like a bearded Hebrew authority delivering a lecture to his confreres. No one without Charles' background of knowledge could have produced such an impressive sequence of nonsense, with all the intonations, pauses and emphases of the dedicated researcher. It was masterful, so patently a parody of his own style that his listening students howled with delight. Only a person of Charles' essential modesty and subtle sense of humor could have carried it off so joyously!

A colleague recently reminded us of certain non-academic occasions when the Leiffers gave a dialogue: Murray presented an interpretation of Mortimer Snerd, Charlie McCarthy's addle-pated side-kick. Dorothy's role was not that of Edgar Bergen, but of Mortimer's "Gran'ma," and Mortimer, perched gingerly on Gran'ma's knee, uttered many Snerd malapropisms, to the enjoyment and relaxation of sometimes serious-minded scholars.

On one occasion, according to Tom Pendell ('41) there was unusual excitement because:

> The Rev. Ernest Lynn Waldorf, elected to the episcopacy way back in 1920, the father of Northwestern's head football coach, and now the massive bishop of the Chicago Area, was a special guest. I do not know how many pounds there may have been of that imposing bishop.
>
> After the meal he had remarks to make about the needs of the pastorate; he requested one or more students to be selected to

respond. For some unknown reason, one of the choices fell on me. I have never been effective as an extemporaneous speaker. I had no idea what to say, and here was this overpowering bishop.

But I underestimated my fellow students. One of them, it may have been Jesse Firestone, whispered a quip. When I was called to make my remarks (I have absolutely no remembrance of what they were, and undoubtedly no one else does either) I closed with my fellow student's observation. "The pastor is called to be the shepherd of the flock. He leads the sheep, he carries the lambs, and sometimes he has to kneel with an obstreperous old ram!"

It brought down the house. The good bishop, all 300 or so pounds of him, left the Commons still chuckling, with some sense of hope for the future of the Church.

The "unusual" often happened at the old Garrett "Commons." Vera Largen Watts remembers one lively evening when, amidst the general hilarity, Chuck Loney made some comment that his fiancee Betty did not like. She declared, "If you say that one more time, I'll put this piece of pie in your face." Chuck, laughing, repeated what he had said and—she did what she said! (P.S. Vera was subsequently present at their wedding, and now, decades later, they are still happily married. Perhaps learning how to give and take pie in the face, with laughter, may be good preparation for a happy home life!)

Those Garrett Banquets

All-school parties were memorable affairs. Sometimes the faculty put on one of the skits. One year their contribution was a "light opera" titled "The Education of Willie Alibi," and sung to the tunes of Gilbert and Sullivan's "Pinafore." Paul Minear deserves major credit for writing the Garrett lyrics. It opened with a faculty chorus, singing and stepping in time to the music:

> We're the Garrett faculty, and our sacred school's a beauty.
> We're sober men and true, and attentive to our duty.
> When the boys go to sleep—from our lectures deep. . . .

A faculty discussion followed, beginning with a recitative by Dr. Hollington:

> Grave and reverend doctors: The Reverend Mr. Willie Alibi hereby petitions with many contentions for more extensions of his cranial dimensions lest he meet suspensions. . . .

After eight of the faculty expressed opinions, Willie (Dean McSloy) sang in his own defense:

I am sincerely sorry
That I am very late again
With term papers and exams. . . .

To which the faculty chorus responded:

But so are his brothers and his sisters and his friends.
But so are his brothers and his sisters and his friends.

Willie's wife (Dorothy L.) then sang a solo in his defense, narrating the many demands on his time at the charge.

The audience, which had been enjoying the program vociferously, broke into gales of laughter as our venerable Harris Franklin Rall launched into the Captain's recitative, with echoes from the faculty chorus. The first part went as follows:

Rall: When I was a lad in the seminary
           I preached every Sunday on an itinerary,
           I fired the furnace and I swept the floor
           But I polished up the apple for the professor—

Chorus: He polished up the apple for the professor—

Rall: I polished up the apple so carefully
           That now I am the teacher of theology—

Chorus: He polished up the apple so carefully
           That now he is the teacher of theology.

Even more hilarious—if possible—was the faculty contribution another year, acting out a play, produced by Frances Smith, called "The Lure of the City." The villain (Frank McKibben) enters a farmhouse "settin' room" and gradually persuades a simple country maiden, Penelope (Dorothy), to flee with him to enjoy the delights of the city. Her "maw" (Georgia Harkness) in night-robe and sleeping bonnet hears a noise and discovers that Penelope has been enticed away. Her distress and yells arouse "paw" (Irl Whitchurch), who comes on stage yawning, attired in his red "long-johns." With the timely intervention of the hero, John True (Otto Baab), Penelope is rescued from "a fate worse than death." A harrowing drama!

After such an evening the relations between faculty members and students are bound to be less formal than in a typical graduate school.

The only unhappy memory we have connected with any of these school banquets was when Minta Nagler had a serious accident. She had been making a new dress to wear for the occasion, and all she needed to do was to get the hem even. She donned the garment and mounted the dining room table in their apartment so that Art could pin the hem. Unfortunately, as she turned she moved too close to the edge of the table, which tipped and she fell to the floor, breaking a leg (her own, not the table's). Of course we were all full of sympathy when we learned of it the next day.

<>

A delightful custom was begun during Dr. Smith's presidency. Soon after the school adjourned for the Christmas recess, a special turkey dinner was served in the Commons, to which all the "Garrett family" was invited—faculty, staff, custodians, spouses, and children. In fact, the children were central in the occasion. We all became well acquainted with one another's youngsters. Always there were Christmas carols, sometimes followed by a little nativity play in which the children took the parts.

Mary Forrer, at that time secretary to the President, recalls, as we do, how important was the fellowship of staff and faculty in the Christmas parties. She remembers how pleasant they were for her two small children and herself:

> There were games, story telling and sometimes a dramatization by the children. One time it was the Nativity story as written by Frances Smith. Phyllis Holter was Mary, my John was Joseph. He still recalls that experience clearly. "I was only ten, but I felt it deeply. I think I almost thought I *was* Joseph."

Then of course there was the Big Event of the evening, when Santa Claus arrived with much jingling of bells and a big pack, from which came an abundant supply of candy and oranges for all of the children. The Santa Claus was generally a faculty member—Charles Kraft or Rocky Smith—or Gus Freeburg, our chief maintenance man. As the number of younger people on the faculty grew, the ratio of children participating likewise increased, until in the 1950's there were about as many children as adults.

VI

A SEMINARY CANNOT ESCAPE
THE POLITICAL WORLD

The Second World War brought many changes in the life of the school. Some were overt and affected the program directly. Others were much more subtle. A considerable number of our students decided that they should enter the military service as chaplains; a few dropped out of school immediately or when their draft numbers came up. Others—the large majority—availed themselves of the government provision that seminary students could continue their school work until graduation. Each year several graduates entered the chaplaincy, but most moved into the full-time pastoral ministry. There were lively debates in halls and dormitories over what role a Christian minister should fill during wartime, and many consultations with faculty members. Quite a few students and a number of faculty members were conscientious objectors.

Northwestern and Garrett were required to name Co-ordinators of Civil Defense. The President asked Rocky Smith to take that post for Garrett. It became his duty to ensure that in the event of a blackout no lights were showing from any of the Garrett buildings. We experienced no air raids in Evanston but there were two or three late evening "alerts," which gave Rocky something besides lectures to think about.

Otto Baab served as a labor mediator for the War Labor Board and was sent to many parts of the country (in non-class time) to arbitrate various labor disputes, as he was a person fully acceptable to both union labor and management.

Many faculty and students regularly went to the Northwestern University Clinic to contribute blood for the blood bank to be used in military hospitals. Some conscientious objectors thought of this as an appropriate way to "save life, not to take it."

One morning during a change-of-class interval, Murray went down to the main entrance hall and was aware of loud talking. Approaching the center of it, I discovered a stranger and one of my advisees arguing heatedly. I interrupted and asked what the commotion was about. The outsider held a pair of handcuffs. When I asked him who he was and what was his business, he produced an FBI identification card with his picture. He stated that the student had refused to register for the draft, and showed the FBI order that he be picked up. At this point he started to put handcuffs on the man. Speaking with as authoritative a voice as I could muster, I first addressed the student:

"You recognize the legality of his action, don't you?"

"Yes."

"Then you will accompany him peacefully?"

"Yes."

Then to the FBI agent I said, "Put away the handcuffs. These cannot be used in this building. He will accompany you peacefully to your office." To my relief the officer, looking a little surprised, responded, "O.K., if you're sure." And without more ado they walked together down the front steps to the agent's car. As I recall, the student was assigned to alternative service after a court hearing, and accepted the assignment.

It may have been true that some men did enter Garrett and other seminaries in order to escape the draft; certainly their number was very small. The admissions office and faculty made a serious effort to keep such persons from seeking what we considered would be an unethical use of sanctuary. However, those of our students who had registered as conscientious objectors were subject to draft call; others came with valid endorsement of church authorities and their Draft Boards to register in the seminary to prepare for ministerial service.

In 1943 Draft Boards ruled that men preparing for the ministry must be in residence throughout the year. Since Garrett in its five-week summer school that year had had an enrollment of 288 from 15 denominations, it was a simple step to plan for two consecutive five-week summer terms in 1944. Three other seminaries (Bethany Biblical Seminary, Evangelical Theological Seminary of Naperville, and McCormick Presbyterian Theological Seminary) were pleased to join us in sponsoring the full summer quarter. We had a faculty of 20, many of whom taught in only one of the five-week terms. The same pattern was followed in 1945 and after that date Garrett continued on its own to offer two five-week terms each summer.

At the close of the war there was a considerable inflow of persons who had been in the various military services. Some came from the chaplaincy; most had been in the Navy or overseas. All were grateful that peace had finally arrived and that they were able to pursue their professional training.

Frances Smith, who was working on her doctoral thesis in psychology at the University of Chicago, conducted in-depth interviews with two sample groups of returned servicemen—ten enrolled in the Northwestern Technological Institute and 20 in Garrett. One fact stood out: in each group there was evidence of serious emotional repercussions from the war. Many were deeply in trouble below a surface of relative self-control, and these fears and conflicts needed to be worked out.

With the war safely (?) past there was some overt tension between a few of those who had been conscientious objectors and the returning veterans. Whether it was due to a self-righteous feeling on the part of some CO's who were more peace-loving in theory than in heart, or to a sense of guilt on their part or on the part of the veterans—or perhaps a feeling of bitterness on the part of veterans that they had suffered while the others had not—it is impossible for us to say. Probably all these and still other factors were involved. At any rate there was internal suffering. Time and gradual rebuilding of self-confidence and trust were needed.

A returned captain in the infantry was in one of my classes in the spring of 1946. He had been in action through some of the bloodiest battles on the Western Front, and had memories that would not be easily erased. In our course on "Christianity and the Social Order" he with many others shared in the discussion of the issues and costs of war and peace. However, not until his senior year did I realize how bitter he felt and how disillusioned with an instructor who, in spite of counter evidence, could still support a position of reconciliation as the road to peace. But some months before his graduation he came to the office to say that slowly and painfully his own position had changed—and he wanted me to know it. We have continued to be friends.

Another veteran and advisee, Buren Stewart ('48) wrote recently:

> We had several conscientious objectors and pacifists in Garrett immediately following World War II. Many of these (I have since thought perhaps out of a feeling of guilt) were more militant in their pacifism than the former servicemen were in their beliefs. Some of these considered us former servicemen just slightly above criminals, and were always taking advantage of every class opportunity to make disparaging remarks concerning us. One day this happened in Dr. Blair's class. He could sense that most of us servicemen had heard enough of this type of treatment. We were forever grateful to him for taking the remainder of the class period to point out that except for those of us ("poor wicked devils") who had served in the armed forces during World War II the chances were that none of us would be free to make such remarks, much less attend seminary. This was the last time we had to suffer insults from the pacifists and CO's. It was interesting that the former servicemen acknowledged that the pacifists and CO's

had a right to their opinions but they never acknowledged that we
had the right to ours.

Such internal and overt tension continued through the years of the
Korean War and after. One man in the 1950-52 period was doing
unsatisfactory work in his classes, perhaps because he thought he
should be involved directly in the Korean struggle. Because of his low
grades he was advised to drop out. He then enlisted and experienced
active duty in Korea. Afterwards he wrote to inquire whether he could
return. He was readmitted and at the end of the second day in the fall
quarter went to his advisor: "Rocky, I can't go on. I'm back in the
same emotional situation I was before . . . . I'll have to leave." To
which Rocky replied, "You can't do that. The faculty gave you a vote
of confidence, and we believe you can make it." After thinking about
it for a bit the veteran said, "O.K., I'll *do* it." And he did. He did have
some problems along the way but he has since had a long and
distinguished career in the ministry. Other similar stories could be
recounted.

Society Moves to the Right

It seems to be the case that during and after great crises, when
people are forced to recognize the instability of human institutions as
well as their own personal limitations, they tend to "get religion,"
especially of a conservative, "fundamental" type. They seek primarily
a faith-affirming, loving, healing resource. Prophetic preaching at
such a time is popular only if condemnation is limited to our
"enemies." As a popular TV preacher recently advised a group of
ministers: "Lay off all that divisive stuff. People want to be 'affirmed.'
Tell them that God loves them, forgives and upholds them, and heals
their diseases. Preach positively and they will love you. Forget divisive
subjects which are sure to get you into trouble. You cannot raise the
budget that way."

This pattern of avoiding controversial preaching was evident during
World War I and for some years afterward. There was a similar swing
of the pendulum during and after World War II. This shift toward "the
old-time" religion and also toward conservatism in politics occurred in
the late 1940's and early 1950's, and expressed itself in several ways.
The meteoric rise in influence of Joseph R. McCarthy, Republican
Senator from "liberal" Wisconsin (of all places), was clearly due to the
vigor of his anti-Communism "investigations." "Patriotic" citizens
also loudly applauded the investigations of the House Unamerican
Activities Committee. Any person of prominence who disagreed with

an inquisitor like Senator McCarthy ran serious risk of being pilloried and of losing his position. One such person was Methodist Bishop G. Bromley Oxnam, who endured extreme inquisitorial probing by the House Unamerican Activities Committee. To clear his record and to demonstrate that he was not a Communist, he asked for permission to appear before the Committee. For one day, "evidence" was presented and accusations made by attorneys for the Committee. Oxnam was permitted to answer questions, but was not permitted to ask questions or make any statements. The distinguished lawyer Charles Parlin sat beside him but was not permitted to speak. Oxnam subsequently wrote of the ordeal in *I Protest*, published in 1954. This was before the United States Senate finally came to grips with the behavior of Joseph R. McCarthy. On December 2, 1954, the Senate voted, 67 to 22, condemnation of him for a number of reasons, including abuse of fellow senators and insults to the Senate during investigations earlier that year, as well as his manner of probing for alleged subversive activities.[1]

When the Editor of the *Christian Advocate*, T. Otto Nall, asked a senior FBI executive how many Methodist preachers were identified as Communists, the answer was an unequivocal "None."

A great deal of political pressure was brought on teachers and professors, from grade school to university, to conform to the standards of patriotism and anti-Communism which were demanded by such persons as Senator McCarthy. In Illinois the "Broyles Bills" were introduced in the Legislature. These "loyalty oath" bills, if passed in their original form, would have called for the dismissal of any person in a tax-supported institution who espoused or taught any system of government other than that stated in the United States Constitution. Under such a law, if strictly applied, a teacher could not have lectured on the British governmental system or that of most other nations. Courses on comparative government and on the ethics of politics would have been legally prohibited.

The legislation would have required teachers to sign a "loyalty oath" in order to hold their jobs. This, in the minds of great numbers of teachers whose genuine loyalty could scarcely be questioned, was an insult to their integrity as conscientious American citizens and as

---

[1] An example of the unreasonableness and unfairness of some defenders of "the cult of loyalty" was given by Alan Barth in *The Loyalty of Free Men* (Viking Press, 1951). He cites the explanation given by a woman who was active in having Owen Lattimore's appearance before a resort hotel gathering cancelled in the summer of 1950: "Just now with the critical condition of this country, anyone about whom there is any question should not be allowed to speak."

teachers of history and political science. It was an effort to use undemocratic and unconstitutional methods to protect so-called democratic institutions, and to eliminate criticism of the self-appointed censors and "defenders of the Constitution."

Some members of the Garrett faculty were profoundly concerned about the Broyles bills. After considerable discussion, they prepared a letter addressed to every Methodist minister in the state of Illinois. It analyzed the dangers of such political action and urged that they and their people exercise their constitutional rights to protest the adoption of such witch-hunting legislation. The letter was signed by Ernest Fremont Tittle, Harris Franklin Rall and Murray H. Leiffer. A number of other faculty members would gladly have added their signatures, but it was decided that three names would be enough. Fortunately the legislation was subsequently defeated, though by only a narrow margin. The Garrett faculty would not have been affected by it, but we felt conscience-bound to speak out in protection of the rights of teachers in publicly supported institutions.

Naturally there were repercussions. President Smith received a phone call one evening from a member of the Board of Trustees, informing him that at the Trustees meeting on the following day another member was intending to speak of the serious "Communist threat" and to declare that at least two members of the Garrett faculty belonged to "Communist-front organizations"—namely the American Civil Liberties Union and the Fellowship of Reconciliation. The caller, whose father had taught at Garrett, said, "Horace, your mettle is going to be tested tomorrow at the Trustees meeting. Mr. X is going to move that two members of the faculty be dismissed because of their political views." The next day this ultra-patriotic member spoke of the "pervasive Communist influence" and named two of us. At that point President Smith leaned forward and said, "Before this matter receives serious consideration by the Board of Trustees, I wish to turn in my resignation." That ended the discussion. This was far more significant than it now might seem. Dr. Smith tended to be conservative politically. However, he trusted the faculty and was a staunch defender of the faculty's right to speak their Christian convictions. The inquisition got nowhere on the Garrett campus. Incidentally, a president who is somewhat on the conservative side of the political spectrum can often do a better job of protecting a faculty member whose political and economic views are "left of center."

A similar incident had occurred at the end of World War I, as mentioned in Chapter IV, when heavy pressure was unsuccessfully brought on President Charles Macauley Stuart to have Professor Doremus Almy Hayes fired.

Indeed it was true that many of us on the faculty were members of the Fellowship of Reconciliation. Dorothy and I had joined it in 1924 and have continued our support of it to this day. But we would strenuously protest now, or at any time during those years, any accusation that we were Communists or disloyal to the fundamental documents on which our nation was founded. I did, in fact, include the "Communist Manifesto" by Karl Marx in a list of required readings, on the hypothesis that a person cannot understand or effectively criticize any point of view without knowing specifically what that view is. Former students have since expressed appreciation for that particular assignment.

As I recall, it was Rockwell Smith who remarked that it would be wiser for us to set forth what we as Christians stood *for* rather than to put in so much time on "defensive action," such as opposing the Broyles bills. He and I decided to invite colleagues to share in a faculty seminar to study the relationship between Christianity and Communism. This we did. The result, a product of months of study and discussion in an effort to speak affirmatively and constructively concerning the issues presented to our society by Communism, was the formulation of a document titled "Christianity and Communism, an Analysis." It was divided into two main parts: a Christian analysis of Communism, in which we compared and contrasted the two systems of thought on a number of points; and Christian principles for action, followed by a bibliography.

Before finalization and publication, however, we invited and benefitted by the criticism of perhaps two-score lay persons with various political perspectives—lawyers, union leaders, business men, and others. After further revisions (during which Otto Baab remarked that only one word of his original paper remained; it was "the"), the statement was published in the *Christian Advocate* on September 8, 1949. We subsequently had it printed in a four-page format and made available at cost. It proved widely popular for use in discussion groups. Numerous business organizations sent us orders for 100 or more copies. It received commendation from many quarters, as diverse as the then Chief Justice of the Wisconsin Supreme Court and Norman Thomas, the perennial Socialist candidate for President. In fact, by 1963 it had gone through 16 printings, a total of 280,000 copies. It had also been reprinted in many lands, including Burma, Chile, Egypt, Germany, India, Japan, and New Zealand, and in many languages, including Arabic, Bengali, Burmese, Hindustani, Portuguese, Spanish, and Urdu.

A small minority wrote sharply critical letters. Some came from self-proclaimed Communists and others from people on the extreme right. An editor of *The Readers' Digest* declined to use it because the magazine was then preparing its indictment of the Methodist Church as part of "The Pink Fringe." In spite of the criticism, it was a project that seemed to fill a real need and we, and also Garrett, were proud of it.

The Theological Pendulum Also Swung

Another interesting outcome of the stresses of the war was the increasing theological bent toward neo-conservatism. That there was much evil in the human soul could scarcely be debated. The social legislation of the 1930's had helped to protect the poor and the weak, but there continued to be as much self-seeking, misrepresentation, and moral turpitude in government and in society as there ever had been. It was quite understandable, at least to a sociologist, that European theologians, whose countries had been devastated and who dwelt in a society demoralized by the appalling costs of the Great War, should assert that man could not save himself, and that only the grace of God could suffice. They were the first to point out how futile had been the best of human efforts to eliminate war and poverty, to transform social structures, and to bring in the Kingdom of God. (Witness the complete failure of the Kellogg-Briand Pact of 1928, in which the nations bravely renounced war as an instrument of national policy.) They told us that only the acts of God could bring about salvation; humanity could not save itself.

Persons like Walter Rauschenbusch who preached the "Social Gospel" were considered naive in thinking that man by himself could bring forth the "Good Society." This was of course a partial and unfair interpretation of what the "Social Gospelers" sought to teach. It is true that they had shown a highly optimistic view of humankind, and would not concede that man was "fatally flawed" in his nature. For them the demand for social righteousness arose directly out of the imperative of the Gospel. They asserted that because of God's love and purpose Christians should exert their best efforts to become effective instruments of His will and should work toward a better world. (How commonly innovators or discoverers of a "new" theory stress the significance of it by greatly exaggerating the differences which separate their new view from the old, "orthodox" view. Almost inevitably there is an unfair and unfortunate denigration of the opponents' position by exaggerating what are conceived to be weak points and overlooking strengths.)

There were many American theologians who concurred with Frank Rall. He had consistently taught that salvation is a matter of the spirit and is God's gift, but that Christians are under command to work for a better world. His position, we felt, was firmly based on the New Testament itself and the teachings of Jesus. In the 1940's and 50's, as it had been in the 1920's and again in more recent years, it was difficult to hold a middle position between extreme right and extreme left.

The new theological trend held center stage for a decade, but was soon countered by the "death of God" theology. We at Garrett considered ourselves truth-seekers. Therefore we were eager to hear all relevant points of view and then to assume responsibility for our own conclusions. So, exponents of both neo-orthodoxy and "death of God" theology were invited to lecture at Garrett.

One indelible memory from the late 1950's: We were dinner guests in the home of a faculty colleague and his wife. Another faculty member from beyond the seas and his wife were also there. The discussion turned to essentials in Christian belief. I remarked that while belief in the Virgin Birth was generally accepted as an important doctrine, it was not a fundamental, a litmus-paper, test of being a Christian. The colleague from overseas immediately and unequivocally announced: "Then you are not a Christian." To which I responded, "Fortunately you are not the final judge of the matter." Incidentally, before a decade had passed, and after he had left Garrett, his theological views became less orthodox than my own.

VII

END OF AN ERA

An educational institution which has served for 100 years is indebted to great numbers of persons for its development. Two of the brightest stars in Garrett history were Harris Franklin Rall and Horace Greeley Smith, both of whom we knew and cherished over many years. In retrospect their retirement—Dr. Rall in 1945 and Dr. Smith in 1953—seemed to span the closing of an important era in the life of the seminary. The intimate fraternal relationship among the faculty members was slowly ebbing away. Our homes were not only dispersed over a much wider geographical area around the school, but our loyalties and interests were also becoming more diverse. In sociological jargon, the faculty, after World War II and especially after Dr. Smith's retirement, was gradually becoming less of a primary and more of a secondary group. This certainly does not mean that conflict or interpersonal tension was developing within the faculty, but rather that the school was becoming more impersonal, like any graduate school within a university. Increasingly it seemed to us (almost certainly many of the newer faculty members would disagree) that those who were joining the faculty tended to view their work as a professor in a large department of Philosophy or Speech might see his responsibility, calling for faithful attention to classroom teaching, writing, and research in his field—but with less personal involvement in the lives of the students, less of what once was considered a pastoral concern. Perhaps as a correlate, there seemed to be a diminished feeling of responsibility for the school as an entity.

In the 1930's, '40's, and into the '50's it was still common practice for many of the faculty to entertain at dinner in their homes two or three other faculty couples. These were intellectually stimulating and thoroughly enjoyable occasions. We all had a common loyalty to the Christian faith and a common purpose—preparing students for leadership in the Church. Further, we were all active as members in some local church, the large majority in First Methodist Church of Evanston.

If a faculty husband or wife became ill, other couples would bring prepared meals, take care of the children, or give other help as needed. While there was some gossip, so far as our awareness extended it was always based on a kindly concern. We knew each other intimately, and none of us wanted to hurt a colleague or to see others hurt him or her. And divorce in a faculty family was unthinkable. Perhaps some moderns would say, "Strange age of innocence." But we liked it that way.

This pattern of relationship was well exemplified by Professor Rall and Dr. Smith and was upheld by them with earnest commitment. We wish to share a few memories about these giants in the life of the school and, more briefly, those who joined the faculty between the dates of Rall's retirement in 1945, and 1950.

Frank and Maud Rall

Harris Franklin Rall was one of many children in a warmly evangelical Christian home. His father, a minister in the Evangelical United Brethren Church, served pastorates over a period of decades in Iowa. Frank's boyhood home was marked by a simple devout piety and, as he later remembered, his father's theological ideas were less important in his own development than the religio-ethical tone which characterized their home.

> Religion was fellowship with God in vital experience, a sound ethical emphasis for which there was to be no substitute, and a deep appreciation of the Church, not as a sacrosanct institution, but as a fellowship and a living instrument which had the right to the unfailing service which both my parents gave it.

After graduating from Iowa State University and four years at Yale, Frank studied in Germany for two years. He received his doctor's degree from the University of Halle-Wittenberg. He then served as pastor of churches on the East Coast, the last being the Lovely Lane Methodist Church in Baltimore, where the Methodist organizing or "Christmas" Conference had been held in 1784. From there he went to the presidency of the Iliff School of Theology in Denver. In 1915 he joined the Garrett faculty as Professor of Theology.

Frank's strong ties to his siblings continued as long as life lasted. A "Rall Round-Robin Letter," including all members of the extended family for three generations, circulated at least annually until the time of Frank's death. There were also family reunions, with as many as 40 to 60 attending, filling a sizable section of a resort hotel for two or three days.

An interesting remembrance of Frank's remarkable combination of pastoral concern and theological wisdom comes from Richard Miller.

The pastor of a large church with which Dick was well acquainted had a physical breakdown and was out of the pulpit for six months. His parishioners continued his salary and sent him to Florida, paying all his expenses. In the same church was a woman whose husband was not well and had to undergo several serious operations. He received no help from his employer, nor did the people at the church seem to be particularly concerned. Painfully aware of the contrast,

> she . . . complained to me one day that she was losing her faith in God and her church . . . the pastor was getting all the attention. I talked to Dr. Rall about it . . . . "What would you do if you were their pastor? Their pastor is ignoring them." I said, "Wouldn't you like to go over and talk to this woman? She's a wonderful person."

> To my amazement he said he would like to talk to her. I had the opportunity to introduce them. She had read his articles in church papers, and knew that he spoke with a good deal of authority. I have never forgotten how he gently but carefully brought her back to a whole new concept of faith . . . . His general approach was, "You can't let people who misunderstand and are unsympathetic be big enough to blot out your God." He stressed that there is only one model in the human race that you dare keep your eye on, and that is Jesus and the way he handled problems. Slowly this lady began to soften. Some time after that her husband died. I talked to her many times as I grew older. And I discovered what Dr. Rall had really done for her. He had not only been a father figure, but he had also brought her to a better understanding of the nature of God and the nature of a congregation or a church.

The Leiffers will never forget a certain sunny Sunday morning in January 1936. We had been living in a one-bedroom co-operative apartment at 725 Simpson Street and felt the need for another bedroom, as our son Don was growing older. The opportunity came when we heard that a commodious apartment in a well-constructed building was available at 721 Foster, across the street from where the Ralls were then living. We had made a down payment on the apartment and on Saturday had been interviewed by the other five residents in the co-op. The next morning on our way to church we saw the Ralls approaching from their apartment, and had a sudden impulse to divulge our secret hope about moving. Maud exclaimed, "You lucky people! For years I've wanted to live in that building. Do you suppose there is another apartment available?" With joy we shared the news that the owners who lived in the other third floor apartment had inquired just the night before if we knew someone who might like to buy theirs. They had to move because two and a half flights of steps were too much for the husband's heart condition. We were happy to get the two couples together, and by the next week the Ralls became our future neighbors across the hall. For over ten years we shared the third floor between us.

Then an apartment on the first floor became available. Frank asked if he could talk privately with the two of us, and sought our advice as to whether they should buy the first floor unit and move downstairs. He said the stairs did not bother him a bit, but he thought they were becoming a little troublesome for Maud. We urged the purchase. In less than a week, Maud asked if she could talk with us some afternoon. She said: "I've been wondering if it might not be wise for us to buy that first floor apartment. Climbing two and a half flights of steps is not good for Frank. We've enjoyed living opposite you folks over these years, but—what do you think?" We said we thought they should buy the first floor apartment, and the sooner the better. They did, and neither one knew the other had spoken to us. After they had moved down the two flights, when a friend congratulated Frank on their wisdom in moving down, he replied, "Well, neither of us was really troubled about the stairs, but it makes it easier for our friends to call on us!"

<>

Both Maud and Frank were short of stature. The people on the second floor, whom they had known for many years, were named "Ball," and were above average in height. So Frank said he advised their friends when calling not to become confused between the "small Ralls" and the "tall Balls" who lived on the second floor, below them.

Unlike many persons who are short of stature, the Ralls enjoyed joking about their height. Frank recounted on a number of occasions how he once stopped to chide two young boys who were sitting on the curb smoking cigarettes. "You boys shouldn't smoke cigarettes, or you won't grow up to be tall men." With a sly glance up at him, one boy replied, "Is that why you're so short, Mister?"

Maud showed equal aplomb. She frequently deplored her difficulty in getting clothes that would fit her and still look appropriate to her age. One day she saw a pretty blouse being displayed in a shop window in Evanston. She entered and asked the clerk, "Do you have a blouse like that which would fit *me*?" "Why, surely. I'll bring some out." Maud slipped on one after another, and the cuffs always hung below her wrists. "My goodness," commented the clerk, "You surely *are* small, aren't you?" "Yes, my dear," Maud replied, "and do you know—there was a time when I was even smaller!"

<>

Maud and Frank were gracious, warmhearted persons, able to laugh at themselves, alert and in full command of the situation, and never stymied for a reply. At the same time they were two of the kindest people we have ever known, always sensitive to the feelings of others.

Students and faculty over the decades have enjoyed the Ralls' hospitality. One colleague, speaking of Maud, said she is "the Perle Mesta of Garrett," to which Rocky responded, "She is the hostess with the mostest." Maud and Frank Rall set a gracious social precedent with their entertaining at dinner, usually followed by lively conversation and some party games, such as Charades. On more than one occasion Maud protested Frank's suggestion that we adjourn to the living room, because, she said, "The conversation around the dinner table is always so delightful." For 40 years, during the time of Dr. Rall's teaching and even after his retirement, he and Maud were central to the life of Garrett.

In light of Dr. Rall's unusual competence as a teacher and also his widely recognized status as a theologian, President Smith asked him to continue teaching beyond the normal retirement age. Frank was author of at least a score of books, and winner of the Bross Prize in 1940, for his *Christianity: An Inquiry into Its Nature and Truth*. Not so incidentally, Ernest Fremont Tittle, pastor of First Methodist Church in Evanston for 30 years, remarked to me one day as we were walking from the church to his home, "You know, Murray, I preach the gospel according to Rall." No higher compliment could be paid.

It was in February 1945 that I had another memorable experience of Frank's modesty and wisdom. He said to me, "We both know, Murray, that as teachers grow older the time comes when it is wise for them to retire—but they may not recognize it. I want you to tell me when you think that time has come for me." My answer was, "You already are tentatively scheduled to teach a seminar this autumn. I think you are highly competent to do that, and have a great deal to offer. You might tell Horace that you plan to retire at the end of that course." And so he did. He was then 74.

With Maud, Frank continued an active interest in Garrett until his death in October 1964. It was probably a year later that at an alumni luncheon in Loder dining room we were sitting across the table from

Maud and George and Agnes Buttrick. George was conversing with Maud, and we chanced to hear him say ingratiatingly, "Do you mind, Maud, if I ask you how old you are?" Maud sat up a little straighter than usual, and responded calmly, "Yes, I do." There was a brief silence before conversation was resumed on another subject. (It was the only time we had known George Buttrick to be at a loss for words.) Later, when Maud and we were together, she said, "Did you hear Dr. Buttrick asking me how old I was? Do you think that was nice?"

Arthur Nagler

Surely in addition to Frank Rall the name of Arthur Nagler belongs conspicuously in the era that closed with the retirement of Horace Smith. He and Horace were members of the distinguished Garrett class of 1910. And they both retired in 1953. In a very real sense the upbuilding of Garrett was *the* life work of each of them. Each was an exemplary and honored Christian minister. Yet they differed in many major respects. Horace seemed by temperament and proclivity to be a born leader; Art was well content to play a loyal supportive role. To speak figuratively, Horace became an able Director of the Band; Art enjoyed a less demanding role and played the flute with faithfulness and beauty. Art was never a policy shaper, and was slow to express his opinion on a faculty matter (unless called on). Yet he, with no effort or intent on his part, exerted great personal influence. He was beloved by all who knew him, faculty, staff, and students. Like Nathanael (Jn. 1:47) he was a person in whom there was no guile.

Art experienced much tragedy in his life. He early suffered from a severe loss of hearing. In the early Depression he and his wife lost their home, on which they had been paying for many years, when the payments could no longer be met. Within a year his wife was killed in an automobile accident. Yet at no time did he make a public display of his grief, or expect any special concessions on account of his sorrow.

Before his wife died, he and a student committee were planning a social event for the student body. The date was set, much work had been done on it, and announcements were posted. A member of the committee has written:

> When we received word of the death of Mrs. Nagler, we expected to call off the party. But he insisted that we not do so. He said the date was several days away, and he felt his wife would have wanted no change of plan. The night of the party he came, sat a while with several small groups, and as he left he said to a few of us who had worked with him on the plans for the evening, "You must know life goes on in spite of human events."

Arthur Nagler was one of the most irenic of men, and there was always a kindly sparkle about him. Dick Miller was the Dean of the School for Approved Supply Pastors held at DePauw University in 1955 or '56 and invited Art to teach one of the courses. Of the 54 men and women enrolled, three or four had serious heart problems. They were given the best rooms on the first floor, and Dick felt he had to explain such favoritism. The explanation evoked the concern of the entire group, especially a small number who were certain—

> the heart problems could be healed by prayer. At first I discouraged the efforts of these men because their evening prayer service was so loud. Those studying . . . were disturbed and asked me to calm the group.

> Dr. Nagler came to our rescue. He listened to the prayer group as they attempted to enlist his efforts to assist their friends to health through divine intervention.

> At last he said, "You folk know I can't hear any sounds without my hearing aid. Do you believe I haven't asked God to repair my hearing? I believe he has answered my prayer. I have found other ways: He has assisted me to endure my deafness. I have even found some advantages, with God's help, in deafness. There is much we are better off not to hear. God knows our needs. God will assist us as we assist ourselves to the best of our abilities."

Some time after his wife's death, Art married Minta Stahl, a gracious, gentle but dynamic woman a few years younger than himself, who had served several terms as a missionary in China. After Art's retirement they took a leisurely bus trip from Evanston to California—the first such experience for either of them. She later told us that the trip was a great success. "It was as much fun as having an eager child on the trip. Arthur's quick glances took in everything, and his exclamations of delight at each new experience endeared him to the other bus passengers." The Naglers retired in Santa Rosa, California.

Some New Faculty 1946-50

As the second World War drew painfully to a close in 1945, troops were gradually mustered out of military service. The enactment of the federal GI (Government Issue) Bill of Rights provided among other benefits both financial and psychological inducement for veterans to take up once again their educational objectives. Some who had not intended to go to college or graduate school, unable to find satisfactory employment, rethought career possibilities and took advantage of the government subsidy. The net result for Garrett was an increase in enrollment and a need to enlarge the faculty. During the years from 1946 to the time of Dr. Smith's retirement in 1953 a total of 16 persons joined the Garrett teaching faculty, and we would like to mention a few of them. Two stalwarts were added in 1946, Richard W. Miller in Church Administration and Gerald O. McCulloh in Systematic Theology.

<>

Dick Miller was a Garrett alumnus ('39) and a man of many talents—alert and sensitive. He had a facility for listening, and people opened up their hearts to him and discussed their problems, justifiably feeling that they could trust and confide in him. Actually he had developed the art of indirect counselling before the psychologists had made it a popular technique.

Something of Dick's skill and method was in evidence when he was a student. A classmate came to him and said, "I guess I'm in trouble. I didn't know that Leiffer expected us to keep a notebook on his daily lectures. The quarter is nearly over, and I don't even have a notebook." Dick said this was difficult for him to understand, since most in the class were keeping notebooks and talking about it.

His friend asked Dick, "What do you think I should do about it?" To which Dick replied:

> It seems to me you can't expect him (Leiffer) under the circumstances to make a great exception for one person . . . . Why don't you look at him as a man who is fair? I am sure he has said in your presence that ministers should be brotherly. They certainly should be honest with each other. You and I also know that he is a professional man. So why don't you go home, dress up as neatly as possible, be sure your finger nails are clean, put on a white shirt and a necktie. Then go in and say to him, "I made a serious mistake. Somehow I missed the assignment of a daily notebook on your lectures. I haven't kept them. I'm sure such a notebook would be valuable, but I don't have one." And simply trust him to do what he thinks would be best. But (I said) it's important that you appear to be a professional man, striving to be better in your profession, and looking to him as a professional guide. A few hours later he came to tell me, "Well, he isn't going to flunk me. But he will cut my grade." And I thought, well, that's Murray Leiffer. He's fair.

Richard Miller was a good listener. He always had ideas and was definitely practical—a well balanced, common-sense type of person, sympathetic but never emotionally overwhelmed in spirit, not given to histrionics or boasting. He made an excellent Director of Student Appointments.

<>

Gerald McCulloh was Scottish in background and very proud of it. He had his doctor's degree from the University of Edinburgh and displayed a Scottish penchant for Philosophy and Theology. Quick in his perception, he was probably the best storyteller on the Garrett faculty. He was a genial, insightful teacher of Systematic Theology who rarely, if ever, lost his "cool." A student in a basic course in theology turned in a term paper on "Jesus Christ as Savior." In his hurried typing the student at one point hit a "q" instead of a "g." The result was the statement: "Jesus has taken away our quilt." The quick-witted professor thought this an opportunity that should not be missed. He circled in blue pencil the word "quilt" and wrote in the margin, "It's all right. He promised to send the Comforter."

Perhaps his most interesting hobby was collecting chiming clocks. He had over two dozen of them, all comfortably ensconced in the living room and hallways of their home. Not all of them were running, but once a year, on New Year's Eve, all were wound and set to chime together. Big Ben in London could not compare! He gave his wife Evelyn high praise for not complaining about keeping them dusted and happy. And she deserved it!

<>

Charles F. Kraft came the following year from a teaching position at Albion College. His doctorate was in Old Testament from the University of Chicago. And that became his teaching field at Garrett. Charles was an activist whose commitment to the Church, to his teaching field, and to Garrett never wavered. As his son Robert remarked to us not long ago, "Dad desired to teach in the seminary. For him, that was the highest. That was where he wanted to be. Garrett was his whole life. I am sure we kids got tired hearing about it. His loyalty extended not only to Garrett as an institution but also to his faculty colleagues." In fact, he bought a copy of every book written by a colleague to include in his personal library. No matter what job he might be assigned by the administration, he did it with verve. He never missed a committee meeting.

One thing deeply disturbed him, especially after he became

chairman of the Committee on Graduate Studies: the pressure of special interest groups to ease the requirements or, to state it more euphemistically, "to introduce more flexibility" so that the PhD degree might be more readily available.

Two delightful stories involving Charles Kraft are recounted by Robert Payne:

> Joyce and I were married at Christmas time of my first year at Garrett. She had been accepted for admission as a student, so enrolled for the second quarter in January. We both took Dr. Charles Kraft's Old Testament course. The first day of class, he was calling the roll from the enrollment cards, and after he called my name he studied the next card and said, "We also have a *Miss* Payne, Miss Joyce Payne." Joyce answered by saying, "Mrs." Then Dr. Kraft, who was my advisor, remembered that I was to have been married over the Christmas vacation. He said, "That reminds me of a story. There was a young man in seminary who was married during the school year and did not go on a honeymoon. One of his professors was in the habit of calling on a member of the class to open the session with prayer. Without knowing that the young man was just married, the professor called on him to offer the opening prayer at the first class session after the wedding. The young man had other things on his mind and was taken by surprise; he said the first thing that came into his mind: a prayer hymn—"Dear Lord and Father of mankind, forgive our foolish ways. Reclothe us in our rightful minds, in purer lives thy service find, in deeper reverence, praise." When Dr. Kraft finished telling that, the class roared with laughter, and my wife was welcomed into the Garrett community.

> Later that same quarter, we had written term papers for that course. I had written on Micah, Joyce on Hosea. On our way home for lunch one day, we were having a good-natured debate over which was the greater prophet. As the debate warmed up with our voices rising for emphasis, we slipped on the snow and both went down into a snowbank. As we picked ourselves up, shaking with laughter, we discovered that Dr. Kraft had been walking behind us and enjoying every bit of our debate. He was laughing heartily over the whole incident. I think it helped our grades in Old Testament that quarter!

When Charles spoke of Amos or Micah, students almost thought they could see the old prophet alongside the professor. Charles was a dramatic, vibrant teacher, who had no trouble maintaining the interest of his students.

Samuel Wong, from Singapore, talked to Dr. Kraft about entering a Master of Arts program at Northwestern, but Kraft—

advised against it because of my deficiency in liberal arts education. After I scored "distinction" in the qualifying exam for the BD program, Professor Kraft himself suggested to me that I might reactivate my interest in the MA program and promised that he would write a recommendation to the Graduate School for my admission. I was amazed that he remembered a discussion held a year earlier, and at his supportive attitude and actions.

Charles and Louise, his wife, when on vacation attended church as usual—preferably that of a student or Garrett alumnus. Al Eliason recalls his surprise and gratification when the Krafts dropped in for a service at his small church in Oconto, Wisconsin.

<>

Ronald Sleeth also came to Garrett in 1947, in the field of Preaching and Speech. His was a joyous spirit, full of fun and yet with a serious turn whenever the subject of preaching the Word came to the fore. He was a West Virginian, having most of his educational work within the state, although his doctorate was from Northwestern University. As Fred Norwood recalls, Ron "was always proud of his West Virginia upbringing, but characteristically always joking about it. When a couple of us were recommending the joys of a camping vacation he rejected the idea out of hand: he had had enough of that back home. His idea of a great vacation was a luxury hotel on the beach!"

<>

Through all this period Ernest Fremont Tittle would usually teach a course on preaching twice a year. Long after, students remembered that Tittle was tough on the class, but he was also tough on himself. "Three things he demanded: 1. State your objective. 2. Prove it. 3. Clinch your commitment. He tore our sermons to pieces and then helped us to put them together in better form."

<>

Glenn Olds ('45) was another alumnus who returned to Garrett as a teacher (Philosophy of Religion). His vivacious, eager manner and rapid-fire lecturing endeared him to the hearts of students. One alumnus wrote that "frankly he intimidated me with his profound intelligence and skills of articulation." However, Glenn was with us for only three years ('48-'51) before moving to the presidency of a college in the East. He is currently President of Alaska Pacific University in Anchorage.

<>

In 1948 a significant new teaching field was introduced in the curriculum with the coming of Carroll Wise as Professor of Pastoral Psychology and Counseling. To be sure, the subject had previously been dealt with directly or at least indirectly in courses in Church Administration, and a number of courses in Psychology had been available by cross registration in Northwestern. Leiffer, when he first came, offered some work in the field of Social Psychology, including a course in "The Church and Social Pathology"—later wisely changed to "The Church and Mental Health," which indicated an important shift in perspective. Carroll Wise, with his excellent training in psychology and his clinical experience in hospitals, was able to open the whole new (yet old) field of human life and struggle to our students who were training for pastoral work. Therefore I willingly relinquished two of my courses which were within his field of special competence.

Not only were Carroll's offerings a significant addition to the curriculum, he also contributed greatly to our students through his personal counseling. As time went on and the need for such counseling increased, others joined him in the teaching and counseling work at Garrett: Ruth Wick ('53-'57) with courses in Religion in Higher Education and Counseling, John Vayhinger ('58-'64), and Morris Taggart ('64-'70). Ronald R. Lee came in 1971, and John Hinkle in 1973.

Carroll was a hardworking and conscientious teacher, and under his leadership a considerable number of persons earned a doctor's degree in pastoral counseling and entered professional service. One of our alumni remarked that "Professor Wise was the self-conscious pioneer, always insisting that what we knew was not quite enough. He knew more about the psyche than most of the rest of us, and rarely would he give up on 'a problem case.'"

So persuasive was his teaching that some students who entered the ministry thought of themselves as counselors rather than pastors. I recall two who announced in their bulletin the "hours when the minister will be available for counseling." One of them told me he could not understand why his members did not avail themselves of his services; and a parishioner of the other man bemoaned the fact that their pastor would sit in his office waiting for people to come to him, but was rarely ever willing to make a pastoral call. Of course, this was not Carroll's fault.

<>

Don Holter joined us in 1949 as Professor of Missions and Christian World Relations. He had his doctorate from the University of Chicago and had served with his wife Isabelle as a missionary in the Philippines ('34-'45), where he had been interned by the Japanese for three years. His teaching at Garrett was much enriched by his knowledge of and experiences in Southeast Asia. In 1958 he was elected President of the newly established Saint Paul School of Theology in Kansas City, where Bill Case, who taught Christian Education at Garrett from '49 to '59, joined him in 1959.

<>

Ernest W. Saunders, with his doctoral work in Biblical Studies from Duke University, came in 1950 in the field of New Testament Interpretation. Attractive in appearance and unassuming in manner, he soon was a valued member of the faculty fellowship. Ernie had a deep commitment to the Christian faith, coupled with an excellent command of the literatures of the early centuries of Christian history and the polish of an erudite scholar. His wide travels and research in the ancient libraries of Mount Athos and elsewhere added depth and vitality to his lectures. As several alumni testify, "He really made the letters of Paul come alive." Another, who himself has a great respect for the spoken word, remarked, "Professor Saunders' lectures were models of elegance and delivered with oratorical skill."

We on the faculty also benefitted. I still recall the clarity and sincerity with which he expounded some passages from Paul's letter to the Galatians at a faculty retreat. Feeling that he did such a good job as a teacher, I urged Ernie not to yield to Dwight Loder's request in 1963 that he accept the post of Dean of Faculty. Other counsel prevailed and he assumed the onerous, though honorific, job. As the years have passed I must admit I was (probably) wrong, for Ernie rendered effective yeoman service in that demanding administrative post even through the difficult "times of trouble" that were already on the horizon. And apparently the addition of that new job did not interfere unduly with his teaching ministry. He returned to full-time teaching for the four years before his retirement in 1979.

Verina and Ernie were gracious hosts to many student groups,

Monica Leaguers, and faculty wives. Together they have conducted travel seminars to Greece and the Holy Land, to the enrichment of what might be called on-the-spot teaching. This he still continues to do.

A few other men were brought to the faculty in the later years of Dr. Smith's presidency, but their major contributions were made in years following his retirement.

Horace and Edith Smith

Horace Greeley Smith was born in 1881, on a farm in La Salle County, north central Illinois. There he grew to maturity, working as a farm boy, doing his share of the planting and harvesting and tending to chores. His love of the horses on Valley Farm was matched only by his appreciation of his parents. He attended the country school and worshipped with his parents in the village church.

Horace's college degree was from Northwestern ('05) and his seminary degree from Garrett ('10). In 1909 he married the sweetheart of his youth, Edith Gorsuch, and with her he shared, with joy, the rest of his life. (He died in 1968.) He soon became a respected leader in the Rock River (now Northern Illinois) Annual Conference of the Methodist Church. He knew both ministerial and lay people throughout the Conference by name, and possessed the attributes that made him both a good pastor and a skilled "political" leader. Fourteen years after his graduation he was elected to the Board of Trustees at Garrett. His entire ministry, apart from the years when he was a District Superintendent, was in the territory surrounding Garrett. He taught one or two courses a year from 1924 to 1932, when he was elected president of the seminary.

In 1932, the year of crisis for Garrett, he was asked to represent the Board of Trustees to serve with Frank Rall and Leslie Fuller on a special committee which was assigned the awesome task of reducing faculty salaries and determining who would have to be dropped from the faculty. At that time he was pastor of the Wilmette Methodist Church. When he agreed to become President at Garrett, he knew that he was giving up an excellent pastorate with an assured salary, and was fully aware how insecure the financial future was for Garrett. Nevertheless, because of his deep loyalty to the school, he accepted the hazards and a sharply reduced salary. Neither then nor in any of the following years did I ever hear him express regret or ask for any sympathy because of his changed circumstances.

To the presidency he brought not only an outstanding sense of commitment but also a pastoral concern for faculty, staff, and students. This was characteristic of his administration. He repeatedly referred to the "Garrett Family," and there was indeed in the faculty and staff a feeling that "all of us are in this together." Some occasionally referred to him as a "benevolent dictator." Perhaps it would be both kinder and more appropriate to think of him as a "father figure," and for hundreds of alumni/ae he was truly a model of the good pastor. Certainly he did not let anyone "push him around." He was by nature cautious and conservative. These traits, so important in those years, along with his many strengths, made him a competent and loved administrator.

Through all this period of economic vicissitude Edith was his close and faithful companion. A statuesque and attractive woman, she was also friendly and gracious. She had beautiful snow-white hair—a "crown of glory," as Horace called it. She was always carefully attired (often in red "because it is Horace's favorite color") and presented a striking appearance. She was a sensible person, with full self-control. Alert and intelligent, she never took advantage of her position as the president's wife. They had three attractive daughters, one of whom died in her thirties, leaving her parents and family deeply grief-stricken.

Both Horace and Edith were proud of their grandchildren and were happy to be with them—an attitude joyfully reciprocated by the children. They called him "Go-Go," because he was always on the move.

Rocky Smith, who joined the faculty in 1940, developed almost a filial attitude toward President Smith. Unlike others on the faculty, he could not bring himself to call him "Horace." When speaking formally he usually said either "President Smith" or "Horace Gamaliel Smith" or in informal conversation, simply "the Boss." For all of us Horace was, by both his formal position and his skills and background, the "head man." Rocky Smith, in his own inimitable fashion, has many a story to tell about "the Boss."

> There was the new student who came to his office, was met by the President at the door, and who on being invited to come in and have a seat walked around behind the desk and sat down in the President's own chair. President Smith continued the interview seated in the visitor's chair, his dignity unaffronted and his sympathetic interest unimpaired.

> On another day a bellicose young man came charging into the office to complain of Garrett's failure so far as he was concerned. After discharging the full measure of his venom on an unresisting

President, he suddenly sprang to his feet and exclaimed: "Do you know what's wrong with you, President Smith? You treat us as grown-up men, and we aren't!"

With complete honesty Rocky included himself among those who might have tried the President's patience:

> When I first came to Garrett, I developed a sense of frustration and resentment. My ego was battered by what I took to be the indifference of my colleagues; and with the unhappy rationalizing facility which is the bane of the academic mind, I found much to criticize and to condemn. In the spring of my first year I could contain myself no longer and thrust myself for audience into the office of President Smith. He invited me to sit down and to talk, the latter invitation being hardly necessary. For 20 minutes I attacked Garrett and its policies, during which his only reaction was an occasional amiable grunt. At the end of that time I had run down and there was a short silence. Then President Smith spoke, "What should I do about all this, Rockwell?" Those words came like a clarifying breeze to a fevered brow. Suddenly I saw myself quite clearly both for what I was, a carping critic, and for what I really wanted to be. My reply was obvious in the light of my new sense of being understood. "I guess I don't want you to do anything. All I needed was to get some things off my chest. I feel better about everything now."

Undoubtedly it was Horace's influence that brought Mrs. Frank W. Howes to the Board of Trustees after her husband's death, and led her in 1935 to establish the Frank W. Howes Scholarships. Each year she entertained "her boys" and a few of the faculty, along with the Smiths, in her home. About once a year she would ask President Smith to conduct a communion service in the Howes Chapel for "her boys" and herself. Even though it meant acute pain because of her arthritis, she insisted on coming to the altar to kneel in participation with them. It was indeed recognized as an honor to be a "Howes Scholar." Mrs. Howes' benefactions were of critical importance, coming as they did in the depths of the Depression.

Convinced as he was of the paramount importance of the Church, and fully confident in the ability of Garrett to do a superior job in preparing young men and women for its ministry, Horace was always on the watch for qualified students. He met Tom and Shirley Kennedy while he and Edith were in Greece and invited them to enroll at Garrett, which they did. (Tom was a research assistant in the Bureau of Social and Religious Research from 1954 to '57.) Just before their first Christmas Dr. Smith showed up at their residence one Sunday afternoon with a fruit cake. He had been given several and wanted to share them.

Many a student remembers with genuine appreciation the President's open-handed welcoming of them. Buren Stewart ('48) has an interesting story to tell:

> I answered the "call to the ministry" while I was in the army during World War II (402nd Field Artillery Battalion, 42nd Infantry Division). While still in the service following the war, I wrote several schools concerning ministerial training. From a large seminary in my own jurisdiction I received a letter written by the Dean, who informed me there had been a war, living conditions were crowded, and things were rough. He closed the letter by saying the seminary only took "honest boys" and they would accept me but under "no circumstances should I bring my wife." (I was well aware there had been a war, as we had gone in during the "Battle of the Bulge" in Europe, and had been in the "Battle of the Rhineland," and other heavy and hazardous engagements.)
>
> President Horace Greeley Smith of Garrett answered indicating conditions were crowded but that Garrett was buying some houses for married students. He encouraged me by saying, "Come ahead, we have never had anyone sleep outside yet." This indicated something of the big heart and spirit of this man who guided Garrett through some very rough years, and made the difference in our attending seminary there.

Buren and Gladys lived in "Aldersgate House" during their years at Garrett.

Eager to increase the number of outstanding Garrett alumni, Dr. Smith sometimes "went the second mile." Tom Pendell ('41) recounts:

> About six weeks before the close of my year at Garrett, I was called in to the President's office for a personal interview. "We would like to have you as a graduate of Garrett," he informed me. I explained that I already had a seminary degree from the School of Religion at the University of Southern California (now the School of Theology at Claremont), and that after three years on special appointment with the Methodist Board of Education as the first executive secretary of the National Council of Methodist Youth I had simply decided I wanted an experience of seminary in the "East" before returning to a pastorate in California, and had chosen courses on the basis of need and interest rather than on graduation requirements.
>
> That did not deter President Horace Greeley Smith one bit. "Get me your seminary transcript," he requested, "and we will see what we can do."

Some days later I delivered the transcript and he began to review the four years' graduate work I had behind me. "Now look, here is this requirement taken care of, this other can be counted as equivalent of such-and-such, this undergraduate course can be given graduate credit, etc." Sure enough, five weeks later I stood capped and gowned with the Class of 1941.

Dr. Smith's affable manner and priceless sense of humor showed up in unexpected ways and places. Let Bob Holmes ('51), a skilled pantomimer, describe an instance:

I . . . worked my way through Garrett entertaining at churches on weekends. I also participated rather regularly in "follies" or the regular weekly Thursday night tomfoolery following the evening meal at the Garrett Commons. So something of a reputation was established.

It all came to a head one day on the occasion of Honors Chapel, that moment when scholarships and fellowships and awards were given to those students who had been outstanding in their academic performance. I, like most of my fellow students, attended out of courtesy to those few who would receive rewards.

Imagine my astonishment when, in the midst of the proceedings, President Smith called my name. My astonishment was exceeded only by that of the assembled multitude. "Bob Holmes? An award? For what, pray?"

I went forward and as I faced my fellow students President Smith gave a rendition of his experiences and perception of me. He had known me and my family since my childhood, since I had grown up in Evanston. (I once hid in his alley incinerator when I played hooky from Orrington School . . . but that's another story.)

He indicated that in my youth he hadn't always been sure what would become of me. He further acknowledged that he still wasn't always sure. Nevertheless, he thought I should not go unnoticed for a particular quality of contribution I had made to the seminary community, and in that light he awarded me a book. I read the title: "The Life of P. T. Barnum." The audience, grasping the appropriateness, exploded. I wondered all kinds of things . . . "A sucker born every minute . . ."

What the audience never knew was what Horace Smith had written on the flyleaf of that book. It read, "A book about a man I greatly admire to one in whom I confidently believe!"

There is no book in my library I treasure more.

Whenever Horace could do so he returned "to his roots" to talk with the old-timers and to revisit the old farm and the cemetery where his parents were buried. One day, on returning through nearby Seneca, he stopped to chat with James Uhlinger ('34), the pastor there, and lamented, "You know, Jim, I walked up and down Main Street, asking if anyone remembered members of my family or friends. I drew a complete blank on the subject. Then I walked out to the old cemetery, and there they all were clustered together—and waiting for me."

Horace read widely and had an excellent memory for quotable sentences from classical as well as modern literature. And he enjoyed poetry. One short poem he liked to repeat was written by Frances Smith, and sent as their Christmas letter by her and Rocky. One line especially in it had an esoteric meaning for Horace. In "whisper of morning" there was a reminder of immortality for him, especially since his daughter Grace had recently died.

New-born Child

Dearest beginning
Whisper of morning
Little green seedling
Turned to the sun.

Noontime is coming
Thunder and nightfall
Burn, little candle-flame
Innocent One.

It was not easy for Horace Greeley Smith to retire. The retirement rule that had been established in the mid-20's, calling for retirement at age 70, was "forgotten." When someone spoke to him about it, he said, "That was for faculty—not for the president." The 100th anniversary of the founding of Garrett was appropriately the crowning of his life's work. Certainly he more than anyone else deserves the credit for the financial recovery of the seminary and the upbuilding of its morale during the perilous Depression years. He was 72 when he retired. But he had the joy of still being President at the time of the 100th anniversary celebration. In all of these events and through the days of struggle and achievement, Edith, his wife, was his close companion.

It was decided, in accordance with his desire, that after his retirement he would have an office on the first floor in the main building. There was, however, a certain poignancy in this arrangement. He was no longer the focal point around which the life of the school revolved. Occasionally a faculty member or a student would drop in to see him, but there were no large important issues awaiting his decision. At times he would stop in at another faculty office to chat. After a couple of years few of the students knew who he was as he walked through the hall. Both he and Edith were acutely aware that, great as had been their contribution, the seminary surged forward without his advice. Observing his unhappiness over this situation, our personal resolve was strengthened to move far away when my retirement became effective. It had long been my policy when I gave up the chairmanship of an academic committee to turn over all the records to my successor and to say, "The job is yours. If you want to talk things over with me—you know where my office is." But rarely was advice asked for.

The great tower of Garrett which has been dedicated to Horace Greeley Smith is not the most important of his memorials. That is Garrett itself, which in a very real sense owes its life to him.

VIII

THE OLD SHIP PLOWS AHEAD

In his valedictory address Horace Smith closed with a quotation from Alfred Noyes:

"Take thou this torch
And carry it out of sight
Into that great new age I must not see,
Into that great new realm I must not tread."

And good Christian man that he was, he did not shed a tear as he turned from the podium and as those of us who knew him best were sure, gave his blessing on those following him who would "take up the torch" and carry it forward with dedication and in joy.

Otto Justice Baab—Acting President

Probably it was wise for the Garrett Board of Trustees to plan an interregnum following the retirement of Horace Smith. He had filled the office of President so effectively and for so long a time that a new person might well have been handicapped under his shadow. Therefore, the Board asked Otto Baab, who everyone knew had no desire to be president, to serve for a year or two while the search for a successor proceeded. He had been on the faculty for nineteen years. With the retirement of Arthur Nagler, along with Horace Smith, Otto was the senior member of the faculty, except for Leiffer. He had demonstrated his ability, unselfish objectivity and integrity again and again. Otto deserved and enjoyed the full respect of the entire faculty and staff. There was a strength and stability in his character that was widely recognized. He curtailed his teaching with reluctance. A modest man, he had no desire for the temporary honorific status involved in the presidency, and kept his own office until he could happily return to it and once more take up his chosen profession.

Other members of the faculty appreciated the burden which Otto assumed, and I believe presented no special administrative problems. At the first regular faculty meeting, one of us moved that he appoint a committee of three, including the senior member of the faculty in terms of age and two others, to prepare a recommendation concerning a retirement policy, to be presented to the faculty and then to the Board of Trustees. After due deliberation, the committee recommended that all faculty and administrative personnel should normally retire at age sixty-five, with the provision that if both the person and the administration wished him to continue on a year-by-year basis, that would be acceptable until the age of sixty-eight. Frank McKibben, a member of the committee, was the first to retire under this rule, which remained in force at least until the time of my retirement—1970.[1]

Otto Baab carried the presidential load to the full satisfaction of faculty, staff and trustees until Dwight L. Loder was elected in the spring of 1955.

Dwight Ellsworth Loder

In 1955 Dr. Loder came to Garrett from the pastorate of the prestigious Hennepin Avenue Methodist Church in Minneapolis. He had been an exemplary pastor and an able administrator, and brought with him a joyful, optimistic spirit. Dwight never claimed to be an expert in theological education, but he did have the attributes needed to give effective leadership to an institution that was well prepared for his coming.

The first time that Dwight Loder visited Garrett to speak in the chapel, after his election to the presidency but before assuming the duties of that office, he approached the pulpit with a slight degree of hesitancy. Sam Sallie ('57) recalls his first words: "I come to this desk with a measure of uncertainty. I hardly know where to start. I feel frustrated, like a mosquito in a nudists' colony!" The boisterous laughter which followed demonstrated the delight of students and faculty at the informality of the new president.

It was at Dwight Loder's urging that the faculty began holding an annual retreat in September. For two or three days we lived together at a Y.M.C.A. camp or some other facility, discussed the academic year that was ahead of us and considered the numerous problems that face a faculty in its professional functioning. More important, however, was

---

[1] The then-President, Orville McKay, asked me to continue as an adjunct professor because of the number of advanced degree students who were working with me, and certain research projects that called for completion. I agreed, provided it involved teaching no more than the autumn and winter quarters and on condition that I had no other responsibilities than my teaching and research, and that compensation be adjusted downward.

the sense of religious dedication and sharing as pastors to our students—pastors in the making. Periods of thoughtful study of one or more New Testament chapters led by one of the Biblical scholars were times of spiritual deepening. We enjoyed one another's company; at mealtimes and between serious discussions, there was considerable jocularity. Some played cards, others preferred to lie in the sun.

In chatting with Vera Watts about the years past, I asked if she had regularly attended these faculty retreats. She replied that at first she was never sure whether she would be invited or not. Then she laughed, and said that the first time she went, Ernie Saunders had come to her office and somewhat hesitantly asked if she could go, "because Glora Wysner of course will be there, and since she has a broken arm she can't get into her girdle by herself. So we need you there."

During the academic year we generally had two or three "Faculty Seminars" in the President's home, or that of another faculty member. One of us would read a paper telling of recent developments in his academic field, another followed with a critique of the paper, after which we had a general discussion of the issue. These were stimulating and genuinely fraternal affairs. Once, or sometimes twice a year, the Loders would invite a number of faculty couples to their home for dinner and a social evening, covering the entire faculty once a year.

While Dwight and his charming wife, Mildred, did not talk about the "Garrett Family" as Horace had done, they reached out to establish a close, friendly relationship with the faculty and staff families. They continued the festive Christmas parties, to which all faculty and staff members, with their families, were invited. Those were joyful, often hilarious, evenings, singing carols and always climaxing with the arrival of Santa Claus, for the enjoyment of the children. Incidentially, twenty-five years earlier when we first came to the Garrett faculty there were only four children of faculty members living with their parents—Charles Whitchurch, our Don, and the two McPherson youngsters. By the time Dwight became President, there were more young members on the faculty and staff. According to our present reckoning, there were at least 29 or 30 children, though of course not all were present in any year. We were a diverse but happy lot, and many stories come to mind as we think about various members of the group.

New Faculty Members Add Zest

During the latter years of Horace Smith's presidency three new colleagues were recruited to the faculty: Henry Kolbe and Ty

Thompson in 1951 and Fred Norwood in 1952. Each of them made his own distinctive and lasting contribution to the school, and stayed with us until retirement.

<>

Henry E. Kolbe was tall, thin and kinetic, a man of many gifts. He hailed from the state of Maryland. His earlier education and college work were in the South: in Virginia and North Carolina (Duke); and his graduate studies in the North: Garrett and Northwestern. He did his doctoral work under the direction of Georgia Harkness. A man of keen perception and unusual command of the English language, he strove for precision in the use of words and in the expression of ideas. His essays on Abraham Lincoln and Carl Sandburg are masterpieces. Perhaps nowhere does his loving tenderness and his aesthetic judgment in use of words show up better than in his "Ode to Martha," his wife, on her birthday in 1977.[2] Martha was a beautiful woman, tall and comely. She was from the South; her college studies and training as a registered nurse had been in Alabama. By 1977 she had become a permanent invalid, suffering from Alzheimer's disease.

One never wanted to miss chapel when Henry was the leader. He always brought a fresh insight, carefully prepared. Some of us still remember when he led chapel in spotlessly clean overalls, in symbolic identification with the working man. Henry's field was Christian Ethics.

A sensitive person, Henry tended to protect himself by withdrawing from the hurly-burly of faculty debate. He usually underrated both his ability and his influence. Sometimes it was difficult to persuade an advisee to take a course with him. However, I was informed by the grapevine that occasionally a student asked to have Dr. Kolbe as his advisor, because that would guarantee that Dr. K. would not be on his examining committee. Yet many an able student appreciated the very qualities that caused a few to avoid his classes. Sam Wong has referred to Dr. Kolbe's emphasis on—

> the importance of clear thinking and concise language in theological discussion. (He) chaired my oral exam panel for the B.D. qualifying exam. His opening question was , "Mr. Wong, what, if any, are the differences in meaning among the words 'authority,' 'authoritarian,' and 'authoritative'?"

---

[2] We have the permission of their daughter, Marte Kolbe Franklin, to print in the Appendix this touching expression of love.

<>

No one could accuse Tyler Thompson of hyper-sensitivity. Tall, good-looking, with a quick smile and ready wit, he consistently gives the impression that he knows his partner in dialogue is also friendly and ready for a pleasant debate on whatever subject is at hand. After completing his seminary training in 1940 he and his wife, Phyllis, left to serve as missionaries in Singapore. The next year brought Pearl Harbor, and within a short time the Japanese were in Singapore and Ty was in a concentration camp "for the duration." Phyllis and Francia, their first-born, were rushed on to the last vessel to leave the port as the Japanese arrived. He came to Garrett in 1951 after a period of teaching in Allegheny College, and remained until his retirement in 1978.

Ty's informal, easy-going manner might cause a person who did not know him well to underestimate the depth of his Christian social concern and the tenacious courage with which he is willing to follow his convictions. Two stories, in his words, are illustrative.

> During the summer of 1959 I was brought under pressure from colleagues in the Democratic Party to run for Congress in the 13th District of Illinois . . . . The Democratic candidate had never received as much as one-third of the vote in the district, and the incumbent (a well-regarded Evanston resident and member of First Methodist Church) had in one of her races obtained the largest plurality of any candidate of either party in any congressional contest up to that time.

> Thus the prospect of a Democratic nomination in the 13th District was not an attractive political opportunity. But it was an educational opportunity—as every candidate for public office is an educator whether or not he or she recognizes it. Small as the prospect of election might be, however, it would be irresponsible to go into such a contest without facing the possibility of election. So I spent . . . time in discussion with colleagues . . . trying to decide whether this activity could properly be brought within the terms of my call to the ministry.

> When I had satisfied myself that it could, I approached President Dwight Loder to see if there were practical considerations which would rule it out. I explained my situation in full, and President Loder responded without hesitation: "If you decide to do this, I'll do everything in my power to protect you in it . . . (pause) . . . And I hope you'll do it!"

> He had to do some protecting, as it turned out. A certain amount of pressure arose from trustees and other constituents. Later on

he told me . . . a trustee called (objecting to my candidacy) and said, "It seems to me it is getting kind of hard to tell the difference between Tyler Thompson and Garrett Biblical Institute."

To which President Loder replied, "Well, if you really want to separate the two, you might work for his election!"

An entirely different issue (racism within The Methodist Church) was involved in the second episode: A mixed group of Black and white persons were turned away from a Methodist church in Jackson, Mississippi, as they sought to enter for a service on World Communion Sunday in October 1963, and were arrested by the police. Some local church boards in the region had passed a rule forbidding the admission of any Black persons to worship services in a "white" church. The Jackson police made the arrests under municipal ordinances forbidding "trespassing" and "disturbing public worship."

During the months that followed there were more arrests until the number had reached over sixty as Easter 1964 approached. All of the black persons and some of the white were Mississippi residents. . . .

Two . . . pilgrimages were planned—independently of each other—for Easter day. One involved two bishops, the other seven white Methodist theological professors (from three seminaries) and two black laymen.

I was a member of the latter pilgrimage, which was planned as a combination of investigation and negotiation, recognizing the threat of arrest but not courting it. We spent the weekend in Jackson, interviewing persons on all sides of the issue. What we learned through the interviews thoroughly illuminated the tragic nature of the situation. What led to our arrest was our response to the attitude of the Jackson District Superintendent, who said to us, "If our own bishop tried to attend one of our churches with a 'negra' (sic), he'd be turned away. And if he persisted, he'd be arrested!"

We were arrested the next morning at Capitol Street Methodist Church, jailed for two days, convicted in municipal court of "disturbing public worship," sentenced to six months in jail and a $500 fine, and released on bond after appeal. Two years later the charges were dropped.

. . . In the aftermath of our pilgrimage we (and others) lobbied the Methodist General Conference of 1964 . . . to remove any lingering ambiguity in the matter. The Conference responded by placing a prohibition against any racial bar in the legislation on the local church.

> For me the whole experience was a dramatic illumination of the responsibilities of a teacher. The professor who recruited me for the pilgrimage had been my student . . . at Allegheny College. His first words to me on the phone were, "I want to get you into trouble."
>
> I didn't yet know what he was going to ask, but I immediately said to myself, "Unless I oppose what he is going to ask on principle, I'm going to have to accept. No excuse based on inconvenience or unpleasantness will do!"

One colleague remembers "the ease with which Tyler slipped into slumber within the first fifteen minutes of a faculty meeting, amazing us all by his periodic return to consciousness and picking up the discussion as though he had been listening throughout." Those of us who knew Ty best were aware that he never wanted to miss out on any worthwhile debate.

<>

In the autumn of 1952 Frederick A. Norwood joined the faculty in church history to follow Arthur Nagler, who was to retire in 1953. Fred, who earned his doctorate at Yale, had been teaching at Baldwin-Wallace. A quiet and modest man, he was the sort of person who never thrust himself upon you, but with whom it was always pleasant to have a good conversation in his office or yours. Fred's excellent history of Garrett, *From Dawn to Midday at Garrett* (1978), tells a great deal about the school and the rest of us, but one looks in vain for information about the author himself, his numerous publications or his distinctive contributions to the school. Indeed, he wielded considerable influence precisely because he had an alert mind and no one could ever accuse him of being self-seeking.

He taught his classes, as he conducted his research work and participated in faculty discussion, effectively, efficiently and without fanfare.

<>

Three years later Samuel Laeuchli, another church historian, joined our ranks. He was a Swiss, with his seminary work in Basel and graduate studies in the Sorbonne, Paris, and Union Theological Seminary in New York. Sam's special interests were in the fields of patristics and pre-Reformation church history—an excellent complement to Fred's concern for post-Reformation, chiefly American, church history. Sam, tall, slim, with clear penetrating eyes, and his wife, Ann, were a most attractive young couple who came with their little girl and boy, so charming and red-cheeked that one might surmise they were the originals for the popular Hummel ceramics. The evening musicales in their home, delighting and enriching us with music that they and their friends provided, will be long remembered by their colleagues.

Sam was an omnivorous reader and intimately acquainted with the ancient literatures in his field. His lectures were works of art, holding the close attention of his students. One of them, Bob Wilson ('55, Ph.D. '58), thinks of him as the typical absent-minded professor, deeply engrossed in his own field:

> . . . One day he came to class wearing two shoes that did not match. Both were black but very different styles. Someone commented that he must have had another pair at home exactly like the ones he was wearing. . . . I took a course on monasticism with Sam. The midterm exam was "Discuss the theological basis for monasticism." I did that but also gave a sociological interpretation which I said was necessary for an adequate understanding. The next day Sam took twenty-five minutes to refute my sociological analysis.

<>

With Will Rogers I can truthfully say about our faculty colleagues "I never met a man (or woman) I didn't like." A marvelous group of persons with such diverse gifts and talents and professional backgrounds and interests that, taken together, they span almost the whole range of human knowledge, vocationally or avocationally.

Beginning with 1957, about three new members were added to the faculty each year. Yet their tenure was far shorter on average than that of their predecessors in the 1930's and '40's. Of the twenty-six who joined us between 1955 and 1965, one died and seven, including Glora Wysner and George Buttrick who came near the end of their professional careers, have retired. Eighteen others moved on to positions elsewhere.

This relatively rapid change in the composition of the faculty inevitably had two effects. There could not be as close a development of "family feeling" as in prior years. And there seemed less sense of loyalty or being part of a long-term heritage. They did add for the time of their tenure significant strength to the academic offerings. And we enjoyed the fellowship with every one of them. Concerning a few we have particularly fond memories.

Edward Ramsdell's able teaching in theology was cut short by his untimely death from heart attack. He, Rocky, and I used to swim together in the Y.M.C.A. pool. For many years after his death his wife, Lucy, lived in Evanston and maintained close contact with Garrett people.

Philip Watson came from England with excellent educational credentials from Cambridge and the Universities of Tübingen, Germany, and Lund, Sweden. He was an authority on Wesleyan theology and a highly competent lecturer in the field of systematics. Philip and his wife, Joyce, were unpretentious and plain spoken. Their lives were beautiful examples of simplicity in meaningful living. John Wesley would have thoroughly approved of them. Philip retired in 1973; they returned to England where their children had preceded them.

<>

In this period, under Dr. Loder's leadership, two of our Garrett alumni (who had studied with me) were invited back to teach—Alvin J. Lindgren and Merrill R. Abbey. Each had a long period of service at Garrett before retirement. Al was always a pastor at heart and with his wide connections and broad experience throughout the church in Wisconsin and Illinois, he did a superlative job in church administration and field education. He and his wife, Alma, soon became an integral and valued part of the Garrett family. He felt it important in the education of seminary students to help them understand the administrative structure of the church as well as the work of the pastor in the local church. Therefore, every four years he organized a seminar, with a full week spent at the General Conference. Students were admitted as observers to the various conference committees, as well as attending the plenary sessions. Each night the class met to discuss the significance of the issues that were involved in the day's experience. He had been an elected member of several of the General Conferences and therefore was well acquainted with procedures and knew many of the leading participants. In 1976 he was elected to membership in the Judicial Council, and enjoyed the rare privilege of serving for eight years on that elite body—which plays a role within The United Methodist Church similar to that of the Supreme Court of the United States. Its decisions on church law are final within the denomination.

<>

I was particularly happy to have Merrill Abbey become a member of the faculty in 1959. We had been friends since his student days, and I had had good evidence of his excellent work as pastor in Madison and Milwaukee, Wisconsin, and also Ann Arbor, Michigan. His presidency of the first Council for Human Rights, 1949 to 1952, in Madison was an indication of his social concern. Merrill is a quiet but shrewdly observant person. A sensitive and intellectually alert man, he is the epitome of the devoted pastor-preacher. His numerous books are witness to his disciplined scholarship, his deep devotion to the Christian faith, and his ability to speak convincingly. Yet he is always humble about his abilities and achievements. Unfortunately, his wife, Lucy, from the time we first knew them, has had poor health. She is very proud of him, and his devotion to her knows no bounds.

<>

We welcomed George A. Buttrick in 1961, toward the close of a long and distinguished ministry at the Madison Avenue Presbyterian Church in New York, 1927-'54, and as Preacher to the University of Harvard and Professor of Christian Morals, 1954-'60. His mind was both brilliant and encyclopedic. The publishing of the *Interpreters Bible* (12 volumes) by the Abingdon Press was his idea, and he was the general editor of the entire project. Only those who have made extended use of this monumental work can appreciate the breadth of knowledge and the studious attention required for the project. He also wrote a number of the commentaries.

George was an outstanding and persuasive preacher and when he spoke in chapel students made a special point of being there. He imparted to the students the joy of preaching. George and Agnes, his wife, had traveled widely and had a tremendous store of interesting experiences to relate. They frequently competed with each other in the telling of them. An evening in their home was a delight to remember.

Reminders of Mortality

When cherished companions retire and move away, or take a position in a distant city, there is always some sense of loss. Far more poignant is it when one beloved member of a fellowship moves ahead of us to the Other Side. As Ernie Saunders recently wrote, "Yes, there is abundant evidence of our frail mortality as human beings while posing as interpreters of the life and thought of the Christian Church!"

We were all shocked when Edward Ramsdell died of a heart attack in 1957, at the age of fifty-five. Again in September of 1958 our circle was broken when Otto Justice Baab, only sixty-two, breathed his last and "put out to sea." How vividly we remember that Sunday. Dwight Loder had instituted, as part of the "orientation week" for new students, a program of special events. A reception was held by the faculty for them on Saturday. Then on Sunday morning we—new students and faculty—attended worship service in a body at First Methodist Church. This was followed by a dinner in the church dining room. After that we took new students, spouses and any new faculty on a four-hour sight-seeing tour of the city of Chicago.

Just as we were going into the church service, wondering why Otto and Eunice had not yet arrived, Henry Kolbe suddenly burst on to the scene and told us that Otto had just died, and he was sure we would want to go to their home. The service was just beginning. We were overwhelmed at the news and left word with Henry that we would be back before the dinner ended, prepared to lead the bus tour. We quickly got our car and drove to the Baab home. Eunice and Otto were like sister and brother to us, and we had long ago assured each other that if either family had trouble the other would be ready to help. We listened and talked to Eunice and a few of the neighbors until we needed to return, as promised, to the church.

The buses were already there when we got back, and we began one of the toughest afternoons we had ever experienced, feeling almost guilty at leaving Eunice. Yet we knew that at that late moment we could not delegate the job to anyone else. When the tour was over and the buses dropped us at the church we got our car and drove out again to be with Eunice. Rocky and Frances Smith and other close friends on the Garrett faculty either had been or were with her. And before bedtime her cousin had arrived from Minneapolis.

Otto, so far as anyone knew, presumably had been in good health, and Eunice told us they had had a wonderfully leisurely breakfast together before he was stricken with an acute heart attack. Soon he was in the hospital nearby, but he died within the hour.

It was our privilege to go to Minneapolis and share in setting up arrangements for the memorial service, to participate in it, and then to conduct the graveside service as his mortal remains were buried in the family cemetery plot near the country church where his father had been pastor and where he had first met Eunice. She as always was courageous and self-controlled despite her deep grief. We have continued to be in close touch with her, as with a sister, from then until now.

It was many days before the faculty and student body recovered from the shock of his sudden departure.

Non-Teaching Colleagues in the Academic Enterprise

When marshalling memories as we have been doing, it is all too easy to overlook some of the people that keep the ship running. The captain on the bridge and the several officers in their respective positions are, of course, essential but so too are those who stand watch, check the gauges, oil the machinery and swab down the decks. In any educational institution such as Garrett there are men and women working more or less "behind the scenes" who keep "the old ship plowing ahead."

Perhaps most important on the list is the secretary to the President. We have known a number of them—all women of exceptional ability. Elizabeth Lee, who had been President Eiselen's secretary, stayed on at Dr. Smith's request, until 1937. Her successor was Beatrice Darr, who held that important post until 1942. She had been a student of ours at the Chicago Training School, and we knew her to be not only completely dependable and discreet but also keen-minded, efficient, and conscientious. She would never betray the confidences involved in a president's correspondence. Beatrice was followed by Mary Forrer, who was the secretary for Horace Smith, Otto Baab and during the first part of his tenure, for Dwight Loder. Mary was a member of First Church, Evanston. Rocky and Frances Smith knew her well, as all three of them were active members of the Fellowship of Reconciliation. Her son, like our Don, was a conscientious objector. After her husband's death (due at least in part to negligence during an operation), Mary needed to work to support herself and her children. She proved to be a thoroughly competent person to serve as the President's secretary. Dr. Smith once remarked that Mary Forrer "holds the portfolio of Diplomatic Relations with the faculty, students and friends." She also possessed a nice sense of humor. She recalls that—

> . . . when I passed the door of Rocky Smith's classroom I often heard him lecturing in a voice both very loud and most enthusiastic. He tells me that one time I asked him, "Rocky, what *do* you do for emphasis?"

> And then there was the time when a workman who was repairing plumbing at Garrett stopped at my desk and said, "You need a new reducing valve." I'd not seen the man before, but I assumed it was a message meant for President Smith. At least I hoped that was the case!

Viola Somerville, like Beatrice Darr, had been a "straight A" student at the Chicago Training School while the two of us were on that faculty. After graduating from CTS she earned her degree from the University of Chicago. While there she met Cyril Bond, with whom she was later married. We were happy to recommend her to Dwight Loder as an excellent person to have on the Garrett staff. After she had been executive secretary in the Development Program for a year, Dwight asked her to serve as his private secretary. She says,

> When President Loder was interviewing me and relating all the negatives of the job (was it to dissuade me?), he said, "You'll be mad at me because I don't tell you what you need to know." I found a "course" in mind-reading and eavesdropping quite effective. It was amazing how necessary that course was in keeping up with one who moved like a shot from a cannon. Little gems picked up were extremely important and most often of a nature that meant "open ears and closed mouth!"
>
> I recall that Dr. Loder told me that I would meet many of the outstanding Methodist leaders who would pass through that door. This certainly was true. Association with the faculty and staff, as well as the students, was a highlight of my 45-year career.

She found, as did her predecessors and successors, that various teachers and others would drop in and sometimes sit down and "spill over" about their own problems or the behavior of others, but she always maintained both her poise and a proper discretion in keeping the confidences that had been shared with her. She was no ordinary secretary but the President's Executive Secretary and proud of it. She was an officer of the Illinois Association of Executive Secretaries and an active participant in its annual meetings.

After Dwight had been elected to the episcopacy the Garrett staff held a luncheon for the Loders, and Inez Larson asked "Vi" to chair it. Viola, who keeps all sorts of records at her finger tips, said, among other things:

> One mark of a profession, according to Justice Brandeis, is that it is an occupation which is pursued largely for others, not merely for one's self. I can't think of any job of which this is truer than that of an executive secretary. If she is worth her salt, she gets her satisfaction out of the teamwork that makes her "boss" more productive and successful.

And that is the type of person that Beatrice, Mary, Vi, and others who have held that sensitive position, have been.

<>

Another post of eminent importance in any educational institution is that of Registrar. Garrett has been particularly fortunate in the women who have occupied that key office. As a matter of fact, for many years a faculty member carried the title while "the secretary to the registrar" did nearly all the work. In 1929, for example, Harold Ehrensperger was the Registrar and Alice Wescott was secretary to the Registrar. At the beginning and close of each quarter, they and Mildred Magill (the switchboard operator) all were kept busy. Between times Alice Wescott attended to the office and kept the records. In due course Alice was given the title as well as the major responsibility. A quiet, reserved woman with a pleasant personality, she tended to the work with few problems and fewer words of praise.

In 1942 Eleanor Tonkin was handed the task of registering students and of keeping the office records of enrollments and grades—a tremendous amount of detailed work which she handled with patience and skill. She also found time to listen to students, a few of whom in every generation have great facility in forgetting the regulations of the school or in drifting into other sorts of troubles. And all of them are from time to time grateful for someone who will listen and who "knows the ropes." Eleanor writes:

> One time one of the "boys" brought in his brother to meet me. After he met me he looked puzzled and then said, "Did you say she's the registrar?" Surprised, I said, "What's wrong with that?" His reply, "It's the first time I ever knew that a registrar could smile."
>
> Another thing which happened frequently, students would come to the office to tell me about some of their problems and worries. I just listened and when they left they thanked me for letting them talk. I even received letters from some of them after graduating, thanking me for listening—they felt someone cared. Dr. Smith even showed me some letters saying they appreciated my listening.

That was Eleanor—a lovely person in appearance and manner that we all enjoyed having as a member of our larger seminary team. When she retired after more than twenty years of service, the office was turned over to Vera Largen.

Vera had come to Garrett-CTS as a student in 1951. A tall, attractive young woman, she came from the South and spoke with a soft southern drawl. She needed employment, and soon obtained a job working as Rocky Smith's secretary, a post she much enjoyed.

> One of my most interesting experiences, during those student years, was serving as Rocky's secretary—that was an education in itself . . . . I managed to convince Rocky that we should change his filing system—in which everything was filed under states; it was difficult when you didn't know where "Bill Jones" was from! I could not doubt its effectiveness for him, however, and his library shelves were no more conventional either. I once (while he was on sabbatical, writing) was able to discover a reference on material he was sending back for me to type—with some notation such as "the book is green, by a man whose first name is William, and it's on the second shelf from the top."

In 1964 Vera was invited to become the Registrar at Garrett. She accepted and was welcomed with open arms. She and Russ Watts were married three years later. After more than twenty years as Registrar she continues to manage that office, with its ever-increasing volume of record keeping, with skill, humor and a large amount of patience and hard work.

<>

The maintenance team when I first came to Garrett was a father and son combination—Gus and Hugo Freeburg, who carried the full responsibility for the maintenance of the main building and the four dormitory structures for many years. They conscientiously worked long hours. One of them would open the building at 7:00 a.m. and they were busy all day long. They were always on the job when needed—early and late, faithful and competent. We truly believe that there was no better Christian on faculty or staff than our dear Gus, a man of absolute fidelity and one who loved Garrett as his alma mater. As Fred Norwood has pointed out: "Maintenance in those days was hard work, without help from machinery or labor-saving equipment." Often on a Friday afternoon or Saturday we have seen Gus and Hugo stacking the chairs in one classroom after another, mopping the hard-worn concrete floors, and then wiping the chairs with a damp cloth. They were delighted when a rotary scrubber, run by electricity, was provided. Many tables and chairs were repaired by them. Then, of course, there were the offices that needed to be cleaned each week. Long hours, hard work, modest pay, and great devotion. May they have extra stars in their crown!

Gus did not hesitate to reprove a student if he witnessed what he considered to be improper behavior. For many years the Garrett Co-operative Book Store, run by the students, occupied a room on the first floor of the main building. Robert De Long ('42) recalled that in the early 1940's, when Ed and Helen Hunt were in charge of the book store, it was a Branch Post Office frequented by many Northwestern students as well as those who were enrolled at Garrett.

A Northwestern student with laundry bag in hand (because those were pre-laundromat days when students still sent their soiled clothes home to "dear old Mom") came down the hall and was confronted by Gus who pointed to the student's lighted cigarette and said with his strong Swedish accent, "Vee don't do dat here!"

Brushing past him, the student is reported to have said, "Oh, you go to hell!"

Without any hesitation, Gus replied: "Vee don't do dat, eider!"

When Gus retired in 1947 Charles Underwood came as an assistant to Hugo. It was not long before he had won an important place for himself in the hearts of faculty and staff. Quiet, unassuming but wisely observant and ever ready to help, his dependability and also his friendship were appreciated by us all. He had a remarkable influence on the students in each generation and carried forward his own unique "ministerial function" that has blest us all through the years.

Charles was always on hand to open the main building at 7:00 a.m. on weekdays and at 8:00 on Saturdays. Al Eliason referred to this dependability in a recent letter:

We watched Charles Underwood as custodian and friend open the main hall door at 8:00 a.m. Saturday when the end of the quarter had been the previous midnight as deadline for term papers. Then the rush to place (technically but not actually) tardy term papers under the professor's office door. Al Eliason ('52) did this only to find Professor Murray H. Leiffer opening his door from the inside! "Did you sleep here?" the amazed Eliason asked.

Charles' counsel was sought by many a person, student or faculty, on subjects far beyond the range of building maintenance. He had the ability to tell a humorous story or, with a perfectly straight face, make a nonsensical request of a student assistant. For example, asking a helper to bring a left-handed monkey wrench from the tool shop, or requesting him to get "that can of striped paint," which the assistant, disarmed by Charles' innocent expression, sought diligently to do, only to discover that there was no such object.

The years do pass and in December 1985 Charles Underwood retired. For some of us old-timers the place will not be the same without Charles' friendly presence.

<>

The person in charge of the Business Office is everybody's friend.
He or she is the one who writes the payroll checks. And the monthly
check is a matter of importance in every household. Prior to 1932 all of
Garrett's fiscal affairs were handled by a Chicago bank. To save costs
during the Depression and because the man who handled the Garrett
account at the bank, W.H. Watt, was retiring, President Smith
requested him to serve as fiscal agent for Garrett on a part-time basis.

The accounts in the 1930's were far simpler and easier to manage
than fifty years later. No need then to make payroll deductions for the
Internal Revenue Service or for Social Security. No "1099" report
forms or other reports to be filed with the government. No pension
deductions from salaries or payments by the school, prior to 1938. No
health insurance forms except for state workmen's compensation. So
the job was relatively simple, consisting of entering the various
receipts, paying the bills, drawing salary checks, and balancing the
books. Mr. Watt handled the whole of it on a part-time basis in a little
office on the third floor.

As years passed, the tasks multiplied rapidly and paperwork piled
up. Advancing age and the flood of work overwhelmed Mr. Watt, and
he resigned in 1950. Another person named Claude Johnston, whom I
do not remember, followed him. In 1957 Inez Larson, who had been
President Loder's secretary for one year, was asked to serve as
Business Manager.

Inez Larson, like Dwight, came from Minneapolis and had been on
the staff of the Hennepin Avenue Methodist Church. She is a comely
woman with a quick mind, and is a pleasant conversationalist. Like
many a person of Swedish background, she enjoys entertaining and is a
"4-star" cook.

Dwight had been much troubled by inadequacies in the Business
Office; Inez, after she had examined the books, was even more
disturbed by the situation. However, she worked long hours and
faithfully and in due course conditions were much improved, to
Dwight's great relief. In 1968, after Dr. McKay had been president for
a number of years, Inez retired.

Sadayuki Mouri, an accountant with a great deal of experience, was
then named Business Manager. By that time the business staff had
been enlarged to match the increased work. A few years later "Suds"
Mouri was named Vice President for Business Affairs and, according
to the catalog, "all fiscal and physical functions: budget, insurance,
pensions, payroll, cashier" were placed under his direction. Benefit-

ting by his excellent training and prior experience "Suds" with the help of four assistants has been able, we understand, to keep all the records in first-class condition. "Suds," an alert, approachable and highly competent person with a keen open mind, has always been ready to answer with clarity the numerous questions that come his way. He reached retirement age at the end of 1985 and his friendly presence is missed.

<>

In a vital sense the library is the heart of any educational institution that is worth its salt. As most educators and all librarians are aware, the literary heritage of the past is enormous and cumulative. Garrett has always had a good library, but for a couple of decades under Samuel Gardiner Ayres it was handicapped by his desire that it should excel in size—to have more "bound volumes" than other seminary libraries. As a result of this ambition he used the help of generations of student assistants to bind up pamphlets (I believe he held the minimum size to 20, or maybe just 12, pages) and counted each as a "bound volume." As one of the assistants testifies, "Some of us became expert at binding those pamphlets at top speed." Further, some of the pamphlets and more than a few of the books (that came "for free") were not germane to a seminary library. The intention was undoubtedly excellent, I presume; the result was deplorable—also very expensive. The Dewey-decimal cataloging system was employed until the mid-1940's. As the years passed and our library grew (legitimately and rather rapidly), that system became increasingly unsatisfactory. Eventually the Library Committee reluctantly decided that we would have to shift to the Library of Congress cataloging system. The latter had many advantages. For one thing the system is susceptible of indefinite development in specialized areas. The job of making the transfer was, however, *enormous*. For perhaps two decades we operated with two different catalogs and sets of numbers.

To us old-timers, the person most firmly identified with the Garrett library is Mabel Gardiner. She had little formal training as a librarian when she came to assist Mr. Ayres in 1924. Library science was still in its infancy. Since Ayres was retired in 1931 we have had several competent, trained librarians—Raymond Morris, Robert Beach, Ray Suput, John Batsel, and now Alva Caldwell. Yet no one of them could excel Mabel Gardiner in dedication or in working knowledge of our particular collection.

She was born in Chicago and, as a girl, moved to Evanston with her parents. Her college degree was from Northwestern. When Mr. Ayres retired, Raymond Morris, an alumnus of Garrett ('29), was employed to head the library. After he left in 1932, the administration asked Mabel Gardiner to assume the full responsibility under the supervision of Ernest Burch, who carried the title of Librarian. In the years that followed, she ordered books as the faculty requested or as she and Dr. Burch deemed necessary, supervised the cataloging, and had the responsibility of overseeing the student assistants. She did not carry a faculty title but, like others on the faculty, never worked by the clock, putting in long hours and often weekends to take care of the countless tasks that fell to her.

Never have we seen Mabel lose her patience with importuning students who made unreasonable requests, or with us on the faculty when we placed additional time-consuming demands on her. She was consistently gracious and accommodating, plain-spoken but kindly. She matured from an untrained librarian into a skilled library administrator, keeping up as well as she could with reading in that professional field. She was always reasonable, but firm when necessary. Her salary was meager and it was not easy for her to meet living costs in a relatively expensive community. We know, because on one or two occasions she confided in us her concern as to how she would get along in her years of retirement. She has been a true servant of the church, and has lived as though she were a member of a religious order—doing all of her own housework. Hats off to women and men who live in such a simple and devoted manner!

IX

(MOST) STUDENTS ARE THE NICEST PEOPLE!

Amid all the cross-currents of thought, conflicting political theories, and serious theological debate, the basic work for which Garrett came into being continued over the decades. Each year brought a new group of questing students, most of them eager to learn, seeking the wisdom they would need as ministers, and hoping also for spiritual guidance and support. A few there were who came with their religious ideas firmly set in concrete. One said to me at the end of his second year, "Well, I just came because I was told I had to get a degree if I wanted to become a full member of the Conference. But I knew when I came what I wanted to do, and I haven't changed my mind and don't intend to." However, the great majority were students in fact as well as in name, earnestly seeking new light from the study of Scripture, and thoughtful discussion and debate. We on the faculty also felt that we were able to learn much from association with the students, as we worked together on religious problems, old and new.

The men and women who came to Garrett represented nearly all components of our population. Sons and daughters of farmers, especially from the midwestern states, were most numerous. Next came those from ministers' families. Many were from homes of other professional people, business men, or those in skilled occupations. But all types of background were represented. We remember one whose father was a saloon keeper, and another who still carries a Teamsters' Union card. After the early death of his father, who had been the driver of a brewery truck, he followed him in that job until he entered seminary.

Some were from very devout homes, often of a fundamentalist slant. Others had little, if any, religious training. A few, unfortunately, came because mother or wife pushed them to choose the ministry. On the other hand, more than one enrolled in spite of strong parental pressure to "follow father" in a business he built up for his son to inherit. In each succeeding year a vastly varied and wonderful new group of alert, friendly, fun-loving folk embarked on their professional training at Garrett. Naturally, there were profound and sometimes heated discussions in the dorms. And a great deal of hilarity. Life at Garrett has never been simply a quest for academic information or spiritual inspiration. Of course, much advice was freely given by upperclassmen to the newcomers. One alumnus wrote two years after receiving his degree:

> When I entered Garrett in 1940, I was promptly "informed" by the "minds" of several of the students which profs were to be chosen in preference to others, which to steer clear of, and, of course, which were the "cinches." As a neophyte, I listened to counsel offered, but did not give any particular credence to it. From the remarks, however, I did begin to think it would be easier for me if I did not choose to major under one Dr. Q.

After a year, he changed his mind and subsequently majored with Dr. Q.

The informal analysis of professors' strengths and weaknesses, their good humor or caustic remarks, their speech mannerisms, the ease or difficulty of getting a good grade with X or Y, are matters of perennial dorm discussion.

During my graduate work in the Sociology Department at the University of Chicago I had adopted the practice of keeping my reading notes, and later my lecture notes, on four-by-six-inch slips of paper. These were filed under appropriate headings and facilitated the rapid organization of data bearing on a particular subject. This technique aroused curiosity and criticism among some of the students, a little of which reached my ears. James Uhlinger, one of my early "majors," referred recently to this practice:

> I recall many interesting classes with you seated at the desk, working your way through long files of 4 x 6 cards. Speculation was rife among your auditors as to what would happen if the file kit for the day were dropped and the card sequence jumbled in a hopeless maze.

Years later Samuel Wong commented regarding the same subject:

> The legendary index cards used by Professor Leiffer in his classes struck many as worn-out notes, but he persisted in their use, having found their efficiency as a learning and teaching device. Trying to impress either the students or his colleagues by adopting the latest fad was certainly not his concern.

An alumnus of fifty years ago remembers:

> The student generation of which I was a part seems to me to have been, first of all, one that believed in the pastoral ministry. We

believed that anyone who was bright enough, and worked hard enough, and was talented enough, could be a good pastor, and that probably the best pastors would be found on a seminary faculty such as Garrett. Our conversations in bull sessions went something like this: "Well, I don't think that professor would have been a very good pastor in a local church. He isn't able to understand what other people are feeling and thinking." Or, "I'd like him as a pastor if I were a parishioner. He seems to have a heart." We were constantly attempting to find the "good pastoral type" as a model.

Occasionally a few conspired to have a bit of fun with a professor. Don A. Williams ('48) recalls one such incident.

> One day in a Rocky Smith course in Church Administration, a student from India raised a hand to inquire, "Is it legal in this country for a man to marry his widow's sister?"
>
> Rocky seriously explained that laws in America vary from state to state, but finally generalized that he thought most places would find it quite permissible for a man to marry his widow's sister. The class enjoyed a laugh on the not-generally absent-minded professor.

Ken Beck ('51) has reminded us of what happened in one of my classes on the first day of the autumn quarter. I do not use the German pronunciation of the diphthong "ei" in our name, but pronounce it "LEEFFER." In calling the roll I came to the name of J. Ray Neiser. After a moment's pause I read "J. Ray NYSER," using the common German pronunciation. At once he said, "*NEESER* would be *nicer*, Dr. LYFER.*" The class cheered approval, while I apologized and grinned.

Once in a while there was a startling experience that almost caught dorm-mates off guard. C. Leslie Palmer ('42) reports one such circumstance:

> Bill lived in the room across the hall from me in the dormitory. . . . One evening all of us, except Bill, had attended a social function and had returned to our rooms. My roommate and I were preparing to go to bed when Bill's roommate banged on our door demanding that we come to his room immediately. We did, and there was Bill lying on the floor in his pajamas. I shook him and aroused him enough to ask why he was lying on the floor. This weak reply came forth, "This just shows you shouldn't try to hypnotize yourself with no one around." I told him to get into bed, which he did. I covered him, intending to let him sleep off his altered state of consciousness (ASC) but made the mistake of

saying to the others, "Maybe he should take a shower," but didn't tell him to do it. I just left him there in bed.

Again, in a few minutes, there was a banging on our door and Bill's roommate urgently calling us to come and see what Bill was now doing. We did.

This time Bill, still in the ASC and still in his pajamas, was in the shower stall leaning in a corner with the water pouring over him. We got him out of the shower, dried off and back into bed where he stayed until morning. We were careful not to make any more suggestions he might pick up and act upon. The next morning Bill was able to tell us the whole story about his experiment with self-hypnosis and how he came to be in the ASC in which we found him.

<>

All kinds of things can happen. Some may be embarrassing to a person at the time but become an entertaining dinner table story later. Such was the experience of T. Otto Nall ('26), who remembered having

. . . invited two young ladies to swim with him and a classmate in the lake behind our dormitory. It was springtime, and I had not worn my bathing suit since last October. Imagine my surprise when I found that some moths had grown fat on my suit. I borrowed a needle and tried to do what I could—with less than satisfactory results. We did not date those girls again!

Otto, who has an enviable memory and is a delightful raconteur, also recalls an enjoyable evening with a hilarious denouement:

We started the Fortnightly Forum at First Church. One evening we had a treasure hunt, with a list of things we were supposed to find, wherever we could. It was dark that night and we had not found the acorn the instructions required. We were on our hands and knees looking under a tree in a vacant lot near Lake Michigan.

A policeman became interested in our search and came over to ask us what we had lost. All together we said: "We're looking for an acorn." He replied: "You won't find any here. That's an apple tree."

Speaking of the Evanston police, the Department had long ago, from time beyond memory, learned to cope with and perhaps to enjoy some of the high jinks of university students. Indeed, a few students who had prior police training were also part-time police officers on the

Evanston force. Many of our Garrett men who tended to be older than those in the university, had been earning their living in various occupations before coming to Garrett. Some had been employed as teachers, especially as high school teachers or administrators, engineers, shoe salesmen or policemen.

An alumnus, who elects to be nameless, told us of an interesting dorm confrontation of over fifty years ago:

> One devoted claimant to knowing and being true to every Word in the Good Book, had the habit of disturbing the entire suite of studying students when it suited him, and "raised Cain" if anyone made a noise when he was at study. The night before the last final exams (which he did not need to take, since he was graduating) he celebrated in his loudest style.
>
> Asked, then begged, to stop, and at length warned by his suite-mates that he must respect their desire to cram, he laughed off their pleas. At length he was told that more was too much. He increased the noise. Against much struggling, he was carried to the lake, to be given a fully-clothed bath. He escaped without ruining his suit, and ran to the police station to complain.
>
> By happy chance, the officer, an N.U. student, knew him and some of his suite-mates. Phoning the suite in private, he asked what had happened, said he had suspected as much, and reported that he would tell the "saint" to apologize to those he had tormented.
>
> A half-hour later, with a benevolent countenance, the Bible pounder entered the suite, suggesting that if the others would apologize he would forgive and forget, and all could be friends. The boys turned it about, and at length he gave in, saying, "O.K., if none of you can be Christian about this, I can." He left the next morning, not waiting for graduation. Some wondered what he would do as the head of a Bible college later, how he would deal with such situations. President Smith reprimanded the boys, but there was a gleam in his eye as he did so. He did not even ask for an explanation. He seemed to know.

Shortly after World War I a former cowpuncher and cattleman fresh from the plains of Wyoming enrolled at Garrett. He brought with him his guns and leather riding chaps. When the circus came to Chicago he was able to get a job as an extra cowhand for a bit of money and a lot of fun.

Frank Coates ('26), who told this story on himself, was a little scandalized by a few of the boys in another suite who occasionally played "craps" for small stakes. Late one evening, dressed up as an "outsider," wearing a red handkerchief tied firmly over his face as a disguise and with one gun in his right hand and the other in a holster, he kicked on their door and demanded that they open up—which they did and were shocked to find themselves victims of a hold-up. Frank commanded, "Gather up that money on the floor and hand it to me." The victims were reluctantly complying when Frank heard two strong voices behind him.

"Put down that gun and up with your hands." Frank looked around and there were two Evanston police officers with drawn guns. Frank, completely shaken, did as he was told.

The policemen, taking his guns and the money, commanded him and also the crapshooters to come with them to the police station where they all, in spite of protestations of innocence on the part of the "hold-up man" and of the "crapshooters," were locked up for a couple of hours while the officers phoned (or pretended to phone) to the school authorities. Then all were released with a great deal of laughter on the part of assembled policemen and much chagrin and relief on the part of a few Garrett students. It developed that one of Frank's roommates had decided to have some fun of his own and to double-cross Frank. So he phoned a police friend, who decided it would indeed be a good joke to "catch the cowboy preacher in the act."

<>

Frequently Garrett had a fine baseball or basketball team which played in the Inter-seminary and the Intramural Campus Leagues. Occasionally, our team either won "the championship" or was a strong runner-up. One year, thanks to several who had been on their university teams, John Shaffer ('62) recalls,

> . . . Garrett had a very good season—so good that it looked as if we would take the intramural championship, which was really offensive to the historically superior teams from Northwestern. They may have put a few "ringers" into the championship game, which we lost, as I recall. The favorite pep call of the students, who started to get interested the year of the "great team," was:
>
>> "We don't smoke
>> and we don't chew
>> and we don't go with girls who do—
>> We read our BI-BLE."
>
> With school spirit like that, how could we go wrong? Anything to prove that we were not too pious to play basketball, or something like that.

<>

Garrett students have been supportive of their colleagues, especially if one of their number has experienced tragedy or just plain bad luck. Virgil Williams ('35) tells of one such experience:

> Dana Boggie, an expert violinist who lived on the ground floor in Building C, had left the window of his room open on a hot day, while he and his roommates were in class. Somebody stole his fancy violin, making his entrance by the window. Everybody was so proud of Dana's personality and ability, we were sure it was not a Garrett student who took off with it. A school collection was immediately set up and the price of a new violin was promptly raised. Dana was so grateful to have another violin, but he moved to a third-floor room!

<>

Arthur Nagler had given his Methodist History class the assignment of putting on a "mock" General Conference. Otto Nall recalls:

> The setting was the venerable assembly hall in the old red brick building on the Northwestern campus, at Sheridan Road.
>
> Several of the most loquacious "delegates" were in the process of counting up the assets and liabilities of the bishops, with the loss rather than the profit side winning.
>
> One "delegate" asked for the floor and, looking towards the balcony, announced: "Perhaps Bishop So-and-So, who will be speaking at chapel today, would like to have his say." There was a great silence and then laughter. Even Arthur's face was red, as those who could see looked to a balcony that was completely unoccupied.

Seminary professors should become accustomed to the unexpected. Three of them (one of them Rocky Smith) constituted the committee to give Lyle Schaller his oral comprehensive examination. After the exam the pattern was to excuse the student for a few minutes while the professors discussed his performance. They had been much impressed by his mature competency, and decided they should recommend to the faculty that he be passed "with distinction." When he was invited back and informed of the committee's decision, his response was, "That's ridiculous! There are a lot of students here who know more than I do." He reported to a fellow-student that he tried to get the committee to change their decision, but gave up when he sensed that he was not being taken seriously.

<>

Perhaps instructors should be careful to keep abreast of the current argot of their students. In that subject I would have drawn a low grade. In those pre-feminist days "bag" was rather inelegant jargon for "girl," but it was not in my working vocabulary. I had seen two members of one of my classes walking toward Garrett with sizable paper bags of what I assumed were groceries. There was a rule against eating in the dorm. One of my then-assignments was to see that the dorm rules were enforced. Next day in class, speaking about social responsibility, I commented that I had seen "two of our men walking toward Garrett, each with a bag on his arm." It was my turn to be startled as the class broke into uproarious laughter at my vocabulary innocence.

That there have been—and probably still are—great and resounding differences in the viewpoints, both religious and secular, of Garrett students should be evident to anyone. An illustration comes in a memorandum from an alumnus of several decades ago:

> One suite had some occupants who had an odd sense of humor and less patience than might be saintly. A rather "holier-than-thou" student in the next suite often came in to correct the theology and morals of some he thought too liberal. Like the "Moral Majority," he had a pipeline from heaven. Four in that pair of suites liked to play bridge, which he knew to be of the devil.
>
> One Sunday night they set a trap for him. With piles of coins, the four sat playing some card game when he entered. He exploded. "You fellows!" he cried, "Not only are you playing cards, you are gambling. You come from your churches, leave your poor wives, and here you are risking your money on cards."
>
> They were all student preachers, so the answer of one of them rang a bell that sent their would-be mentor out of the room in a rage. "You get us wrong, XX. We're not gambling with *our* money. This is from the missionary collection we took today."

<>

There have been many happy courtships and marriages among the students at Garrett. Naturally every courtship is unique. Two of them stand out in our memory. Stanley Fixter ('51) and Margo Orr both enrolled for the first time in the summer school of 1948. Hiel Bollinger was teaching that summer and she came as his secretary. Both Stan and

Margo were attractive young people and each was engaged when he/she enrolled. However, they quickly began to enjoy each other's company. After three weeks and some serious forward-looking discussion, she phoned her mother and asked if she could make a long dress for her. "Why, surely, what kind?" "White satin with a train." Over the phone came the comment, "You're crazy." "Well, I'm twenty-four years old and will bring him down for you and Dad to look over." And, after thirty-eight years of happiness together they are serving the Christ United Methodist Church in Ft. Collins, Colorado.

Stan had intended to become a Y.M.C.A. secretary and was working for the Evanston "Y" while attending seminary. He says:

> When I was at Garrett I was aiming for the Y.M.C.A.—and was sort of confused in my relationship with the church. Garrett was as supportive and understanding as could be. I remember Horace G. Smith saying, "Stan, I spent time with the Y.M.C.A. in my early days. . . . The Y.M.C.A. is good as long as you are in program. As you go further in the Y you have to go into administration. And that's when you will wish that you were in the church." And that's exactly what happened to me. . . .
>
> Years later, after serving in the Y, I talked with Bishop Glenn Phillips. He said, "You've worked up to a good salary in the Y. Maybe you'd better stick with it." I said, "No, I can't get away from the call. . . . The folks in the Conference welcomed us with open arms, and Garrett had been the same way."

It was in January of 1953 that George Weber enrolled for a class in Church and the Urban Community. One of the assignments which could be chosen in that course was to spend two or three days on Skid Row on West Madison Street, unshaven and dressed in old clothes, so as to identify as much as possible with the men on the street and seek to view the world through their eyes. We had early in the quarter gone as a group to visit some of the missions working with the homeless men, talked with the superintendent, had a meal at the Christian Industrial League and attended the service there. George was one of those who that year elected to become better acquainted with the area. He talked with the men as one of them, spending most of his time on South State Street and staying overnight at the Pacific Garden Mission. He also became well acquainted with William Seath, Superintendent of the Chicago Christian Industrial League, just off West Madison Street.

George was so intrigued with the problems of these men that he took time out from seminary and obtained a job at the Christian Industrial League, and in the process met Supt. Seath's daughter, Wilma. They fell in love with each other and that December were married, making excellent copy for the newspapers. The Chicago Sun Times headlined:

Love Bloomed in Skid Row; Wedding is Sober Occasion

Wilma Seath, 18 and George E. Weber, 25, were married Sunday in the chapel of the Chicago Christian Industrial League. . . .

Thirty of the thousands of men the League has lifted out of the gutter were among the guests. As members of the Presbyterian mission's own Alcoholics Victorious, they joined the others after the ceremony in drinking—fruit punch. . . .

The bride is the daughter of the Rev. and Mrs. William Seath. . . . The Rev. Mr. Seath has been Superintendent of the League for 23 years, and his daughter virtually was reared in the Skid Row neighborhood.

The bridegroom is a Garrett Biblical Institute student, who came to W. Madison dressed like a bum to make a survey. Later, in more conventional attire, he went to the League to interview men being rehabilitated.

There he met Wilma. . . .

We have been in touch with George and Wilma over the years. He has been a good and faithful pastor for more than thirty years. In a recent note from Wilma, she said:

As the young bride of a seminary student I really needed some special companionship—a sharing in the new role I found myself in, and the Sunday evening get-togethers in your home did the trick.

I remember them fondly, even after 33 years of parsonage life, so you see the impact they made. As to details, I can only recall warm feelings and uncomplicated friendliness in what was a time of much uncertainty. I can only hope we have provided similar experiences in our own home for other young people facing new and challenging opportunities.

<>

After World War II an increasing proportion of our students were older than "pre-war" and more were married. Frequently, a student's wife got a job in town. Every year from six to ten of the girls who had teaching credentials were able to secure positions in Evanston or other suburban schools. Some with nurse training or secretarial experience found positions without much difficulty. Others got jobs in one of the stores. Consequently, many of the couples wanted to live in Evanston. Occasionally, two couples joined forces to rent an apartment.

It was out of such a beginning that Garrett housing for married students developed. Two couples rented an apartment on Foster Street in a three-story building east of the "L" station. Later they persuaded a third couple to join them. They soon discovered that the building as well as a similar one next door were for sale at a reasonable price. Within the year Garrett bought and refurbished both buildings. Each was capable of housing three couples on each of the three floors. For over a decade these buildings provided relatively adequate housing for "young marrieds." An occasional couple, for one reason or another, could not "take the heat" of such sharing of facilities, but for the large majority it offered a good environment for learning the arts and skills of living together—and at a relatively low rent. Incidentally, from time to time young people from other than white American stock enriched the fellowship. We heard only good and happy reports of such co-operative living from all sides.

An enthusiastic account of co-op life comes from Robert J. Payne ('50):

> One of the rich memories we have of our years at Garrett was living in one of the co-op houses, Aldersgate House, at 820 Foster Street in Evanston. Three couples shared each of the three floors, each having their own room and sharing the rest of the rooms with the other two couples. (That was also true at Charter House, next door.) Each couple had their space in the kitchen and pantry. Sometimes two or three couples would be eating dinner at the same time at the same table, each having their own meal. We would admire each other's menus sometimes, and our wives often exchanged recipes. Sometimes we would cooperate on a dinner for all three couples. Once a month we had a "house meeting," including dinner on one of the floors, where each couple would contribute something to the dinner. Sometimes we would all wash dishes together (the three couples on our floor), and the husbands, drying the dishes, would frequently ask, "Is this ours? Where does this go?" At one point, we entertained the couples from Charter House, and a special part of that occasion was our singing a song of greeting to them composed by Eugene Bonham. Incorporated in that song were some of the expressions familiar to co-op living, e.g., the two cited above, and in addition, "Would anyone like to use the bathroom before I take my bath today?"—and the reply, "If I may. . . ."

Occasionally, we would have an open house for the Garrett faculty. We heard repeatedly, "I don't see how you couples live so close to one another like this and get along so well." We became very close to the other couples with whom we shared the first floor at Aldersgate. We shared many things with one another. Our dinner table conversations were twofold in content: the men discussed courses they were taking or had taken, experiences they had in common; and the wives would contribute experiences from their different places of employment. Sometimes we would talk late into the night, sharing thoughts, experiences, humor. We went to Aldersgate the second quarter of my first year in seminary, directly from our wedding. It was a wonderful way to begin married life, and there was no adjustment problem whatever for us. Some couples who had lived by themselves in apartments or houses before coming to Garrett had a little more difficulty adjusting to co-op living. But I think all of us who were together at Aldersgate at that time would recall our experiences there with happy nostalgia. We certainly do!

<>

Every year many enduring friendships have been formed among students. Surely one of the most tested and durable was a fellowship of five student couples who, in 1940, entered on a group ministry in the economically-deprived hill country of southeast Ohio: Joseph and Carol Bell, Glenn and Margaret (Leonard) Gothard, Paul and Ruth (Bradley) Mekkelson, Roger and Rachel (Lohman) Ortmayer, and Gene Hibbard who later married Mary Emma Painter. They had met while at Garrett. Joe writes: "We found our common bond in the position of pacifism and in organizing a branch of the Fellowship of Reconciliation. That led to our desire to work together after leaving Garrett." Together they served twelve small churches. Each couple had the primary responsibility for the ministry in one or more of them but each was also co-ordinator for a work area (such as youth programming) across the entire parish.

They not only shared in planning the church programs—but also their problems and joys. They shared their salaries and even their debts, and paid them off together. When, after five years, they went their several ways, it was all by mutual agreement and in love. The ten of them have remained steadfast friends over the years, meeting usually once a year for a few days of continued sharing—in Florida or California or some place in between. Three of the men have recently moved on "to the Promised Land," yet close ties of Christian love continue to hold them all in a committed fellowship.

<>

Life may and should be beautiful and joyous for us all. But for everyone, clouds, dark and threatening ones, blow up from time to time and sweep across our sky.

Not all students find attending seminary to be an easy undertaking. For some, health is a serious problem and much courage and perseverance are frequently called for. For example, Carl Keightley had developed tuberculosis after attending college and spent four years getting over it. He was still weak when he came to Garrett, unable to sit up for more than a short time. Therefore, he had a table built on rollers that would move back and forward over his bed. He attests, "I wrote a lot of papers in a prone position in those days." His roommate, Bob Townsend, said, "Carl is the only student who ever went through seminary on his back." Yet, as his advisor over those years, I can testify that he never complained about his health or used it as an excuse for a late paper. In fact, I do not think I knew of his handicap.

We on the faculty often have been unaware of the serious health condition with which some of our students had to contend. Their bravery and faith were an inspiration to those who knew them. That was the case with Ernest Fradenburgh. The son of an Appalachian coal miner, he was a gentle, light-hearted person with a whimsical sense of humor. In his senior year, Ernest came to my office on appointment, obviously with something important to talk over. "After I graduate I want to have a church that nobody else is willing to serve." After discussion he decided he would welcome an appointment to some small church in Alaska. At his request, I got in touch with Bishop Bruce Baxter who, in due course, assigned him to Seldovia, a settlement of less than 500 on the south coast of Alaska. The village boasted one church and three saloons. We kept in close touch with Ernest and Isabelle, his wife. His letters were filled with stories of life in that isolated community and the rather pathetic efforts of some of the local women to keep the little church functioning for the sake of the children and themselves—as a counterfoil to the rough, hard life of those who had come to "strike it rich." The life of the town centered on the saloons.

One of Ernest's stories which we still recall described a funeral service that he conducted at the church. Some of the pallbearers who had fortified themselves more than adequately with whiskey had trouble carrying the coffin out from the church. When going down the front steps, two of them lost their grip and let it drop. The rough-hewn coffin split open, to the dismay of the small group of attenders and the pastor.

Ernest had not done as good work in his senior year as earlier at Garrett, and I was aware that he was not in the best of health. However, it was not until he began his ministry in Seldovia that he told us he was suffering from a serious case of multiple sclerosis. He served in Seldovia for a year and a half. Rapidly impaired health forced him and his wife to return to Seattle for hospitalization. When he seemed to be improving somewhat, he pleaded with the Bishop, "Please let me go back to Seldovia. It's my baby—the only baby I'll ever have." And he did return, since no one else was available, but for less than a year, inasmuch as his health continued to deteriorate. At their request, we corresponded with the Superintendent of Pittman Community Center, Tennessee, a Methodist institution in the coal country of Appalachia, with which we were acquainted, and secured an invitation for the two of them to live at the Center. She would be able to teach and he could be cared for by a missionary doctor who lived at the Center. It was the kind of community in which he had grown up, and he felt at home there. Ernest could no longer write us, but in October 1947 we received a poignant letter from Isabelle, which read in part:

As Ernest cannot write any more, I shall have to thank you for both of us for your thoughtfulness. We appreciate the spirit behind your check even more than we appreciate the actual money. The encouragement of his friends means much to him right now.

He is much the same as he was at Garrett, but his wit and humor now come out less frequently. He can no longer be out of his bed for more than a few minutes at a time. He cannot walk, he cannot write, he cannot see. I believe he minds losing the use of his eyes most. He can still use his hands some . . . only a spirit like Ernest's could remain cheerful and hopeful in the face of (his disease).

You might be interested to know that the first serious effects of this disease were becoming evident when Ernest was still in seminary. How he loved to play ball there at Garrett, but he had to quit because he couldn't see the ball. He didn't study more because he could read only a little before his eyes went bad. He was afraid to mention his illness because he wanted so badly to graduate. Now that his health has become so impaired, he is very happy that he finished his seminary work. . . .

X

RESEARCH AND OTHER FORMS OF LEVITY

Garrett from its inception has been interested in the Church as a fellowship of believers. After the First World War increasing emphasis on the importance of the community in which local churches found themselves led to the introduction of courses in rural and urban community life and institutions. Two men were added to the faculty in 1920 with the expectation that they would promote the study of churches and their ministry to the community. Clare J. Hewitt, a pastor in the Rock River Annual Conference, was named Director of Rural Field Work, and Frank Orman Beck, who had been Survey Director of the Chicago Welfare Department, became Director of City Field Work on the faculty.

Albert Z. Mann replaced Hewitt in 1927, and I followed Beck in 1929. We worked closely together and developed co-operative research programs in rural and urban communities. In 1932, when Mann left, I tried to cover courses in both urban and rural fields. In a sense it was a holding operation until the school could again afford an increase in faculty size.

Nevertheless, some research studies were continued with student participation, especially in urban fields. Taking advantage of my background in community studies at the University of Chicago, where I had been a research fellow for two years, we sought to analyze different types of urban churches and their communities based on ecological, economic and ethnic factors. We worked out techniques for analyzing church and community population age and sex composition, which could be used in discovering strengths and weaknesses of a local church. They have also proved valuable in forecasting trends in church and community, and have been widely used by others in later years. Many studies of this nature were made during the 1930's as class assignments and, especially, in summer seminars for urban ministers. The Department of City Work of the Methodist Church provided modest scholarships to cover expenses for pastors, who spent five weeks studying their own churches.

It was through these summer seminars, which brought urban ministers together, that we decided there was something distinctive about the churches in cities of "in-between" size, neither town nor metropolis, which deserved research study. Therefore, we deliberately sought out pastors who were serving churches in cities between 25,000 and 200,000 population as participants in the urban seminars. One result of these studies, supplemented by research work during the school year, was the publication of *City and Church in Transition* in 1938. In addition, during the 1930's, we, together with students, had completed some eighteen studies of individual churches and their communities, eight studies relating to the ministry as a profession, eight articles dealing with research methodology, and thirteen miscellaneous magazine articles. We also authored *In That Case—A Study of Ministerial Leadership in Problem Situations* (Willett Clark, 1938).

The coming of Rocky Smith to the faculty in 1940 was a great boon. It was a genuine relief to turn over to him not only a panel of academic courses but also responsibility for research work in town and country communities. While I continued to carry a normal teaching load and the directorship of the summer school, it was possible to accept an occasional request for large-scale research projects.

Some Early Church-wide Studies

The first major inquiry from an agency of the general church came in 1941. The 1940 General Conference of The Methodist Church was deeply concerned over the decreasing number of persons entering the ministry and had authorized the Commission on Courses of Study together with the seminaries of the church to make a study of ministerial resources and recruitment. Knowing of our research facilities at Garrett, those responsible asked us to undertake the task. It would be a pioneering project since no similar study had been made.[1]

This first study showed that the age distribution of Methodist ministers who were then serving churches forecast a serious shortage in the profession five and ten years down the road. Murray was asked to present the report to the General Conference of 1944. Being aware of the size of the audience (about nine hundred delegates, plus other officials and guests in the balconies), we prepared two large charts,

---

[1] The challenge of this significant undertaking, which had to be of a church-wide nature, led us to adopt the name Bureau of Social and Religious Research. It was under that name that we conducted an expanding number of projects.

twelve feet in length, simple and dramatic, showing the effects of time passage and ageing. One presented the age distribution of Methodist ministers, and the other the inadequacy of the recruitment and training program of the Church. In the current five-year period (1943-47) it was estimated that 3,275 persons would be lost to the effective (i.e., active) ministry, whereas in the previous five-year period, 1938-42, only 2,284 had been recruited.

In process of reporting to the Conference, part of the summary was quoted: "More than one-third of all ministers now in service will die or retire within ten years." There was a highly audible gasp from the assembled delegates, as they looked around at their ministerial colleagues. When the report was concluded, Mrs. J.D. Bragg, President of the Woman's Society of Christian Service, asked for the floor and made an impassioned speech which began:

> We have had presented to us this morning, I think, the most significant report which will probably come before this General Conference. . . . I did not realize the significance of it until it began to unfold before us from this platform. . . . I would like to have the ears of the lay men and lay women. . . . This is a condemnation upon us, the Mothers and the Fathers of The Methodist Church, that we have not taken seriously enough the great need. . . . I stand condemned before it. . . .

The Conference voted that the study of Retirement and Recruitment be continued. This the Bureau did, and we reported again to the General Conferences of 1948 and 1952.

It was in the same quadrennium, 1940-1944, that the Publishing Agents of the Methodist Church were also confronted with a couple of problems. The first involved the publication of the "General Minutes"—an annual compilation of data including much general information about the church, and statistical tables which presented many items concerning the membership and finances of the several churches in each of the Annual Conferences. The book was too large and too expensive to continue publishing in its then form. At their request we undertook the task of "streamlining" it. We recommended the deletion of certain items and simplification of the statistical tables, to increase the usefulness of the volume while cutting its overall size.

After the Publishing Agents accepted and put the recommendations into effect, they presented a much harder and more controversial problem. Three Methodist denominations had united in 1939 and their three books of law, or "Disciplines," had been "fused" in 1940, in a fashion that satisfied almost no one. We were asked to "rationalize" it. There were overlappings, contradictions, a very unsatisfactory index, and some important omissions. For example, the legislation concerning local churches and church membership was scattered under the legislation governing the various boards of the Church with no major section on either Church Membership or the Local Church.

After the two of us had read all the materials carefully, we asked for whom the book was designed: the board secretaries and the bishops *or* pastors and lay people? The Publishing Agents at once saw the point, and agreed to a complete reorganization of the book with a new paragraph numbering system, similar to that used in cataloging library books, so that new materials could be added without revising the whole numbering system. We also discovered that there was no general agreement on the meaning of several important frequently-used terms. So, with the help of many persons in different parts of the country, we rather laboriously developed a glossary. All these things over a period of three years were prepared, discussed with the Publishing Agents and others, sent to the Board of Publications and eventually were adopted by the General Conference of 1944. The pattern then established is essentially that which is in use today.[2]

The Publishing Agents had a further request, that we serve as consulting editors in preparing the Discipline. This we continued to do for a number of quadrennia, even though it required that each of us get new glasses after each quadrennium!

The Bureau Grows Up

As the years passed, the work of the Bureau received steadily wider recognition. Many requests came to study churches faced with community changes, to undertake feasibility studies for the establishment of new churches, to analyze the programs and financing of church-community service agencies, to conduct city-wide religious census studies. Some of these involved only one church, others covered all the churches in one or several denominations in a community or city, and sometimes a whole metropolitan area.

[2] An ancillary recommendation which we made to G. Bromley Oxnam, Secretary of the Council of Bishops, after the General Conference of 1944, was that the General Conference should elect a Co-ordination and Correlation Committee, which would function during the Conference sessions and call attention to apparent conflicts in legislation proposed by different legislative committees, to avoid the enactment of conflicting or unco-ordinated new legislation—which unfortunately occurred at the General Conference of 1944. The Council of Bishops agreed and called on the General Conference of 1948 to establish such a committee of three, asking Murray to serve as one member of it. There has been such a committee at each subsequent General Conference. I was a member of it through 1960.

So the Bureau grew up in informal fashion, in response to requests for help that came from various sources. Operating the Bureau might be called a labor of love. The time which Dorothy, Rocky and Murray gave to supervision, preparing and presentation of reports, was in addition to regular teaching responsibilities. The school provided no budget, but did make available a large, well-lighted room and two large tables for the Bureau laboratory.

When studies were requested by various agencies, we estimated the costs of student time (for many years one dollar an hour, portal-to-portal), materials, transportation, etc., and hoped that the agency would be able to meet the full bill. A real help came from the Department of City Work, which began in the late 1930's to contribute some funds for work scholarships.[3]

Gradually there were two important developments in the Bureau. With the growing number of projects, and a larger inflow of funds, it was possible to increase the size of the Bureau staff, and to buy equipment which facilitated our assembling and utilizing data. The staff also had access to the full array of IBM equipment at the University, which acquired increasingly sophisticated apparatus as it was developed.

The growing interest of staff members in research, and improving relations with University personnel resulted in a greater desire to work for Master of Arts and Doctoral degrees in the field. This involved their taking courses in the University in related departments—Sociology, Anthropology, Economics and History. Consequently, they were in residence at Garrett-Northwestern for a longer period of time than most seminary students. Four or five studies might be in process in the "lab" at the same time. While one or two persons might have primary responsibility on one job, they also shared with others and in the weekly staff meetings. Working together over long hours in the laboratory, gathering data on the field, and presenting the final report to agencies, the staff developed a fellowship which was far more than vocational.

A pleasant rapport existed among the members of the staff. Some

[3] *The Story of Research in Sociology of Religion*, at Garrett, including the Bureau of Social and Religious Research, was published in 1972. It listed in the index 287 reports, chiefly the product of staff research. Others, however, were Master's or Doctoral theses produced by staff members, or research articles or books written by Rockwell C. Smith or the Leiffers. The wide spread of research activities is indicated by the number in our various categories: Churches and Their Communities, 115; the Ministry as a Profession, 50; Church Structures and Their Functioning, 23; Opinion and Attitudinal Studies, 22; Research Methodology, 35; Miscellaneous, 42.

"seniors" were usually on hand to assist and offer counsel to neophytes. There was much friendly joking with sometimes a bit of horseplay in the Bureau "lab," especially in evenings and on Saturdays when people were tired, as we often were. Perhaps illustrative of the collegial spirit are comments made by Jim Davis ('56, Ph.D. '64) and his wife, Nan.

> Our memories of Garrett center around learning experiences with our primary mentors, the Leiffers. . . . Under Murray Leiffer's direction we learned to "feel" the pulse of a church while we laboriously painted age-sex population pyramids of the church membership and community census data. . . .

> After a recent successful church adult mixer and progressive dinner, we flashed back 32 years to remark how closely the planning mirrored principles from Dorothy Leiffer's course in "Recreation in the Church Program."

> Much of the Leiffers' direction and guidance was done in their living room or over supper, and always included any spouse or "intended." The mentor-student relationship was such that they were always "Dr. and Mrs. Leiffer" face to face, while we called them "Uncle Murray and Aunt Dorothy" behind their backs. They pretended not to know for 25 years. They baptized and loved their students' children and we have a wonderful new grandson named Murray.

Many of the Bureau alumni (as they called themselves) have entered into teaching or have been elected to positions of responsibility on boards and agencies of the Church. At most recent reckoning, at least 23 became professors in colleges, universities or theological seminaries (three have already retired!), eight others are in administrative or research positions within the Church. Many students, when they were enrolled in the basic course "Communities and Their Churches" (either with rural emphasis under Rocky Smith, or the urban, with Leiffer), chose as team project a delimited study of their own charge. These persons were not counted on the Bureau staff, but they got a sense of the high morale of the staff members. One of the great rewards of our years of teaching at Garrett has been the fellowship with these staff people, which has continued even into the years of our retirement. There was a brotherly concern and respect for one another. Recently, a letter from Robert Wilson, now Professor of Church and Society at Duke University Divinity School, described a recent meeting of an advisory group that had been convened at the request of a major board of the church:

The experience of working with both of you and the other students in the BSRR was significant. The friendships begun there have continued. Just last May an advisory group for the Board of Discipleship was meeting in Nashville. We were sitting around a circular table at lunch. Present were Ezra Earl Jones, Alan Waltz, Lyle Schaller, Doug Johnson, Warren Hartman (a former EUB) and myself (all Bureau men except for Hartman). The matter under discussion involved coordination and data sharing by the Board of Discipleship and the General Board of Global Ministry. The details were discussed and a working arrangement quickly agreed upon. Lyle commented, "We have just seen what may have been one of Murray Leiffer's greatest contributions to Methodism." He went on to point out how well the group worked together and the high level of mutual trust that the members had. This he attributed to our common experience of working with Leiffer at Garrett. The group agreed with Lyle.

The Bureau undertook an increasing number of church projects. For example, a religious census study, undertaken on behalf of various denominations and covering several communities in northwest Chicago, yielded marginal data that permitted writing articles on "Mixed Marriages and Church Loyalties" and "Interfaith Marriages and Their Effects on Religious Training of Children." Another project involved a church-wide study of the attitudes of lay leaders and youth concerning the ministry. It was published under the title *The Layman Looks at the Minister* and was described at some length in *Time* magazine.

In 1954-56, when opinion polls were still in their infancy, the Bureau was asked by the editors of the *Christian Advocate* magazine to undertake a nation-wide study of the current attitudes of Methodists on a variety of subjects. The study, in which the whole lab staff participated, resulted in a series of seven articles in the *Christian Advocate* which created at the time much interest on the part of readers in the Church and beyond. A syllabus was prepared by the magazine for use in local discussion groups.[4]

Staff members talked the same language, and acquired a stern respect for accuracy. Approximation will not suffice in coping with hard data. And an error by one person in reading or recording census tract information may seriously jeopardize the value of an entire research project. Sam Wong, who was on the staff from '64 to '67, had his first taste of research work as he assisted us in several studies when

---

[4] Four of the topics discussed were: "Methodists Don't Do That—Or Do They?"; "What Are Our Sources of Spiritual Strength?"; "Segregation in Churches"; "Vocation and Conviction."

the two of us taught at Trinity Theological College in Singapore. He recalls:

> It was in Singapore where I first worked for him (Leiffer) as an interpreter and a research assistant. I was asked to locate on a map of Singapore the Chinese Methodist churches and I did so. The visiting professor scrutinized the work and began making changes stating that Telok Ayer Church was to be plotted on a specific corner at the junction of two streets and not at the approximate position I indicated. That was my first lesson in precision work.
>
> Both he and his wife enjoyed looking up words in the dictionary. On the numerous occasions I visited them at their Foster Street apartment and their cabin in Estes Park, I almost never left without their looking up a word or two in their Oxford Unabridged!

A natural result of our work in the Bureau was the development in all of us of an increased appreciation of the local church. Our research required close and informal contacts with pastors and lay people of all types. The discussion of their problems, successes and disappointments, together with our commitment to assist in discovering the opportunities and resolving the difficulties facing a congregation, developed an empathy in staff people which has influenced their attitudes and increased their effectiveness in later years of ministry. In fact, Rocky and we would assert that the most valuable contribution of the Bureau to the life of the church was not the 280 or more studies which were completed, but the training of the 65 research assistants and others who were in our classes.

Dorothy and the Recreation Course

When Dorothy married Murray and joined him at Garrett in 1924, she became one of the "student wives," a Monica Leaguer, and before long a candidate for an M.A. degree. One of the first Leiffer purchases was a small portable Remington typewriter, on which many reams of term papers, theses, and personal and office letters were typed. There always seemed to be things she could do to "help" Murray, ranging all the way from preparing "company meals" to making digests of significant sociological treatises.

When in 1929 Murray joined the Garrett faculty, it seemed just natural that she should have a desk in one corner of his office, and a reasonably efficient desk typewriter. That was the beginning of a lifelong "secretarial" job. There, at no cost to the school, she handled all the secretarial work for the Bureau, the summer school, and related projects, as well as our extensive professional and non-professional correspondence. She also has shared in the professional writing. When a president of Garrett suggested that her name should be added to the payroll, her response was: "Thank you, but I like the arrangement as it is." To be sure, she did receive compensation when she taught a course on "Recreational Leadership in the Church." This was a half-major course offered once or twice a year from 1939 to 1965, when she "signed off." Incidentally, this became one of the "talked-about" courses, and we still hear references to it.

In that early period the pastors of small churches, rural or urban, were expected to be somewhat adept at all aspects of church programming, especially for the youth, and it seemed logical that they could improve their performance by having a course in recreational leadership. That reasoning appealed to Dorothy, who agreed to conduct such a course. Her assignments were designed to be practical: making a card file of games, folk dances, relay races, and so on, at least 200 cards; taking one's turn at planning a party, also at leading the group in a lively game; helping the class to plan a party for the student body, and participating in leading some parts of it. In the 1940's the typical class consisted of 25 or 30 young men and five or six young women. They were good sports; some men wore an arm band to designate themselves as women when we needed partners in a Virginia Reel, for example. It was evident that some of the fellows really appreciated being placed in such a leadership position and having to carry it through.

One memorable party, titled "The Ides of March," was planned and prepared for the entire student body and was held in the library (much smaller then). We decided that a Roman theme was called for, and we had the idea that an organ grinder and his monkey would add atmosphere at the beginning. We knew there was such a pair who performed periodically on Sherman Avenue and Davis Street, and got in touch with the man to make a deal for him and his monkey to join our party from 7:30 to 8:00 o'clock on the evening of the affair. They were a success! Among others who arrived during that half hour was President Smith. Dorothy wondered what his reaction would be and was pleased that he did not seem to disapprove. Suddenly the little monkey, in bright coat and cap, jumped off the hand organ and scampered over to where Dr. Smith was standing. Before we knew it, he had climbed up and was sitting on the President's shoulder. We all held our breath, wondering what he would do next—and how the President would take it. The little fellow stretched out his arm and softly patted the top of Dr. Smith's bald head. The crowd cheered! A yank on his leash from his master called him back to his headquarters, and Dr. Smith relaxed with a chuckle. We on the committee breathed a sigh of relief and turned to the next event.

The course in recreational leadership drew enrollments of 35 to 50 for several years and was enjoyed by practically everyone connected with it. We had two sessions per quarter at the Leiffer apartment (with refreshments). We still run into former students who recall the happy experiences we had in the class, and there were gratifying "testimonials" as to the values derived from the "practice." When, in the mid-sixties, the seminarians seemed to have become more sophisticated, Dorothy decided she should stop while things were still going well. It had been a real learning experience for us all—including Dorothy.

Field Trips

Like some other seminaries, Garrett had an orientation week, to help entering students get acquainted with the school, the faculty, the curriculum, and one another. To familiarize them with the resources and diversity of Chicago, we would engage four or five large buses to accommodate the entire group—new students and faculty, also spouses and children. We, and others as needed, with our megaphones, lectured informally in our assigned buses. We traveled through various parts of the city, pointed out and described places which they might visit to advantage "on their own"—the Art Institute, Field Museum of Natural History, Museum of Science and Industry, Oriental Institute. We might stop for a visit at Hull House, the oldest social settlement in Chicago, or for an afternoon musical program at the Rockefeller Chapel at the University of Chicago.

In the urban course and the one on "Racial and Cultural Groups" two or three field trips, were conducted, with a much more delimited objective. It might be an afternoon and evening in the Polish area, visiting two of the large Polish Roman Catholic churches, the Polish National Catholic Church, talking with the priests, eating a meal in a Polish restaurant and perhaps attending an evening program in a local church.

On another day the class would visit a number of social settlements, such as Chicago Commons and Hull House. When Jane Addams was living we might "sit in" on the Hull House staff meeting and she would talk with us about their problems and achievements. In a city such as Chicago the possibilities were endless and the learning opportunities for us all were great.

Walter MacArthur is a minister who is also an artist. Writing about some of his Garrett experiences, he said:

> . . . What I remember most . . . were serendipities that came along in the course of routine study. Along with Truth, which unfolded for me under his guidance, came one day an appreciation of Beauty. On one of several field trips to a variety of social-impact programs in the heart of Chicago, time was made in our schedule to visit a Roman Catholic church in which were some magnificent stained glass windows. We had been looking "down" at the sordid conditions of the inner city. It was distressing and depressing. Then, to walk into the silence of this lovely church and "look up" at the glory of light streaming through the fragments of glass which in their arrangement gave forth not only a unity, but a revelation of wholeness. It was truly a "thing of beauty" and has been for me across the years a "joy forever."

<>

Field trips are intended to be educational experiences. But some are more instructive than others. In May 1951, we took my class in "Urban Churches and Their Communities" by chartered bus to Chicago's south side. Our first stop was at the headquarters of the Chicago Urban League on South Prairie Avenue, where Franklin Lane, Director of the Employment Department of the League, met us. He described in some detail the difficulties facing Blacks, especially young persons, in getting jobs.

Then under Mr. Lane's guidance we visited the headquarters of the largest Black-owned insurance company in the world, and also the editorial offices of *Ebony* and several other magazines designed by and for Black people. Mr. John H. Johnson, the editor, talked with us at length about the problems he faced and the excellent response his publications were receiving.

Next we went to visit the Mecca Garden Apartments, which had been built early in the century when this was a "high-class" residential community. It was a large, four-storied structure, built as a hollow square with a garden in the middle, occupying the entire block. The apartments were designed to face inward toward the garden, and there was a balcony with an ornate railing on the garden side of each floor which ran around the entire building. The units were then large and commodious, with only limited access from the bordering streets.

The driver parked our bus beside the apartment near the corner on 31st Street. Mr. Lane led the group across the street, to tell us about the history of the structure. The wealthy clientele had long since moved south, and the apartments had in recent years been subdivided into smaller units. The restructured units each consisted of two or three small rooms. The "garden" was no longer well maintained, and the apartments were in poor repair. Now the residents were low-income Blacks, many on relief.

As he was talking a car drove up past our bus, parking right at the corner. Its occupants, three young Black men, began bantering loudly with two or three women who leaned from the windows of the first-floor corner apartment and invited them to "come on in." At that moment a police officer appeared on the scene and ordered the men to turn the corner to the left and get out! He was short in stature and swarthy in appearance, probably of southern European heritage, certainly not a Black. The men in the car swore at him, paying no attention to his orders. He immediately drew his gun. Two of the young fellows tumbled out of the car. One of them—a tall, well built man—went to the rear of the car and took out a tire iron (it looked like a two-foot section of a car spring leaf) and confronted the officer. A vigorous, angry shouting match followed, and tension was red hot.

Mr. Lane, aware of what threatened to become a dangerous, perhaps deadly fight, said to the group, "Let us move quickly into the apartment house." I felt that the presence of our bus might have been a contributing (though surely minor) factor, and urged Dorothy to "help Lane round up the group quickly and get in the building. I'll join you soon."

Walking over to the cluster of mutually threatening men, I said, "Cut it out. It's my fault for having the bus there." The vituperative yelling went on. To get attention, I tapped the tall Black man on the back—and when he seemed not to hear me, I hit him harder. Simultaneously in as loud and commanding a voice as I could muster, I ordered the cop, "Lower that gun!" After I repeated my demand (and to my great relief) he did lower the gun. His gun hand was still shaking. Then I turned to the Black men and, in an equally firm voice, said, "Now, get in your car and drive on. Any direction, but go!" Again to my relief, they got in and, still yelling at the officer, drove straight ahead.

I then realized that I was shaking too. When I turned to go toward the Garden Apartments, there right in back of me was Milton Weisshaar ('52) towering six inches above me. Later I discovered that Clyde Bachman, another member of the class, had stood at a little distance and had taken several pictures of the whole fracas.

It was with great relief that we turned to join our group. And to my surprise and delight I saw my Dorothy standing at the entryway to the

（略）

complex, where she had been keeping a nervous watch over what was happening at the corner while she also tried to keep track of the location of Mr. Lane and the class.

We felt there was something of a lesson for us all—beyond that concerning race relations: that there is, in unanticipated ways and places, hazard and the threat of violence. The seminary and its people do not live in a cloistered and protected world. Lives and well-being are in jeopardy all about us.[5]

Mention has been made of an optional assignment in the course on "The Church in the Urban Community." It involved two students, going together, unshaven and dressed in old clothes, living for a couple of days in the "homeless man" area, talking with the people who "hung out" there, attending a session in one of the missions, and staying for a night in a mission or a "flophouse." Each was to take no more than a dollar with him—enough for a round-trip "L" fare and a couple of cups of coffee.

Two such men, A.G. and D.S., after spending a long and fatiguing Saturday on Madison Street and much of the night trying to sleep on benches in the Chicago Northwestern Railroad Station, went to an early service at the Chicago Temple, to see what kind of a reception they would have. The reception was not cordial and there was no food! So, still without breakfast, they got on the "L" and came out to Evanston. The Leiffer apartment was on the route from the Foster Street Station to the Garrett dorms.

About nine in the morning we had finished breakfast when the

---

[5] (We had not recounted this story to anyone until we told it to Rocky and Frances Smith in August 1986. They thought it should be included in these "Reminiscences." In fact, Rocky offered what was to us an interesting sociological interpretation—which we asked him to write out. Here it is:)

The important insight for me in this account is that Murray's sociology proved more than "skin deep." In an incident fraught with acute personal danger, to which he reacted according to his own observation with almost paralyzing fear, he nevertheless behaved in a manner reflecting his informed social understanding. His first move was to get the attention of the angry contestants by speaking in a firm voice, by tapping the young Black man on his shoulder, and, when that did not secure his attention, thumping him on the back. The moment he had the attention of both parties, he delivered a plain and direct command to the person in primary authority, the police officer: "Lower your gun!" When the policeman did so, Murray turned immediately to the young men and ordered: "Now get in your car and leave!" Without Murray's prior command to the police officer the young men could not have left without seeming to run away, but the police officer's acquiesence to the command made it possible for them to beat a retreat. Murray did not fall into the trap of trying to adjudicate the dispute. He simply offered a way out that respected the dignity of all concerned and allowed them to save face and perhaps to save lives as well. (R.C.S.)

doorbell rang. Murray responded by pressing the "buzzer" which unlocked the front door, and called down from the third floor, having no idea as to who might be arriving that early on a Sunday: "Good morning, what's up?" In a gravelly voice came the response—"Will you give a couple of bums some breakfast?"

Up they came, looking indeed like two men "off the street." They had plenty to tell us about their experiences and were able to eat a very substantial breakfast. After they had "licked the platter clean" Murray asked, "How about a piece of pie?" Dorothy had baked one the night before and over half of it was left. We've never seen people enjoy pie more.

Research - an Exportable Commodity

We were invited to conduct research seminars dealing primarily with urban church problems, by a number of other schools: University of Southern California in 1942 and 1951; Iliff School of Theology, Denver, 1955; Texas Christian University, 1958; School of Theology at Claremont (California), 1959; Trinity Theological College, Singapore, 1961; Union Theological Seminary, Manila (Philippines), 1965. Each of these was a broadening and learning experience; we discovered at first hand how similar are the problems of cities and of churches. People behave in amazingly similar patterns in spite of differences in language, ethnicity and underlying culture.

After a semester of teaching in Manila (1965) we traveled north to Japan for adventures of a different kind. The Kyodan (the—more or less—United Protestant Church of Japan) had established a "Leiffer Committee" and laid out an ambitious series of lectures for us. Murray was invited to speak to the faculty and student body of most of the seminaries and in several churches, fifty-two talks in all. Dorothy was asked to speak to some women's groups. Twice we were the luncheon guests of the City Council of Sakai, a rapidly growing suburb of Osaka where I talked and answered questions about city planning and community development. We were also asked to speak to community gatherings in a public school in Sakai, to one in Yamato, and another in Sendai. A number of these were morning-through-afternoon sessions where we discussed church planning and urban evangelism. We enjoy recalling the sessions in Sendai when, after my lecture, the woman who was president of the Women's Clubs of the Prefecture challenged the vice-mayor, who was presiding, about the mishandling of the sewer extension project. She declared, "This is the first time we've ever had a chance to discuss these important matters with you—and it won't be the last." The details which she and others present volunteered made the urgency of the issue very clear to us. One of the Buddhist monks who was present assured me that he saw eye-to-eye with me about community involvement of religious leaders. "In fact," he added, "you would make a good Buddhist."

We both learned much from our friends in Europe, Singapore, Manila and Japan.

We never traveled abroad without some professionally related responsibilities being included—until after retirement. In 1969-70 we made our last "professional" trip abroad. It was to South America, where we had a dozen alumni-friends and the Board of Missions had indicated a desire for an objective report of the progress of our mission work in several Latin American countries. I had also been elected to the Judicial Council of The Methodist Church in 1964, and during the 1968-72 quadrennium served as president of that body—through a crucial period. Since several autonomous (national) Methodist Churches were being established, the Judicial Council asked me to represent it there ("but at no cost to the Council"). This double opportunity to visit our southern neighbors we were happy to accept, again an exciting set of learning experiences.

And Then There Were Other Opportunities

In unanticipated fashion, one project often led to another. The Bureau studies of the attitudes of lay persons toward, and their expectations of, ministers resulted a few years later in the conducting of a series of "Round Tables" in different parts of our land, under the aegis of the *Christian Advocate*, on the general topic of "Protestantism, What Is It?" Among the participants in the first one were: Kermit Eby, labor leader; William Hoeft, an editor of *Time*; John McNeill, church historian; Paul F. Douglass, church survey expert; Bishop G. Bromley Oxnam; Bishop John S. Stamm, President of the Federal Council of Churches, Harris Franklin Rall *et al*. That series, in turn, led to a nationwide opinion poll (and seven articles) on "Finding Out What Methodists Think," which, in turn, was followed by seminars on race relations. All of these cast light on our studies of the movement of population groups and of churches in cities.

Perhaps it was such an array of experiences in coping with controversial issues that evoked a unique request. The General Conference of The Methodist Church in 1952 had instructed three of its agencies (the Boards of Temperance, World Peace, and Social and Economic Relations) to develop a plan for uniting the three into one, presumably stronger and maybe less expensive, structure. By 1956 no progress had been made and the General Conference of that year requested the Co-ordinating Council of The Methodist Church to bring in a specific plan for the merger in 1960. That Council, stymied by the reluctance of the three agencies to budge from their independent status, came to us in 1957, asking that Murray take over the thankless task. With reluctance I did, with the understanding that Dr. Edwin Garrison, chairman of the Council, would give full support as needed.

Our procedure was simple: I asked the General Secretary of each of the three agencies to name a senior trusted member of his staff to work with the other two staff persons and me, on a plan of union. The four of us had a number of lengthy meetings. The rules I established were (1) each man was to feel perfectly free to talk over with his superior anything and everything that went on in our meetings. He could quote *me*, but not what he or others said. (2) Each was to speak freely his own personal opinions, out of his broad knowledge of his agency and its experiences. (3) All were to recognize that compromise was essential and no person or agency could win a complete victory. A detailed plan for merging the three agencies was evolved, presented to the Co-ordinating Council and, then, to the General Conference of 1960, at which the new General Board of Church and Society was established, with a few minor changes from the proposal of the committee of four.

<>

While this study of agencies was moving along smoothly, the Bureau was conducting a broad study of the district superintendency in The Methodist Church. Three-fourths of the district superintendents and bishops participated in the study, and over half of a carefully selected sample of lay men and women responded, not only filling in a detailed questionnaire, but also writing additional comments. The result: the first published study on *The Role of the District Superintendent in The Methodist Church* (1960). A similar study was conducted by the Bureau a decade later, with even broader participation. Two volumes developed out of the latter project—in 1971 and 1972. In 1969 the Bureau published another parallel study of ministers in five Protestant denominations, titled: *Changing Expectations and Ethics in the Professional Ministry.*

However, the most interesting and, in a sense, the most demanding of all our research undertakings, was a quietly conducted and highly confidential one.

The General Conference of 1960 of The Methodist Church instructed the Co-ordinating Council to undertake a study of "the effectiveness of our general superintendency (read: episcopacy), including the number and size of areas." The Council assigned the responsibility to its Committee on Structure which called together six recognized research persons to propose a methodology.

We suggested a series of projects: a background report on the history of the episcopacy; a study of the attitudes of ministers and laymen toward the episcopacy; a similar study of the attitudes of district superintendents; and "a study of the Methodist episcopacy as it is now functioning and how it might be developed to the greater advantage of the church." When the final decision was made by the committee as to research assignments Dorothy and I were on sabbatical, teaching in Manila. Our friend, Edwin R. Garrison (who had been elected bishop in 1960 and was President of the Co-ordinating Council and chairman of the Committee on Structure) wrote to ask if I would accept the fourth assignment. This was perhaps the crucial—certainly the most uncharted and delicate—part of the study.

We recognized how significant for the church such a study could be, the amount of effort it would require, and the possible negative attitude of some bishops toward any such unprecedented study. After deliberation and prayer I replied to Bishop Garrison that I would undertake the task on one condition: that the Council of Bishops itself would elect one of its members from each of the (then) six Jurisdictions and one from the Central (i.e., "overseas") Conferences, to serve on a Consultation Committee with me.

In April of 1962 the Council of Bishops elected such a Consultation Committee. It was indeed an all-star group: Gerald H. Kennedy, chairman; Eugene Slater, secretary; Charles F. Golden, Nolan B. Harmon, John Wesley Lord, Richard C. Raines, and Friedrich Wunderlich. Edwin Garrison also sat in on all sessions.

When the chairman asked what I proposed to do, I responded that I would like to have a two-hour private and strictly confidential interview with each bishop. Also that I would ask each of them to keep track of his time for a typical four-week period, recording his activities on a daily time sheet. Then Jerry Kennedy asked, "What would you do, Murray, if the bishops said they did not wish to cooperate in the study?" That possibility had not even dimly occurred to me, but the Lord gave me the right answer, and I passed it on at once: "In that case, Jerry, I would be delighted. I never asked for this job and would be happy to drop it. All I would need to do would be to report to the

Co-ordinating Council which could inform the next General Conference that the bishops did not wish to cooperate in the study. And that would be that." Bishop Raines at once said, "Well, we can't do that," and the rest concurred.

I requested the Consultation Committee to meet with me for a half day or more before each Council of Bishops gathering, at which time I would review developments and ask for their critical guidance. To my amazement and delight, the eight bishops who represented different points of view on numerous subjects, took the responsibility seriously; attendance at the semi-annual sessions was almost perfect, and participation was frank and completely unrestricted. I had promised that I would discuss each emerging conclusion and recommendation with them before presenting it to the Co-ordinating Council. I knew I needed their critical input at each stage of the study; however, I told them I would not feel bound by it.[6]

In November of 1963 the entire set of 34 recommendations was made to the Committee and the Council. Two were dropped, the bishops agreed to accept informally another, the others were presented to the General Conference with a supporting vote of 27 to zero on the part of the Co-ordinating Council. The 31 which went to the General Conference (one involving a constitutional amendment) were adopted in practically unaltered form, to the apparent considerable satisfaction of the body. Later in the week both Leon Hickman, who (as vice-chairman of the Co-ordinating Council and a delegate to the General Conference) presented the report to the Conference, and I were elected by written ballot by the Conference to the Judicial Council.

---

[6] In carrying forward the study I did have a confidential interview with each of the 68 bishops—every active and several retired men. The heads of Church agencies were also interviewed. All interviews were taped, making possible later careful review. The first two private secretaries who transcribed a tape made numerous serious errors. To my great relief Dorothy, who knew both the bishops and the church, offered to do the transcribing. The total resulted in approximately 2,500 pages of single-spaced typing. This irreplacable file was deposited in the Garrett Library in 1964, with the written assurance that it would not be made available to any person until 1990, and then only to qualified research historians.

XI

PART OF A TROUBLED WORLD

Economic depression, war, political reactionism, and social insecurity produce shock waves which beat upon the thinking and life of the student body and faculty of a seminary as on the rest of the world. The decade of the '60's was a traumatic one for people everywhere. Indeed, it is debatable whether our planet could be called peaceful at any time since World War I. The Armistice of 1919 brought nominal peace, but aggressive actions were followed by retaliation and further aggressions by more retaliations, with all comers claiming morality to be on their side. And so it continued, through the Depression of the '30's, World War II in the '40's, and the Korean War in the early '50's.

Nevertheless, in retrospect there was a relatively quiet interlude from the close of the Korean War in 1953 until the end of the decade—except for the increasing political activity of Blacks across America, who felt that this was the time when they should achieve full and fair treatment in all aspects of life. In the autumn of 1953 Dwight Eisenhower was elected President, and the plea for "back to normalcy" was loudly voiced throughout the land. The millenium had not come, but there was almost a decade of relative calm. This coincided roughly with Dwight Loder's presidency at Garrett, and he was well suited to deal with the school's needs and the social pressures at that time.

Under Loder's leadership the faculty was considerably enlarged.[1] The students benefited by study under professors with a wider variety of religious and cultural background and more diversity in training and perspective than in any prior period. However, these newcomers

---

[1] Colin Williams came from Australia and was with us from 1955 to '58, Samuel Laeuchli from Switzerland, 1956-67, William Hordern from Canada, 1957-66, and Philip Watson from England, 1959-73, all in the historical and theological fields. Each was a stimulating scholar in his own area, and each brought an ecumenical perspective. Not all new faculty were from abroad. Alvin Lindgren came in 1957, Merrill Abbey in 1959, and Paul Hessert in 1963; all three were Garrett alumni. Alvin and Merrill stayed until retirement. Others who came during Dwight's administration (for more than a short period) were John Vayhinger, 1958-64, Richard Ford, 1958 until his death in 1978, Grant Shockley, 1959-66, Glora Wysner, 1960-68, Albert Sundberg, 1960-82, Charles Ellzey, 1961-77, Jameson Jones, 1961-66, and George Buttrick, 1961-69.

tended to remain at Garrett for shorter periods, resulting in somewhat less cohesiveness within the faculty. Well trained, erudite scholars who join a seminary faculty come with a professional commitment to teach. Perhaps they could no longer be expected to have a pastoral as well as professional attitude toward the students, a dual relationship which characterized most of the faculty at Garrett during the decades before the 1950's. This contrast was accentuated in the case of Garrett because prior to 1950 most of the teachers lived within walking distance of the school. It is understandable that the sense of a "committed" or "called" community would be diluted with the passage of the years. Classroom instruction may have been improved, but that is not what we are considering here. Garrett continued to be a community, but not so closely knit, more like a community in transition.

Racial Tensions: The Seminary and the Wider Community

Evidences of unrest in academia as well as in the general society in this country were numerous. The Supreme Court desegregation decisions of 1954 and '55 were still being ignored in many parts of the country, and the Black leadership was becoming increasingly disillusioned at the slow progress that was being made in achieving civil rights.

Groups of young Black people began "to assert their civil rights" in many communities of the southeastern states in the later 1950's. Young Blacks, often accompanied by a few whites would enter a lunchroom, take seats at the counter or at a table, and refuse to leave until they were served or the police removed them. Let Chomingwen Pond ('61), a white Garrett student, give her report of one "happening" in the spring of 1960:

> The lunch counter sit-ins were in full swing in southeastern United States that spring of 1960, and Evanston's fledgling CORE (Congress of Racial Equality) chapter decided it was time to take direct action in support (of the lunch counter sit-ins in the S.E.). In accordance with CORE policy at the time, we informed the local police just when we planned to picket Evanston's Woolworth store in sympathy with our Negro (the term "Black" did not come into favor for another six years) brothers and sisters who were denied service at Woolworth lunch counters in Dixie. The police in turn reminded us of Evanston's anti-picketing ordinance.

We went ahead anyway. Saturday afternoon found a small group of us, mostly seminary students with some local citizens, walking back and forth with our signs in front of the dime store, not sure whether Saturday night would find us in jail or not. About mid-afternoon a car pulled up and parked nearby, and Murray Leiffer stepped out to join us on the picket line. We were thrilled! In those days faculty members just didn't *do* such things, and to have the active support of one of our seminary professors was a big boost to our morale!

The police kept an eye on us for a time, but since we did not physically try to prevent anyone's entering the store, they did not arrest us. We did hear later, though, that Rocky Smith, Dean of Students, was furious with us. "Next time you plan something like that," he was reported to have said, "let me know before the banks close so I can have bail money ready!" (That idea had never crossed our minds!)

<>

Northern cities presented about as many obstacles to integrating Blacks and whites in churches as did those in the South. On Chicago's far South Side, the South Deering community, which included the Trumbull Park public housing project that at first housed only whites, offered a classic example of the difficulties facing a church (and its leadership) which adopted an "open-door" policy, welcoming all who wished to respond to its ministry. It was white Garrett students who spearheaded the transition at the South Deering Methodist Church. "Chomee" Pond, an astute, courageous Garrett activist, wrote her Master of Arts thesis, "Grace Did Much More Abound," telling the story in fascinating detail. Here is a brief but vivid account of part of the struggle, which she recently wrote for this book.

June 8, 1958 was a great day for South Deering Methodist Church. For two and a half years since the old church burned, the congregation had met in the gym of the Trumbull Park Field House. Now they were to break ground for a new building.

The past five years had been stormy ones for the small community on Chicago's South Side. In 1953 a handful of Negro families, desperate for decent and affordable housing, had moved into Trumbull Park Homes public housing project. They were the first Negroes to live in the area, which was miles from Chicago's "black belt." Community residents had reacted in fear and violence.

Neither of the community's two churches, Roman Catholic and Methodist, had done much to help their people deal with the situation in a Christian manner until the Rev. David K. Fison accepted appointment to the Methodist charge shortly before his graduation from Garrett in the spring of 1956. Carefully and courageously, he had offered his services to anyone, Negro or white, who would accept his ministry. That brought the wrath of the local racists down on him, his family and the congregation.

But "where sin abounded, grace abounded the more." Despite threats, harassment, and the unrelieved tension of daily life in South Deering, loyal Methodists found the strength to remain faithful, to welcome Negro families into their fellowship, and to attract other whites. Garrett students and faculty took a keen interest in the little church and helped in a variety of ways, especially by conducting a religious census of South Deering in 1957 and in working with the youth of the church.

Now, financial gifts from the Chicago Temple and other Chicago area Methodist churches made it possible to start work on a new building. Invitations to the Ground Breaking Service had gone out to all of the groups that had expressed interest in the church, reminding them that the larger the crowd of supporters, the less likelihood of violence by the opposition.

It had rained all night and most of the morning. Heavy clouds continued to blanket the sky as the day went on. It would be unpleasant for the congregation at the outdoor service, but it might also discourage the opposition from coming out.

The service was set for 3:00 p.m. One o'clock came and went. The public address system rented for the open-air occasion had not arrived. Two o'clock. Three o'clock and still no sign of it. Later it was learned that the driver of the sound truck had arrived in South Deering about one o'clock and had asked a policeman for direction to the church site. "Get out of this community with that truck! You'll only cause trouble if you stay," the policeman had answered. The driver left.

At three o'clock the service started. About 250 members and friends of the church, representing some twenty religious groups from all over the Chicago area, many from Garrett, lined the rope that marked the outline of the new church. Across the street about thirty boys in T-shirts and jeans, and a few men and women watched the proceedings. Uniformed police were everywhere.

Though it was Sunday afternoon, a cement mixer filled with rocks was kept running in the alley across the street from the church site. Nearby a man with a noisy power mower cut the same patch of lawn over and over again. A woman on a bicycle pedaled in and out of the congregation, ringing her bicycle bell, but when she was ignored, she finally stopped. Part way through the service a fire engine quietly raced by. (We wondered if someone had called for it, hoping the siren would disrupt the service.) But nothing disturbed the congregation, not even the aerial noise bomb which exploded directly overhead during the main address.

The ceremony opened with the advancing of the colors by the church-sponsored, interracial Boy Scout troop. Just as they finished, the sun broke through the heavy clouds to shine brilliantly until the very moment of the benediction when the rain began again.

Church dignitaries spoke. Dr. John Hager, Superintendent of the Chicago Home Missionary and Church Extension Society of The Methodist Church, brought the main address.

Finally, Pastor Fison read the words of institution. "By the Grace of God the South Deering Methodist Church will now raise a new steeple to the clouds to the Glory of God . . . . We will erect on this site a Christian church for all people, where the Gospel of Christ is proclaimed and where His teachings of love and brotherhood are lived."

The congregation responded, "Let us rise up and build."

The Boy Scout troop had made 100 wooden shovels for the congregation to use to break ground, but there were not enough to go around. Mrs. Fison sensed a man at her shoulder and asked if he would like to share her shovel.

"You know I don't," he said coldly.

Only then did she turn and recognize the husband of one of the members who had left the church because of its racial policy. . . . Ground was broken, ashes of the old church scattered, and a model of the new church unveiled. H. Bernard King, one of the first Negroes to move his family to Trumbull Park Homes and a long-time Methodist, struck the bell from the old church, sending its glad message throughout the community.

The man behind Mrs. Fison paid no attention. Loudly and persistently he was whispering, "Does he (Pastor Fison) still think he's man enough to do it, Mrs. Fison? Does he still think he's man enough to do it?"

The congregation answered with the closing hymn. Said Mrs. Fison, "I sang just as loud as I could,

>   "A mighty fortress is our God,
>   A bulwark never failing;
>   . . . .
>   And though this world with devils filled

Should threaten to undo us,
We will not fear, for God hath willed
His truth to triumph through us."

Six months later the congregation held its first worship service in
the new building, and on Easter Sunday 1959 Bishop Charles W.
Brashares consecrated it "to the glory of God . . . the honor of
His Son . . . the praise of the Holy Spirit."

The church continued to grow in size and witness. By 1975 the
congregation was about a third white, a third Black, a third
Latino, with a bilingual Latino pastor and H. Bernard King as Lay
Leader.

The Garrett community was most aware of South Deering
Methodist Church as a congregation pioneering in racial
inclusiveness, . . . in February 1958 it was . . . the only Methodist
church in the nation successfully serving a public housing project.

What If? - A Story About Martin Luther King, Jr.

On August 28th of 1963 there was the amazing Washington
demonstration in support of civil rights. It was then that Martin Luther
King, Jr. made his memorable speech: "I have a Dream that this
nation will rise up and live out the true meaning of its creed, 'We hold
these truths to be self-evident that all men are created equal.'"
Progress toward a just society continued to be slow. The Selma-to-
Montgomery Civil Rights March, led by Dr. King, occurred in March,
1965; it started with three thousand and ended with twenty-five
thousand marchers, guarded by four thousand troops dispatched by
President Johnson. That summer the appalling Watts riots exploded,
resulting in many deaths and vast property damage. In November 1963
President Kennedy was assassinated. In 1968 Martin Luther King, Jr.
was also assassinated.

We have wondered in what ways and to what extent history would
have been changed if Martin Luther King, Jr. had accepted an
invitation to join the Garrett faculty which was extended to him early
in 1958, ten years before his tragic death. After giving an address in an
Evanston synagogue, he met with a Garrett faculty committee at the
University Club. We unanimously supported President Loder who
had invited him to join our faculty. He asked for further time to mull it
over and, on August 5th, wrote a regretful declination to Dr. Loder.
Sections of the letter are included here, with Dwight's permission, as
part of the historical record.

Dear Dr. Loder:

For several months now I have prayerfully and seriously thought through your offer to serve on the faculty of Garrett Biblical Institute. As I said to you before, there has been something of a pendulum swinging in my mind between an affirmative answer on the one hand and a negative answer on the other. . . .

. . . so I feel a moral obligation to share with you the decision that I have presently made. As you know, I am deeply entrenched in the rising tide of racial conflict here in the deep South. My congregation and members of the community are also involved. And they look to me to guide them spiritually and otherwise, as they move with uncertainty through this maze of racial tension.

I have a deep sense of responsibility at this point and feel, for the next few years at least, that my place is here in the deep South doing all in my power to alleviate the tensions that exist between Negro and white citizens. I have started on this challenging venture of love and non-violence, and I am all too aware of the fact that this philosophy has not been spread enough throughout the deep South. I am hoping by the Grace of God to be able to carry this approach far beyond the bounds of Montgomery, and this will take both time and hard work.

In the light of all of these considerations I reluctantly decline your gracious offer. . . . I cannot begin to express my appreciation for considering me for such a significant position. This offer certainly left me with a deep sense of humility and gratitude. . . .

I ask the prayers of all the folk at Garrett in the search of the true Christian solution to this sometimes heartbreaking problem of race.

Sincerely yours,

(signed Martin)

Martin L. King, Jr.

A Change of Leadership at an Awkward Time

It was in this period of mounting global unrest that Dwight Loder was elected bishop and therefore left the Garrett presidency in September 1964. In February '65 Orville McKay, who for fourteen years had been the pastor of the First United Methodist Church in Midland, Michigan, was elected to the presidency. Considering the unease in society in general, and in academia in particular, it was an inauspicious time. Fred Norwood recounted in his history, *From Dawn to Midday at Garrett*:

> Loder's had been an efficiently operated, tightly governed administration, which made possible the noteworthy advances in terms of both financial structure and faculty personnel. Orville McKay introduced a more relaxed, more democratic, more pastoral administration, with emphasis on the last. "Mac" wished to project a presidential administration of enablement, encouragement, cooperative spirit, and above all democratic openness.

This spirit of "democratic openness" was certainly in harmony with the times and was what a restless student body was demanding. Whether it was most apposite to the existential needs of that stressful period we are unsure. What we do know is that it was not an easy time to serve as president of Garrett or any other institution of "higher" education. McKay was an open, friendly person. He and Mabel were an attractive, handsome couple, able to mingle in any type of social group and seemed to be at home. They had the skill of making the one with whom they were talking feel he was important to them. We enjoyed their friendship as did the rest of the faculty.

"Mac" was already in office when we returned from Japan at the close of a sabbatical (December 1964 to August 1965). We sensed an unease in the social atmosphere like a sharp change in barometric air pressure before a storm. Tensions within the society, as well as within the Garrett community, had increased. Perhaps we were anticipating such because in Japan we had witnessed the student "takeover" of Doshisha Theological Seminary in Kyoto. Murray had been scheduled to give some lectures there, but two weeks earlier the school had been "closed down" by the students. A small group, communist led, we were told, insisted they had the right to determine who would use the seminary dormitories, and then made additional demands. We did meet with the seminary faculty in an off-campus location!

Our first awareness of the changed climate at Garrett—after nine months' absence—came when we entered the main door. To the left at that time was the switchboard, located in a small cubicle. When we greeted the operator, a pleasant middle-aged woman, with a cheery "Good to see you again," she smiled wanly and shook her head: "O, Dr. Leiffer, you'll hardly know the place. It's terrible the impolite way some of the students talk, and the words they use. If there's a nasty way to say a thing, that's the way they do it. You'd think they want to make you angry."

Unrest in Academia

By 1968 the Vietnamese War had begun, when U.S. planes bombed North Vietnam bases in retaliation against attacks on U.S. destroyers in the Gulf of Tonkin.

The Vietnam conflict greatly exacerbated the tension and fears of youth. Our nation had been indirectly involved in Vietnam since 1955, and became directly so after 1964. Over 180,000 of our troops had been sent there by the end of 1965; American casualties were mounting. Anti-war demonstrations became commonplace on campuses across the country. The sit-in at Columbia University by the Students for a Democratic Society (SDS) in April 1968 again reminded us of the one at Doshisha. In May 1970 four students protesting the Vietnam War were shot to death by National Guardsmen on the Kent State campus, Ohio. The President's Commission on Unrest condemned the shooting as "unnecessary, unwarranted, and inexcusable."

Perhaps it was inevitable that young people, growing up in a disorganized and disorganizing society, which had no clear conception of any generally acknowledged set of values, would become disillusioned and bitter. In fact, some of them referred to themselves as "the lost generation," and denounced the wobbly standards of their elders—i.e., "all those over 35." Of course, the majority of youth did not join in this indictment of the established, yet they could not be uninfluenced by the small, aggressive, loudly vocal minority who were sure that they spoke, and had the right to speak, for the whole of their generation. These latter were quite ready to throw both history and tradition into the discard. They asserted, "Let's make a fresh start. All we can rely on are our own experiences, and each of us has the right to do his own thing."

Garrett had its full share of problems to face. In the late 1960's we had a small but determined group of dissidents. Many of them showed their disdain for the "establishment" by unconventional dress and behavior. A favorite costume of this minority was a well-worn T-shirt and a pair of jeans cut off just below the hips and fringed, sometimes decorated with suggestively pointed cloth arrows or other symbols which had been sewed on. They might be wearing tennis shoes or none at all. And their bodies were not always well washed. The protesters were an odd agglomeration, anti-war activists, feminists, "anti-establishment persons" who disliked the faculty, the President, the curriculum, the grading system, or all of them.

Black students had their own protest agenda, and might or might not join in with the others. They demanded to be heard and insisted they had the right to set the agenda, including redefinition of the purpose of the school in which they had enrolled.

The behavior of this relatively small group of rebellious students seems in retrospect to be unbelievably insolent. Morale in both faculty and general student body was adversely affected. Perhaps for the sake of history we may be justified in presenting a few specific stories—now scarcely credible—from those years:

In 1969 a student, enrolled in a course on "The Prophets" with Charles Kraft, interrupted the professor during a lecture and said, "We've heard enough about those old fellows. Amos and Hosea are all out-of-date. They have nothing to say to us today."

An experience of Professor Edward P. Blair, one of the ablest of New Testament scholars and widely sought then and now as a lecturer by various lay groups and other seminaries, was even more traumatic, but highly illuminative. His account:

> The course was "Community and Christian Life in the New Testament Period" (winter quarter of 1969). I had some 68 students, all first year, and two assistants.
>
> A month before the course began I called in the assistants and about five students who were going to be in the class, for a full discussion of the course content, the method to be pursued, and class requirements. I was aware of the surging drive for freedom on the part of the students and wanted to be sure that the course would allow maximum independence and relevance to the contemporary situation. Their wishes were structured in.
>
> About three weeks after the course began, we came to the end of a segment on First Corinthians. I asked the students if someone would like to summarize the main thrust of the section and we would talk about its relevance to the contemporary church. No student wanted to attempt this. I then turned to the two assistants. Both declined. I therefore stood up and took about ten minutes in summary. I saw hostility arising, for what reason I could not determine.
>
> After the class R.H., one of the chief rebels, followed me down to my office. He said to me, "There is a lot of hostility in this class and it is focused on you." I responded, "You are not telling me something of which I have been unaware. I have known from the beginning of the course that you and many others have wanted no part of Biblical study and have been making no preparations for our daily sessions." Then he attacked me for "lecturing to the class" for ten minutes and standing up to do it, to boot! I responded somewhat heatedly that I felt that after completing a Ph.D. in New Testament, and some thirty years of teaching the New Testament, I had the right to take ten minutes—and to stand

up if I wanted to—to summarize the material when no one else in the group wished to attempt it. "You want to put a chain on me and set me in a corner, speaking only when you allow me to speak," I said. I continued, "You had a part in structuring this course and now you and your associates do not want to participate in carrying out what you helped to structure. You are now going to see something you probably have not seen before: you are going to see a professor resign a course." "You can't do this," he replied.

I went to the phone and called up the assistants. I called in several of the rebels. We all marched up to the Dean's office (Ernie Saunders) and I informed him I was resigning the course, that I would not teach students who did not want to learn and had no respect for professors. I said that the students had abridged our *human* and our *professional* rights and that the condition in the school was intolerable. I told him that even if it meant the end of my professional career I would not continue under these conditions and that I was taking my wife and leaving town for the remainder of the week (it was then a Wednesday). I gave him our phone number where we were going and left.

That night President McKay called us. He said that he had just returned from a trip out of town. Almost his first words were, "Ed, I congratulate you for having the guts to stand up to those students. They have been kicking my shins blue for months. I want you to know you have my 100% support."

The next evening Ernie called. He told me that he had spent almost an entire day with the students and they finally had agreed that they were putting professors in an impossible position and that they were ready to apologize, if I would come back. I responded that of course I would return.

I met first with the Group I (Biblical and historical) professors. After briefing them from my perspective on what had happened and a three-hour or so discussion of the total school situation, they said that they would support me in my stand.

At the first opportunity the two assistants and I met with the entire class. Several spoke in apology. They said that they did not realize what they had been doing to their professors, that there was no use being in Garrett if professors were not allowed freedom to be themselves and make their contribution. They requested that we begin again. I told them that my life had significance only as we shared understandings and worked together and that I would completely disregard what had happened. We opened the meeting for suggestions for reshaping the course.

The rest of the course was remarkably creative. It turned out to be one of the best courses I ever had at Garrett. A large number of the class members came into my office and told me privately that they had not been in sympathy with the rebels but that they had been intimidated by them and afraid to speak up in opposition. I think this was indeed the case.

Now this whole episode must be seen in context. During this period the students had pressured the President and the faculty to allow them to sit in faculty meetings as auditors. Consequently, many faculty members never spoke in opposition to student pressures, such as not to record grades (or at least F's), to do away with Comprehensive and Preaching exams, to allow credit for work taken during the student strike and subsequent cancellation of classes, to turn over all scholarship funds to minority groups, to build a special (easier) program for Blacks leading to doctoral degrees, to drop requirements in the historical fields in the M.Div. program, etc. Two or three of us spoke out, but many were wholly intimidated by student presence and pressure.

The students . . . broke up a meeting of the Board of Trustees and went from person to person in the attempt to feed each with rice (the food of poverty), with the intent to make the trustees out as "fat-cats." They insisted we invite a Chicago Communist alderman to have a part in the Rall Lectures. In his first words he insulted President McKay and the Rall Committee (of which I was chairman that year) by actually giving a "Bronx-cheer" in response to information given him privately that President McKay and some of the Committee members had opposed his coming. Some of the rebels sat on the floor and at times pounded on the walls of the chapel and hooted. The Communist even grabbed the microphone from my hands when I tried to adjourn the meeting, due to the lateness of the hour (the Communist spoke an hour when he had been invited to speak thirty minutes), and called for a student vote on whether or not we should adjourn. He insisted they must be allowed to remain and discuss. We had kitchen staff waiting to serve us in Loder Hall. I called the Rall Committee together (it included several students as well as faculty members) to the stage and the decision to adjourn carried by one vote. It was a shameful exhibition of intolerance and hostility, one that I shall never forget.

Students on campuses across the country were caught up in a frenzy of protest action against the Vietnam War, and centered their bitterness on sharp criticism of academic life and "traditional" educational procedures. They wanted to topple all "authoritarian structures." There were countless faculty meetings, wrangling over curriculum changes and forms of governance that students insisted must be changed. They (i.e., the small dissident minority—the others did not speak out) demanded full participation in all levels of decision making. The faculty was divided, Dean Saunders recalls:

> . . . Many faculty were insistent on the centrality of subject matter; others, sharing student views, contended for the need to focus on persons in the educational process. In one heated debate, the door of the meeting room opened and a group of solemn-faced students marched in carrying a makeshift coffin, marked with a sign reading "Body of Knowledge." Without a word they made a slow circuit of the room as we watched somewhat uneasily and made their exit. It was one of a number of scenes of symbolic action, dubbed "guerrilla theater," which was played out over these months. We settled back to work again, but the students had made their point without a spoken word, and we listened in a different way.

<>

Yet even in those difficult times there were numerous occasions of fellowship that eased the tension. There was a memorable evening when, during the administration of Orville McKay, august members of the Garrett faculty with their spouses gathered at popular Fanny's Restaurant for a feast of spaghetti and informal social exchange, weighty matters for the moment set aside. A lull in the conversation developed into a definite pause, and out of the pause came a voice, powered by Rocky's lusty lungs, in a familiar phrase of hymnody: "Come Ye That Love the Lord." In a split second the banquet table burst into song, raising Fanny's rafters in a way that must have been a shock to other diners. Fifteen minutes and several gospel hymns later, the waiters were stepping more lightly in and out of the private dining room, and faculty concerns of the morrow were gratefully lifted to the Mercy Seat.

1968-69: A Sad Year for the Nation and for Academia

Martin Luther King, Jr. was assassinated on April 4, 1968; later that month students paralyzed Columbia University for two weeks. Senator Robert Kennedy was assassinated in June; the Democratic National Convention in Chicago in August was one of the most turbulent in the nation's history, and violence erupted as police and troops clashed with over ten thousand anti-war demonstrators.

A year later Garrett was "invaded" by subterfuge by a radical wing of the Students for a Democratic Society. President McKay told me he did not know of their coming until he had a phone call from a minister in Michigan, stating that his daughter had received a handbill at the high school urging her to come to Garrett and participate in a peaceful demonstration in Chicago. I only learned of their presence when I saw some SDS people leaving Loder Hall as I was heading for my office. I went instead into the Commons and found the women in charge both angry and in tears. They described the influx of at least two-score young men and some women who barged into the serving area that morning. Some paid for their food and others did not, since "society owed it to them." They had taken over the gym the night before. "They won't let anybody go down there," said one of the women. There were two "guards" at the head of the stairs who challenged me. I replied, "I am the senior professor at this school, and I am going down." As I proceeded I heard one guard say to the other, "Oh well, the old guy can't do any harm." The gym was a mess, with some mattresses scattered about and a cluster of youth in a huddle at one end. My comments to a man at the entrance were of no avail, and I left. Later we saw some men returning from Chicago, their arms greased (so they could pull away if they were grabbed by police) and carrying heavy chains.

But all that is now long past. The hates and fears are forgotten, and many of the protesters are by now, I suppose, middle-aged neo-conservatives.

I never experienced such harassment as did some of my colleagues because my students were nearly all seniors or graduates. However, it had been my custom over many years, when I had an eight o'clock class, to begin the session with a very brief prayer. A few of the students grumbled about this as not being a proper academic procedure, but the practice was not changed.

One day during the protracted Vietnam crisis, immediately following a chapel service, the president of the student body called a meeting of students to determine how they might collaborate with Northwestern activists who had for two days blockaded Sheridan Road, shutting off all traffic. Fewer than a tenth of the students remained, and I believe only one faculty member. With inflamed rhetoric (largely about ending the Vietnam War!) it was proposed that the chapel pews be contributed to the big bonfires that were planned. With enthusiasm it was so voted. The fact that they were only a small part of the student body did not inhibit their acting for the entire group—concerning property that none of them owned or had paid for. Before the motion was put a couple of men had started to unbolt the pews. The chairman acceded to my request for permission to say a word. My comments were brief: "These pews were paid for, not by us, but by people in many churches, small and large. They were put here for the use of our predecessors, for us, and for those who will follow us. They are ours only for the time we are here. You have no right to destroy these pews and to deprive future generations of students who might think differently than you do about chapel furniture." Having said that I left the chapel. The pews were all unbolted but stacked against the walls, where they remained for some months.

It was the age-old problem of recognizing that there must be limits to freedom. Over two millenia ago Heraclitus said, "The problem of human society is to combine that degree of liberty without which law is tyranny and that degree of law without which liberty becomes license."

<>

When President McKay was invited to become the pastor of the large United Methodist Church of Janesville, Wisconsin, he decided to resign his position at Garrett and opt for the type of pastor-preacher ministry that had been his life's vocation. He had served at Garrett with distinction and courage for five tumultuous years. We regretted his leaving but bade him "Godspeed."

The Central Objective of Garrett Remains Constant

Shocking as were such discourteous and threatening attitudes for faculty and many students, they may not have been any more subversive of a genuinely educational process than when students are either lethargic or so closely identified with the status quo that they complacently accept the materialistic conventions of our secular society. For young men and women to be apathetic in the presence of serious injustice—whether it be ethnic or economic or other—is tragic. We have lived long enough to see how quickly youth may lose their vision and become conventional time-servers, even in the ministry. We wish to testify that there is an in-between course which is neither overt rebellion against the elders and the so-called establishment nor quiet acquiescence to the policies and practices of those currently in power.

Quarter after quarter and year after year through the "time of trouble" the faculty and staff of Garrett continued to perform, to the best of their ability, functions which have historically been theirs. Over a period of fifty years we had witnessed the deep Christian commitment of colleagues and students, through depression and war, and did not fear that the central loyalty to the Christian faith would fail. We knew men and women in every graduating class through this period who have shown great effectiveness in their Christian ministry and have been faithful ministers in the church. They have accepted the challenges and hazards with joy and courage.

The testimony of Thomas Merton is relevant: "It is a glorious destiny to be a member of the human race, though it is a race dedicated to many absurdities and one which makes many terrible mistakes. Yet with all that God Himself gloried in becoming a member of the human race."

Witness and Tragedy

Bruce and Eugenia Johnson ('64 and '62) were two Garrett young people, friendly, attractive, and deeply committed to the Christian ministry. They elected to represent the cause of Christ in one of the most difficult parishes in America, at the Armitage Avenue Methodist Church on the North Side of Chicago. Seventy years ago this was a pleasant, middle-class, largely German and Scandinavian community two miles north of the Loop, but by September 1969 it had become a high-crime-rate area, gang-ridden, with an alarming rate of unemployment and broken homes, where drugs were readily available. The Johnsons sought to bring the ministry of the Word, peace and mutual understanding in that strife-torn neighborhood.

On a Monday morning in September 1969, the postman on his rounds found their little four-year-old boy sitting on the front steps, still clad in pajamas, crying. He questioned the child who sobbed, "My mommie's asleep and she won't wake up. I pounded her." The postman got the help of a neighbor and together they entered the home, where they found the two parents brutally murdered, their three little children unharmed. Evidently Bruce had been talking with some drug-crazed caller. A half-emptied cup of coffee was at his side and a pipe on his lap. Evidence showed that the caller had suddenly stabbed Bruce repeatedly. There was no indication that the young minister had resisted the assault. The murderer then viciously and repeatedly stabbed Eugenia to death, as she lay in bed in the adjoining room.

The awful shock of this wanton slaying overwhelmed the entire neighborhood, the city, and Garrett, too. On the evening of the memorial service for the young pastor and his wife two long processions wound through the streets of the community, joining near the church, led by Bishop Thomas Pryor. It was an odd assemblage that marched through the streets of that poverty-stricken neighborhood. A reporter wrote:

Some were smartly dressed suburban matrons, others were from the hippie community nearby. Several young mothers from Appalachia were walking, carrying children with torn clothes and runny noses. . . . They represented suburb and inner-city, rich and poor, black, brown, and white. Black Panthers, Young Lords (a Puerto Rican street gang), Comancheros (another street gang) were either in the march or impromptu marshals keeping the parade in bounds and orderly. . . .

Fewer than a third of the 1,500 marchers could crowd into the sanctuary to join in the memorial and celebration service for Bruce and Eugenia.

. . . There never had been a service quite like it before. A young Latino deeply moved his hearers when he declared, "Bruce came down from the mountain tops of the rich to be with the poor. He was not a regular minister . . . but he was a 'slick-talking cool' the way we do in the ghetto. Sometimes we read about Jesus Christ and forget what he came for . . . to free men's souls, to free men spiritually and physically. . . . Most people are like boats in the harbor, always tied up to the dock. Bruce and Eugenia left the harbor and tried to cross the water."

A fellow minister in the same neighborhood told the congregation that "Some in the community have been saying, 'The Johnsons opened their front door to death Sunday night,' but we know this is not true. Years before they had opened themselves to death in baptism, had opened their lives to Christ. Anybody who has learned how to do this can live any place, any time, anywhere.

"The lesson we learn from their lives is that before we can live, we must get death out of the way . . . . Our cities and our world are full of people who are full of death."

The impact of the deaths of Bruce and Eugenia was indeed traumatic. It gave ample evidence of the quiet courage of two young people who dreamed of a day when all persons would live in peace with freedom. Their deaths were a declaration of faith in the Way of the Lord. While we at Garrett mourned their death we also rejoiced in their valorous, unflinching dedication to the reconciling power of love. Their intrepid life-giving witnessing to their firm belief in that power came right in the middle of Garrett's "time of trouble" and was a powerful reminder to us on the faculty that within every class which we had the privilege of teaching there were youth—perhaps unconventional when judged by middle-class folkways—who were dedicated to giving valiant witness to the "Jesus-Way."

<>

We left for Latin America in November of 1969 and returned in March of 1970, earlier than anticipated because of the death of our son. That June Murray reached retirement age. However, at the President's request he agreed to remain as an adjunct professor for not more than two years. Therefore, our relationship with the school was only marginal, for the first time in 41 years!

XII

GARRETT: AN INCLUSIVE COMMUNITY

So far as we know, there has never been segregation of any type at Garrett. While the school was located in an upper-income suburb, it welcomed anyone, regardless of race, who was academically qualified and desired to prepare for the work of the Christian ministry. Had it not been so in 1923, we would not have enrolled there as students. The annual catalog which listed the names of all the students gave no statistical breakdown by race or sex, although it did present statistics by home state or country, and by denomination and academic institutions where they had previously studied. The doors were open to all qualified persons, male or female, white, black or brown. In the 1950's the school was criticized because it had not kept any data on the basis of race! The faculty had followed that policy because it wished to avoid even an appearance of racial differentiation. There never had been separation in the dormitories or in the thinking of the faculty.

William Holmes Borders, for many years the pastor of the largest congregation in Atlanta—the Wheat Street Baptist Church—is an alumnus of Garrett. His home was in Georgia. He was graduated from Morehouse College and came to Garrett in 1929. Some years ago he told me that one of his first classes was with Dr. Rall. The second day of the term after a brief lecture, Dr. Rall called for student participation and asked, "Mr. Borders, what do you think about this?" "That," says William Borders, "was the first time any white man had called me 'Mister,' and I've never been quite the same since!" It made him almost speechless, but it gave him a sense of self-respect, especially coming from a person of Dr. Rall's renown.

It would be difficult indeed for young people today to realize the strain that was placed on a Black person coming from the deep South in the 1930's or '40's when he or she entered a predominantly white school in the North. One illustration stands out clearly in our memories. Garrett awarded scholarships in the urban summer seminar, with the deliberate intent of bringing pastors from all parts of the country, and sought to have a few Negroes among them. Each summer term we had a "tea" on the first afternoon of classes, and invited all of the faculty and students to attend. This was before Loder Hall had been built, and the teas were held on the first floor of the Administration Building, the west half of which had previously been used to house the Bennett Museum. There were no offices or classrooms on the entire floor on the west side of the building. I registered a young Negro pastor from Texas, and urged him to be sure to attend the tea. I did not see him there but, looking around, located him in the Library, and asked him to join me in having a cup of punch and some cookies. This he did. However, he soon disappeared. Seeing him the next day, I asked him why he left the tea without more chance for conversation. With hesitancy, he said apologetically, "I had to leave suddenly because I became sick at my stomach. I had never before in my life eaten with white people."

A testimony from a white man written concerning the same period, makes clear the early inclusiveness at Garrett. Vance Rogers ('41) referred to:

> . . . the emphasis at Garrett on equality, affirmative action, equal employment opportunities, and all of the other standards under the current civil rights legislation.

> Garrett was way out in front of society and of other institutions in recognizing an individual for his value as a human being. Specifically, Garrett was integrated long before that was the accepted standard in society as a whole.

> Chester Kirkendall, a Black from Mississippi, enrolled at Garrett when I did. We became close friends and shared many experiences.

> I recall being asked to leave more than one restaurant in Evanston because they did not serve Blacks. This was humiliating for him and for me, and it certainly left a continuing imprint on my life as to the worth of individuals.

> Chester went on to graduate as I did, and, ultimately, he became President of Lane College in Jackson, Tennessee. I became President of Nebraska Wesleyan University in Lincoln, Nebraska. Our paths crossed again as college Presidents, and this was during the turbulent period in which there were numerous expressions of discontent with the status quo.

> Chester and I decided to arrange for a student exchange. Specifically, four or five white students and a faculty member or two from Nebraska Wesleyan would exchange places with a similar group from Lane College. This proved to be a most worthwhile decision . . . avenues of opportunity to understand

one another were opened, and, by and large, it created an extremely
favorable environment in this whole area of human relations.

So far as I can recall, the first Negro to teach on the
Northwestern-Garrett campus was Horace Mann Bond, President of
the Fort Valley State College of Georgia. He taught a course on "The
Negro in American Life" in our Summer School of 1944. And this was
a matter of comment on the campus!

When teaching a course in Christian Ethics, no matter what its title,
it was inevitable that Murray would give major attention to race
relations. During my youth, when I lived on 125th Street in Harlem, I
was the one who was in the minority. In each of the three public
schools which I attended there, "Anglos" were liable to have a rough
time. I had been beaten up by Jewish youngsters in Mount Morris
Park, chased on 125th Street by an Italian boy with a gun (probably a
toy, but a real threat to me), and roughed up more than once by young
Blacks. So I developed quite a sympathy for the underdog. For the two
years that we were teaching at the Chicago Training School on the
South Side of Chicago, we also lived in an almost entirely Negro
community and know that it can be a pleasant experience.

The first course I taught at Garrett specifically on race relations, was
"Racial Groups and Cultural Life," in the spring of 1936, 50 years ago.
It was not easy to add this course to an already sizable portfolio in
Social Ethics, courses in rural and urban fields, Sociology of Religion,
and the research program, but I felt "called" to do it. Leaders from
various racial and cultural groups were regularly invited to speak in
that course, in the basic course in Social Ethics, and in the courses on
Urban Life. Frequently, we would have such a person and his wife at
our home for dinner and then invite the students to come over for the
evening. There the discussion could be more informal and frank.

In the basic course, after giving a number of illustrations of gross
injustice done to Black people, some of whom we knew personally, it
would be pointed out that beneath the friendly response to whites by
Negroes, there was often a feeling of bitterness about the injustice
done by the whole white-dominated society. Naturally, my own
deep-seated Christian philosophy was stressed, that only insofar as the
whites began to seek reconciliation with persons of other ethnic groups
would a genuine and honest communication be possible between the
races. Further, I regularly warned, we whites must expect that in the
future there will be much white suffering in the process of achieving a
true reconciliation, and that some who have thought they were free of
prejudice and who have sought to effect reconciliation will be

distressed to hear themselves denounced as hypocrites. Because of the long tradition of white dominance and the power that whites held, persons of color at that time could not risk showing their real feelings. Other instructors sometimes dropped into our classroom, to sit through a lecture. On one such occasion, a Black professor who was there spoke to me privately after the class, and said, "Murray, I don't think you are right. We Negroes do not feel bitter, the way you have indicated." Some years later he gave evidence that bitterness had "risen to the top" with him. From our perspective this was appropriate and inevitable, but such release of suppressed tensions comes only at a heavy price to all who are involved and the hurts will not soon disappear.

In the recent 1986 decision of the United States Supreme Court in the Michigan School District case, Justice Lewis Powell voiced a similar warning to "liberal" whites: "In order to remedy the effects of prior discrimination, it may be necessary to give special protection to a group previously discriminated against." He then added that "innocent persons may be called upon to bear some of the burden of the remedy."

It has been our great good fortune to have opportunity to know and to share with people of many different races on a personal level, so that we usually felt we were forgiven for being white, and we communicated as friends, color differences being wholly forgotten.

Reconcilement is Good for the Soul

The pains of reconciliation are not limited to the relations between Blacks and whites. Within our student body were men and women from almost every racial and cultural group. Especially at the start, tensions might run high. A painful adjusting was described recently by our esteemed friend, Jacob Quiambao, a Filipino, currently teaching at Wesleyan College, in Macon, Georgia:

> World War II was just over and I was bitter against the Japanese because they invaded my country and I fought them in battle. I was in that infamous Bataan Death March and at the O'Donnell Concentration Camp as a prisoner of war. Almost immediately after the War, I came to the U.S. to study at Garrett. One of my classmates was Peter Ahn, a Korean young man who fought on the side of the Japanese. One day, Peter said to me, rather naively, "Jacob, I was in the Japanese Army and early in August, 1945, I got my special order to go to the Philippines and I was going there, but the war ended." Suddenly, my hostility rose to the surface and I said seriously, "Peter Ahn, had you gone to the Philippines then, I would have shot you!"

Shortly after this incident, a representative of the Dempster League asked me if I would join a deputation team to speak in the churches on "Forgiveness and Brotherhood." I knew then that Peter Ahn would be on the same platform with me, and how could I talk on forgiveness when I was anything but forgiving? So, I declined the invitation, but the young American guy who was a Dempster League officer said, "Think it over, Jacob." That night I struggled and prayed hard, and the following day I went to school early to look for the young American, and when I found him, I simply said, "Yes, I am joining the deputation team."

A small, but meaningful part of Garrett's reconciling ministry.

One of the ablest persons we know in bridging racial barriers is Claude-Marie Barbour, a French Huguenot woman who came to Garrett in 1971. In the early '60's her first assignment as a missionary was in Lesotho, in Southern Africa, sharing the life of a mountain village of Bantu people. There she began to practice a policy of learning from those among whom she was living before assuming an ability to teach them. This idea has become the core of her understanding of the mission task and of her teaching: "Mission in Reverse." Later she lived with Black orphaned children in Soweto near Johannesburg, and was made to suffer physically there because of her commitment to justice and racial equality. Then in Scotland she founded the Women's International Center of Edinburgh, committed particularly to the welcoming of immigrant women and children from Pakistan, India, and Sudan.

A scholarship from the World Council of Churches brought Claude-Marie to the United States in 1971. In a Garrett seminar conducted by Rockwell Smith she met a number of Black pastors. One of them invited her to accompany him each weekend to his church, the Koinonia Missionary Baptist Church, located in an underprivileged area in Gary, Indiana. On graduation she took an apartment—the only white woman in a Black neighborhood—and for a year became a full-time volunteer worker in that church.

Claude-Marie was the first woman to earn a Doctor of Sacred Theology degree at Garrett ('73); her thesis was "A Comparative Study of African Traditional Rites and Christian Initiation Rites." She is an ordained Presbyterian minister. In 1976 she joined the faculty of the Catholic Theological Union of Chicago. Today she is tenured and the first woman to become a full professor on that faculty. Claude-Marie founded Shalom Ministries, Inc., a Christian ecumenical community of men and women involved in a ministry of justice, peace and healing in strife-torn communities in the United States and in the Third World, committed to live simply, as followers of Christ.

Covenanted and affiliated members live in the poverty-ravaged Kenwood/Oakland community of Chicago, and among the ethnically diverse multitudes of street people in "Uptown" Chicago, and in various places over the world. Members are today working in some fifteen "Base Communities," sharing in ministry, problems, and income, in places as diverse as the Rosebud Indian Reservation of South Dakota, Argentina, Cameroon, Chile, Uganda, and Uruguay.

An Encompassing Inclusive Fellowship

After teaching at Garrett one summer, Dr. O. D. Duncan, Professor of Sociology and Rural Life at Oklahoma State University in Stillwater, wrote President Loder:

> . . . my brief stay at Garrett always will be one of the bright spots in my long career of 40 years as a teacher. Not only did I find the cool bracing air from Lake Michigan refreshing, but the human association was also delightful and challenging. I liked especially the friendly democratic atmosphere. I experienced no feeling of rejection on account of either my southern background, my religion, my field of specialization, or my bucolic personality. To me that was priceless.

The openness of the Garrett fellowship extended not only to people of both sexes and all races, but also to Buddhists, Jews and Christians— Protestant, Catholic, and Orthodox. After World War II two Orthodox Polish rabbis attended classes at Garrett to increase their understanding of the English language especially in the matter of religious terminology.

One of the ablest doctoral candidates among the many that Rocky and I had was Samuel Teitelbaum, a rabbi with a rabbinical degree from Hebrew Union College-Jewish Institute of Religion. Sam responded to a note in our Christmas letter to friends last year, inviting them to share their reminiscences of Garrett. He wrote:

> I, Samuel Teitelbaum, a Jew, a rabbi, am truly part of the heritage of the Garrett-Evangelical Theological Seminary, a Christian institution. My memories of that school of higher religious learning are long, long memories, particularly its personnel, its faculty and students. I remember with special nostalgia my very helpful teachers in sociology and sociology of religion, Professors Murray H. Leiffer and Rockwell C. Smith. These two were not only my principal instructors but also my patient guides in all the facets of my graduate studies. They and I became not only colleagues but close mutual friends. They and Garrett, as a whole, were indeed a veritable boon to me and my career.

. . . I found nothing but courtesy and graciousness at Garrett, from its students and faculty alike. I felt thoroughly at home in its environs and ecumenical atmosphere.

. . . I feel constrained to admit to an aberration. I had been, until very recently, an inveterate pipe-smoker. During my Garrett-Northwestern days I was wont to walk about the Garrett halls puffing away at my pipe and producing a voluminous cloud of smoke. Strangely enough, not one person spoke to me about this violation of the Garrett custom. But one day it dawned upon me when I became aware of the fact that not a single other person ever smoked in these halls, that I was "sinning." Immediately I spoke to Murray, with some embarrassment, about this infringement. In fact, I had not refrained from smoking in his office—but he had said nary a word to me. This time, smiling genially, he reminded me of the Methodist tradition against smoking, though no one would place restrictions upon me. I promised to "sin no more."

Garrett has indeed been an inclusive fellowship unless persons elect to exclude themselves.

Merlyn Northfelt Comes to the Presidency

In spite of the long-term record of the inclusive spirit of Garrett, the untoward events of the years 1965 to 1972 created a divisiveness and unease greater than anything we had experienced since we first knew the school in 1923. Of course, such unhappiness as characterized both the disturbers and those who sought tranquillity reflected the fact that all of society was in disarray. It was in the middle of this time that Merlyn W. Northfelt was elected to the presidency of Garrett. His whole ministry had been in Northern Illinois and, perhaps prophetically, the assignment in which he had been serving was titled "Co-ordinator for the Northern Illinois Annual Conference of The United Methodist Church." The staff under his leadership was recognized nationally for its creativity and effectiveness. Typically, he elected to delay his inauguration until the following March, even though he took over the Garrett responsibility in September of 1970.

Merlyn, an alumnus of Garrett ('46), was well acquainted with the Board of Trustees, on which he had served as a member for many years, and with the faculty. He is a sturdily-built man, with an amazing measure of stamina, both physical and psychic. He came with creative ideas and administrative skills, which was fortunate because he was faced immediately with many problems calling for quiet and firm action.

Merlyn was a good listener and part of his strategy was not to be rushed into hasty decisions. Faced as he was with loud and insistent demands from various small but determined minorities, this was both appropriate and wise. An excellent illustration of his handling of a difficult problem was described in a letter to us:

> One of the oddest experiences was in the early seventies when some of the radical students insisted that the "art display" in the main hall show both pictures and clay models of (sex objects). This, of course, was connected with the feminists' disdain for Freud. I had ordered these displays out of the main hall where the public was more apt to come. As a response to my action, some of the students kidnapped our priceless, full-size original oil painting of Barbara Heck. I was sent an anonymous note that the painting would be returned when I, the President, would cease and desist censoring the art displays and allow the return of the (exhibits). They—the students—really wanted me to get angry—and respond with some rash action or statement. Instead, I played it cool.
>
> After a few days some students who claimed to be innocent asked me what I intended to do. Again I played it cool and told them that the painting was insured for a large sum. That if she was not returned in a few days I would notify the insurance company and they would probably send an investigator. The students passed the word—and the next morning when Charles Underwood opened the doors in the front hall, there was Barbara properly hung in her regular spot on the first landing on the stairs going to the second floor. Of course, I did not pursue the matter further, nor did we celebrate her return.

In his inaugural address and his subsequent development of seminary policy, Merlyn made a three-fold commitment for future expansion of the total Garrett enterprise. As printed in the 1973 catalog, these were: (1) The Church and the Black Experience, (2) Peace and the World Community, and (3) The Role of Women in Christian Community.

There had, of course, been Black members on the Garrett faculty prior to Merlyn's coming. Grant S. Shockley taught in the field of Religious Education, 1959-1966. Edsel A. Ammons ('57) was Professor of Church and Urban Society from 1968 until his election to the episcopacy in 1976. The big increase in Black representation on the Garrett faculty came in 1970-72, with the arrival of John H. Cartwright in Christian Ethics, Hycel B. Taylor in The Church and the Black Experience, Philip A. Harley ('56) in Church Administration, and Charles H. Marbury in New Testament. Dr. Marbury later served as Dean of the Seminary. Other Black professors have more recently been added to the faculty: Larry G. Murphy in History of Christianity, Peter T. Nash in Old Testament Interpretation, Edward P. Wimberly in Pastoral Care, and Henry James Young in Theology and Ethics.

In the years since 1972, there have been at least four Black members on the faculty at any one time. Matching the increase in the number of Black faculty was a determined effort to recruit Black students through the use of scholarship funds and other financial assistance, resulting in larger numbers of Blacks in the student body than previously, averaging well over forty in recent years.

The second of President Northfelt's major concerns, "Peace and World Community," was far less tractable. He did indeed succeed in reducing the discord within the Garrett community but even he, with all his skills, was limited to personal and institutional witnessing to the desire for peace and sharing with kindred spirits in the age-old struggle toward its attainment.

Concerning the third objective—improving the "Role of Women in Community," it was possible to deal more concretely. Here again faculty and student recruitment have played a determinative part. The number of full-time women on the faculty has increased from one or two in the 1930's through the 1960's, to six at the present time. And the proportion of women in both total enrollment and in the basic Master of Divinity degree program has grown until now it is about equal to that of men.

Northfelt himself ranks as the most important achievement during his administration the harmonious merging of the Evangelical Theological Seminary, which had been located in Naperville, and Garrett in Evanston. This had long been on the horizon, but no progress was made until Merlyn arrived on the scene. I remember proposing in the late 1940's to Horace Smith that, since the two denominations represented by the two schools (Evangelical-United Brethren and Methodist) were involved in serious merger talks, the two seminaries located in the same general area should also begin overtures—starting with consultation before new faculty positions were established. However, Horace dismissed this as impracticable. When the same suggestion was made to Dwight Loder about 1960, his response was similar. Later a formal commission established by the General Conferences of the two churches made the same recommendation—only with more authority. The commission also recommended the uniting of the two seminaries in Ohio and of two on the East Coast. These latter proposals fell on deaf ears.

With able cooperation of the Evangelical leaders, especially that of Paul Eller, President of Evangelical Theological Seminary, and with

Merlyn's special skills as interlocutor and mediator it was possible to move steadily toward the co-ordination of the faculties, the Boards of Trustees and the assets of the two schools. In 1974 the two schools were merged into the new Garrett-Evangelical Theological Seminary. To be sure, scores of co-operators were needed. The registrar, Vera Watts, had her own set of distinctive problems, working with students from (1) former Garrett, (2) former E.T.S. and (3) those in G.-E.T.S. As she remarked, it was sort of like (a marriage) "his," "hers," and "ours." But only one who understands how huge are the problems of loyalty to heritage, economics, property and, most important, personnel can fully appreciate the logistics involved in the achieving of "An Inclusive Seminary." No wonder some staff people still refer to "Merlyn, the Magician." We, looking on from afar, joined in the applause. Merlyn retired in 1980.

EPILOGUE

Those who follow us must cope with much more difficult forces in a more fragile world than confronted us: exploding population, rapid exploitation and destruction of earth's limited resources, nuclear energy with all its ramifications, not the least of which is the threat of nuclear war. In addition there is the appalling increase in the availability of *power*, psychological as well as physical—the compulsiveness of television, conjoined with the ability of relatively small economic and political groups to shape and control public opinion.

These dynamic pressures within society are more vast than anything which we knew 50 years ago, and we view with deep sympathy and concern both students and teachers who must wrestle with these new realities.

There is a temptation, when faced with massive difficulties and "impossible" barriers, to become despairing and perhaps even cynical. But this is the way of non-faith and darkness. Men and women of faith have long attested that the best way to combat despair is to declare one's trust in the goodness and power of God. Surely it is true that the more hazardous the situation the greater is the need for people of courage and hope. And this is one of the functions of a school such as Garrett-Evangelical—to enable men and women to discover the importance of our roots in faith, and to empower us to become effective partners in the struggles for righteousness which most surely lie ahead.

It has never been easy in past generations or in ours to live out in action the faith we profess. Nevertheless that is the goal toward which we must strive. And with the help of the Lord we must seek to become spiritually self-disciplined. No one else can do it for us. Nor can we *do* it for another. For ourselves we have sought to develop a few guidelines:

> Do not be overwhelmed by the evening news. Another issue will appear tomorrow—and next year. Norman Cousins wisely commented: "No one knows enough to be a pessimist."

> Rejoice in human uniqueness; it is one of God's amazing gifts. And do not fear differences of opinion. It would be tragic if all

members of the faculty were Republicans or Democrats or Socialists. Dialog is essential to avoid indoctrination.

Resist the idea of inevitability. Inevitability is the hallmark of Marxism, not Christianity. Avoid negative existentialism. No one can close the book on human history.

In every age and culture there have been and are certain personal attributes worth cultivating in ourselves:

Be a person of integrity. Jesus said, "let your 'yea' be 'yea' and your 'nay' be 'nay.'" (Mt. 5:37) Tell the truth, even though it be costly.

Be patient—with husband/wife, children, parishioners. We all are fallible and limited in experience and understanding.

Be compassionate—especially with those who suffer.

Be gentle—especially with the young. Allow them time to learn.

Be simple. Do not be caught up in the desire to consume. Ostentation and conspicuous consumption—they are the trademarks of the modern pagans.

Be loving—that is the Priceless Ingredient.

There is something precious in the fellowship of committed Christians. Martin Luther King, Jr. had a dream—certainly not for himself nor even for his Black comrades and fellow sufferers—but a dream of a redeemed society in which all of us regardless of sex, race, or ethnicity, will be cleansed of our petty self-seeking, our feelings of frustration and aggression. Salvation may come from those who have suffered most—but not just because of their suffering—rather because of their vision, their courage, and their hope.

We gratefully follow the leadership of King, of Paul, and of the One in whom they have placed their trust and to whom they have pledged their faith—Jesus of Nazareth.

<>

Ours has been a long and adventurous life, full of wonderful opportunities far beyond our deserving. And now, octogenarians, we realize we are moving toward another Commencement Day. We have already filled out application forms for enrollment in the Postgraduate School of the Spirit. With a bit of nostalgia—but no eagerness to take the courses over again—we look back at our still incomplete education in this amazing, beautiful, and mysterious school of life, with both wonder and gratitude. We do not know what form our graduate courses will take, but we are content to leave that with our Counselor and Registrar.

APPENDIX

Our colleagues over the years have been creative spirits and we have rejoiced not only in their friendship, but also in their writing. Here are four selections, by as many persons, which we have greatly enjoyed. We believe they are not generally known and are happy to have the privilege of including them as part of the "Reminiscences."

I

THE STORY OF CREATION

Harris Franklin Rall

In the beginning God was creating the heavens and the earth. And the world was without form or light. Through boundless spaces there wandered tiny electric particles, separate and solitary. And there was chaos and night.

And God said, Let there be island universes. And the Spirit of the Eternal moved upon chaos. Through the unmeasured distances, here and there, the electric particles gathered together, masses that turned on themselves and formed into spirals, mothers of suns yet to be. And it was evening and morning, the first age.

And God said, Let there be stars. And the vast island universes broke into star clusters, and shaped themselves into stars. The electric particles were drawn together in ever closer union, in fierce turmoil and inconceivable heat; and the suns shone forth, and there was light. And it was evening and morning, the second age.

And God said, Let there be planets. And it came to pass that one great sun in its course swept near another. From that other it drew forth a great tidal wave of flaming matter; and from this wave great jets spurted forth, and tore themselves away, and started on their separate orbits around their sun. And planets were born, and the earth planet. And it was evening and morning, the third age.

And God said, Let there be atoms and elements. Out of electric chaos in a myriad suns the atoms appeared. In the cooling earth planet, the ninety-two elements were shaped. And out of the elements were formed earth and air and water and the countless physical structures of the world. And it was evening and morning, the fourth age.

And God said, Let there be life. And God took the elements that he had made; and God shaped the living cell and all forms of lesser life and higher, of life vegetal and animal, simple and ever more complex, moving slowly upward through ascending levels. And it was evening and morning, the fifth age.

And God said, Let there be man. And God chose one of the lesser creatures of the earth. And God bade him to walk erect, that he might have hands to shape tools and rule his world, and eyes that could look forward and upward. And God touched his brain and kindled there the restless quest for truth. And God touched his lips that he might speak and have fellowship with other men in love and toil, and hand on greater treasures for a later greater race. And God quickened into life the soul of man that he might know the meaning of life, that he might set high goals and rule himself, that he might hunger for the infinite, that he might commune with the Eternal. And it was evening and morning, the sixth age.

And God saw everything that he had made. And God said, it is not yet finished; and God rested not from his labors. And God called man to know the purpose of the Eternal, and to enter upon the fellowship of creative love, and to know that his labor was not in vain in the Lord. And it was the morning of the seventh age.

II

TO MARTHA ON HER BIRTHDAY

October 20, 1977

We have belonged together; far away and long ago;
Yesterday and today, now and here;
And through all the years between.

He who is the Father of us all
Placed two new lives within our care,
And in His grace he has given faith and love and hope:
Faith in the light when days were dark;
Love strengthened through shared adversity and joy;
Hope for the future hid behind the bend of time.

How shall I say it new, now we and the year are old?
What need to speak at all, when deep within
The wordless silence of the heart truth is known,
Surer far than that which comes in mask of words
Which part reveal and part conceal life's full rich meaning?

The touch of hand in hand,
The light of joy that flashes in the eye,
The warmth of nearness, the living memory
Of shared labor and joy, tears and promise,
In time that has been and is no more:

These manifest the truth of life enwound with life,
Of love that has withstood the strains of all the years
And *will* stand under the stresses of these latter days.
Accept in faith the time that is and is to be
And beyond that the timelessness of eternity.

For time and timelessness are one in Him
Who holds us in His hands, sustains us in His grace,
And brings to us His peace. Amen.

(Henry E. Kolbe, Janesville, Wis.)

III

ACADEMIC PROJECT

"Too hard a journey for three old professors"—
"Scarcely appropriate"—their colleagues said,
"A student assistant could have handled the project."
But the old teachers followed as the Star led.

Though the night was dark, a lamp warmed the stable
And the straw gave comfort to age-stiffened knees
As they knelt in the glow of the cradling manger
Offering gifts from their scant treasuries.

"Nothing to publish:" the Dean's reaction;
"Clearly irrelevant!" the young men said.
But the three old teachers would always remember
Star light and lamp light on a baby's head.

Frances and Rockwell Smith
Christmas 1973, Carlsbad, New Mexico

IV

MIRACLES

Miracles of knowledge:
of what to look for, where to cut,
of what to take and what to leave alone;

Miracles of understanding:
of what body and soul can do alone,
of what help they need, in medicine or word;

Miracles of care:
of the pastoral presence, the friendly visit,
of the well-chosen card, the gift of food;

Miracles of imagination:
of shared experience in fear and hope,
of lovely blooms or fruit, clever gift, surprise;

Miracles of work:
of family, friends, or colleagues
    who gladly lift my load,
leaving me peace to go among dragons,
    to fight, to listen, to wonder, and to mend;

And Miracles of prayer:
of unexpected hope, love, joy, courage,
of sudden sharing, tears, and strength against despair;

All Miracles from God:
all coming like spring scents on the wind,
from a God so shy
    the gifts all come unsigned,
so quick to give